THE WORKINGS OF LANGUAGE

From Prescriptions to Perspectives

EDITED BY
REBECCA S. WHEELER

Westport, Connecticut
London

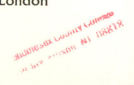

Library of Congress Cataloging-in-Publication Data

The workings of language : from prescriptions to perspectives / edited
   by Rebecca S. Wheeler.
      p. cm.
   Includes bibliographical references and index.
   ISBN 0–275–96245–8 (alk. paper).—ISBN 0–275–96246–6 (pbk. :
alk. paper)
   1. Language and languages. 2. English language. I. Wheeler,
Rebecca S., 1952– .
   P106.W663 1999
   400—dc21   98–50239

British Library Cataloguing in Publication Data is available.

Library of Congress Catalog Card Number: 98–50239
ISBN: 0–275–96245–8
       0–275–96246–6 (pbk.)

First published in 1999

Praeger Publishers, 88 Post Road West, Westport, CT 06881
An imprint of Greenwood Publishing Group, Inc.
www.praeger.com

Printed in the United States of America

The paper used in this book complies with the
Permanent Paper Standard issued by the National
Information Standards Organization (Z39.48–1984).

10 9 8 7 6 5 4 3 2

Copyright Acknowledgments

The editor and publisher gratefully acknowledge permission for the use of the following material:

Chapter 1, "The Language Mavens," by Steven Pinker was originally published as "Grammar Puss: Fallacies of the Language Mavens" in *The New Republic*, January 31, 1994. Reprinted with permission from *The New Republic*.

Chapter 9, "Speaking of America: Why English-only Is a Bad Idea," by Geoffrey Nunberg was originally published as "Lingo-Jingo: English Only and the New Nativism" in *The American Prospect*. Reprinted with permission from *The American Prospect* 33 July–August Copyright 1997 The American Prospect, P.O. Box 383080, Cambridge, MA 02138. All rights reserved.

Chapter 11, "Metaphor, Morality, and Politics: Or, Why Conservatives Have Left Liberals in the Dust," by George Lakoff was originally published in *Social Research* 62.2 (Summer 1995). Reprinted with permission from *Social Research*.

Chapter 14, "Life on Mars: Language and the Instruments of Invention," by Mark Turner and Gilles Fauconnier was originally published as "A Mechanism of Creativity" in *Poetics Today* 20.3 (Fall 1999). Reprinted with permission from *Poetics Today*.

Chapter 16, "Women and Men in Conversation," by Deborah Tannen, *The Washington Post*, June 24, 1990, copyright Deborah Tannen. Reprinted by permission. Fee waived as a professional courtesy. Originally titled "Sex, Lies and Conversation." This article is based in part on the author's book *You Just Don't Understand* (Ballantine, 1990).

Contents

Contents

Introduction

As a linguist and English teacher, I regularly see consequences of our early and not-so-early language training. Often, as people first learn of my profession, they back into a cognitive corner: "Oh, I'll have to watch my grammar," they worry. Or, "I'm not so good at grammar." Or, in a more aggressive stance, they commiserate, "You must hate the way people butcher the language these days." Others may bemoan how "Southerners get their words wrong" or speakers of Black English are just talking "garbage" and are "too lazy to get English right." Many people believe that they can know a person's intelligence or his or her very worth through the language he or she speaks. Such language concerns are shared not only privately, but also publicly at high governmental levels. Indeed, in response to a perceived multilingual menace in the United States, the U.S. House of Representatives even passed an English Language Empowerment Act in August 1996.

It is my hope that this volume will help undo common misconceptions about language. It arose out of my musings and discussions with English-faculty colleagues in which we identified what we hoped a graduating English major would come to know about his or her language. In addition to delving into expository and creative writing, literature, literary theory, and literary criticism, I hoped my students would emerge with a greater understanding of what language is and what it is not.

The contributors to this volume speak to common misinformation on language and help to soften the rules-and-regulations approach to language correctness. If there is a single theme, it is this: when you encounter intense, aggravated claims about language, pause. Indeed, dark claims about language serve as a signal that it is time to step back and look for the fuller picture of what might be going on.

Part I, "Ways of Talking," treats language prescriptivism, the origins of North American dialects, Black English, Ozark/Appalachian English, and sign language. Steven Pinker's chapter, "The Language Mavens," responds to popular anxieties about language. Setting the stage, he observes that language is a human instinct, that all societies have a complex language, and that children develop language without conscious effort or formal lessons and by the age of three speak in fluent grammatical constructions. Yet despite all this, alarmists, the "language mavens," wail that Johnny and Jane can't construct a grammatical sentence between them. Pinker explores the contradiction, locating the roots of such Chicken Little thinking about language in the eighteenth century when intellectual and social currents in London brought about handbooks and style manuals. The early authors of these manuals, given market forces, each tried to outdo the other by including greater numbers of increasingly fastidious rules that no refined person could ignore. Pinker unpacks the folly of a range of well-known prescriptive rules and concludes by showing the logic, elegance, and natural patterns of evolution within the language we all instinctually command.

Where do the many varieties of English in North America come from? Where does African American English come from? In "North American Varieties of English as Byproducts of Population Contacts," Salikoko S. Mufwene argues that all North American varieties of English exhibit traits that are novel and traits that show the influence of neighboring languages (languages in contact). He shows that the English settlers who initially came to America spoke widely different varieties of English. In America, these dialects evolved as speakers came into contact with speakers of other languages (from Europe, Africa, and elsewhere). Indeed, regarding the source of American dialects, Mufwene shows that the mixing of English dialects alone was sufficient to produce new English varieties in North America—in particular, Black English. The other languages just made the scenario more complex; when speakers from other countries came to America, the degree to which they influenced American dialects was directly proportional to the degree to which they were integrated with native English speakers. Mufwene offers a vivid and animated historical account of the origins of North American dialects, with particular focus on Black English.

In "African American Vernacular English Is Not Standard English with Mistakes," Geoffrey K. Pullum addresses a very common view of the English spoken by many (not all) African Americans in relatively segregated black communities. It is widely regarded as just ordinary English marred by ignorant mistakes and carelessness. Pullum argues that it is possible to make out a difference between getting things wrong and following a different set of rules, and he reviews a number of pieces of evidence that African American Vernacular English actually has a different grammar from Standard English: it follows rules just as intricate and systematic as any other language, but they are not the same rules as the rules for Standard English. What's more, he offers clear evidence that at least some African Americans who have written about this language—known in the press since 1996 as "Ebonics"—actually do not know it.

Rebecca S. Wheeler's chapter, "Home Speech as Springboard to School Speech: Oakland's Commendable Work on Ebonics," examines the furor in the United States that erupted over the Oakland, California, school board's Resolution on Ebonics. In December 1996, Oakland recommended that teachers use African American Vernacular English (Black English) in the classroom to help students learn Standard English, yet you'd never know this from the venomous accusations and autonomic reactions that erupted at all levels throughout the United States. Wheeler demonstrates that it makes good sense to use home speech (such as Black English) in the classroom as a stepping stone to help students learn school speech (Standard English), and that Oakland's core insight on Ebonics was indeed commendable.

In "Southern Mountain English: The Language of the Ozarks and Southern Appalachia," Bethany K. Dumas examines linguistic characteristics of Southern Mountain (Ozark and Southern Appalachian) English and briefly traces their history. She then explores evidence for the highly stigmatized nature of what is sometimes called hillbilly talk and suggests that the topic provides a focus for discussing the damage caused by prescriptivist attitudes toward language variation.

In "On the Other Hand: American Sign Language, Signed Englishes, and Other Visual Language Systems," Lynn S. Messing provides an introduction to signed languages and artificial signing systems. She shows that American Sign Language is in fact a real language and possesses the properties common to all languages, but that it is also distinct from other signed and spoken languages. She discusses some of the variety found in the language and reviews the most promising attempts to develop a writing system for it.

In Part II, "Englishes, English-only, and Languages in Danger of Extinction," the contributors examine the spread of English around the world, the English-Only movement, and the loss of languages.

In " 'From Out in Left Field? That's Not Cricket': Finding a Focus for the Language Curriculum," David Crystal explores the implications of English as a global language. He finds that the emerging reality of English as a global language, and of new varieties of the English language, illustrates in a powerful way how the notions of language variety and change should be at the core of any language curriculum. The chapter argues the case for the development of an all-inclusive, linguistically informed, dynamic curriculum in which global trends are seen as a perspective for understanding regional or national realities, and the principles of language variation and change are seen as a means of interrelating historical, social, psychological, and literary curricular issues.

In "Investigating English around the World: The International Corpus of English," Gerald Nelson and Bas Aarts report that the spread of English around the world has been one of the greatest linguistic developments of the twentieth century, mounting to an estimated 350 million people speaking English as a first language and four times that number speaking it as an official second language. Yet the very ubiquity of English brings its own questions: Is it meaningful to speak of English as a single language, or should we simply speak of British English, American English, Indian English, Kenyan English, and so on? Which variety should language teachers, say, in Japan and China teach? Which variety will be most useful internationally in twenty years' time? To answer questions such as these, linguists have turned to computer technology. In this chapter, Nelson and Aarts describe the International Corpus of English, a project that is collecting and computerizing large databases (corpora) of naturally occurring samples of English from twenty different countries or regions around the globe. Based on this work, researchers will be able to produce the first-ever linguistic map of the world.

Geoffrey Nunberg's chapter, "Speaking of America: Why English-only Is a Bad Idea," demonstrates that the English-only story is nonsense from beginning to end. Nunberg explores why the English-only myth is so seductive and finds that language trails symbolic baggage in its wake and frames the notion of national identity in a particular way. He argues that the English-only movement has been successful because it provides a symbolic means of registering dissatisfaction with a range of disquieting social phenomena—not only immigration but also multiculturalism, affirmative action, and even public assistance. Yet ironically, with English becoming a world language, and with 97 percent of Americans speaking English well, never was there a culture or language so little in need of official support.

Mari Rhydwen, in "Language Loss, Our Loss," explains why the current rapid loss of the world's languages is considered detrimental not only to speakers of these languages but to all of us. She starts by imagining a world in which those of us who speak dominant languages are threatened with cultural genocide and goes on to document the causes and extent of language loss, comparing it to the comparable loss of biodiversity. The chapter concludes by describing the benefits of linguistic and cultural diversity and makes a plea to foster it.

In the final part, "Language and Politics, Prejudice, the Media, Creativity, Humor, and Gender," the contributors explore a variety of issues in which language is a key player. George Lakoff's chapter, "Metaphor, Morality, and Politics: Or, Why Conservatives Have Left Liberals in the Dust," is an overview of a book-length study of liberal and conservative conceptual systems. It asks what unifies liberal and conservative positions on a wide range of issues such as abortion, taxation, gun control, welfare, education, the environment, and funding for the arts. The answer is surprising. At the center of liberal and conservative worldviews are opposing models of ideal family life that are mapped onto the political domain by a common metaphor, the nation as a family.

Rae A. Moses writes on "Language as a Weapon of Hate." She describes how the design of language makes it a ready weapon of prejudice. She reviews some of the ways that scholars have studied discrimination and prejudice and then demonstrates how the design features of language contribute to its powerful impact in communicating racist and sexist hate. The study of the language of discrimination also helps us understand the ubiquity of prejudice and the importance of our human capacity to speak.

Colleen Cotter, in "Language and the News Media: Five Facts about the Fourth Estate," looks at media and news language from a sociolinguistic perspective. She points out that the news media has its own culture and its own language patterns at the same time it participates in the communicative routines of the wider society in which it is embedded. She views the media as providing insight into language behavior and processes of linguistic change as well as being a vehicle for the display of agendas and identities, actions that are accomplished through language and the reciprocal interaction of author, audience, and text.

Mark Turner and Gilles Fauconnier's "Life on Mars: Language and the Instruments of Invention" deals with the aspects of creativity in human language. Conceptual integration—"blending"—is a basic cognitive operation for creating new meanings out of old. Recently, it has been argued that conceptual integration is the central mental capacity of human beings, the one that effectively separates them and phylogenetically did separate them from other species. Language is in central ways both an instrument and a product of conceptual integration.

Victor Raskin, in "Laughing at and Laughing with: The Linguistics of Humor and Humor in Literature," introduces humor as an important testing ground both for linguistics and for literature and as yet another area of fruitful cooperation between these disciplines within English departments. Humor research has established itself firmly in the last decade or two as a highly powerful multidisciplinary field, and both linguistics and literary studies have contributed richly to humor research. The chapter focuses on ways in which the two disciplines can interact even on complex and very fashionable theoretical issues while focusing their attention on humor.

When Deborah Tannen's book *You Just Don't Understand* was published in 1990, the idea that women and men have different ways of speaking was not the commonplace it now is. It was that book that brought this concept to the forefront of public awareness. A surprise hit, the book remained on the best-seller list for nearly four years and was translated into twenty-four languages. It is an unusual case of a linguistics crossover book: a book written by a linguistics professor that is read by a general audience. Tannen's "Women and Men in Conversation" is based on the material in that book. In it, Tannen suggests that we can better understand frustrations that occur in conversations with members of the other sex if we think of male-female communication as a kind of cross-cultural communication. With the caveat that not all women and men speak the same way, and that there are many influences on speaking style other than gender, Tannen shows that women's and men's styles can be traced to their childhood socialization in same-sex peer groups. Girls tend to play with a best friend and use language to reinforce their closeness, while boys tend to play in larger groups, where the activity creates closeness and talk is used to maintain independence and negotiate status. These differing foci result in contrasting interpretations of the same conversations.

Denise Troutman's "Breaking Mythical Bonds: African American Women's Language" highlights the social construction of language within African American women's speech community. Four features of language used particularly by African American women are described and illustrated through concrete examples.

I hope that *The Workings of Language* provides you grist for your language mill, enabling you to turn away from common fatalistic incantations about the state of our language. Alarmist and reductionistic, superficial language prescriptions blind us and bind us. We lose sight of the real complexities involved, and we forget to notice the fertile arenas in which language flourishes in our every day. All on its own, no prescription needed.

Rebecca S. Wheeler

I

WAYS OF TALKING

1 ———————————————————————————————————

THE LANGUAGE MAVENS
Steven Pinker

Language is a human instinct. All societies have complex language, and everywhere the languages use the same kinds of grammatical machinery, such as nouns, verbs, auxiliaries and agreement. Normal children develop language without conscious effort or formal lessons, and by the age of 3 they speak in fluent grammatical sentences. Brain damage or congenital conditions can make a retarded person a linguistic savant or a person of high intelligence unable to speak. All this has led many scientists to conclude that there are specialized circuits in the brain, and perhaps specialized genes, that create the gift of articulate speech.

But when you read about language in the popular press, you get a very different picture. Johnny can't construct a grammatical sentence. As educational standards decline and pop culture disseminates the inarticulate ravings and unintelligible patois of surfers, rock stars and valley girls, we are turning into a nation of functional illiterates: misusing "hopefully," confusing "lie" and "lay," treating "bummer" as a sentence, letting our participles dangle.

What is behind this contradiction? If language is as instinctive to humans as dam-building is to beavers, if the design of syntax is coded in our DNA, why does the average American sound like a gibbering fool every time he opens his mouth or puts pen to paper?

The most benign explanation for this apparent contradiction is that the words "rule" and "grammar" have very different meanings to a scientist and to a layperson. The rules people learn (or, more likely, fail to learn) in school are called "prescriptive" rules, prescribing how one *ought* to talk. Scientists studying language propose "descriptive" rules, describing how people *do* talk. Prescriptive and descriptive grammar are simply different things. To a scientist, the fundamental fact of human language is its sheer improbability. Most objects in the universe—rocks, worms, cows, cars—cannot talk. Even in humans, speech comprises an infinitesimal fraction of the noises people's mouths are capable of making. I can arrange a combination of words that explains how octopuses make love or how to build an atom bomb; rearrange the words in even the most minor way, and the result is a sentence with a different meaning or, more likely, word salad. How are we to account for this miracle? What would it take to build a device that could duplicate human language?

Obviously, you would need to build in rules. But *prescriptive* rules? Imagine trying to build a talking machine by designing it to obey rules such as "Don't split infinitives" or "Never begin a sentence with 'because.' " It would just sit there. Prescriptive rules are useless without the much more fundamental rules that create the sentences to begin with. These rules are never mentioned in style manuals because the authors correctly assume that anyone capable of reading the manuals must already know them. No one, not even a valley girl, has to be told not to say "Apples the eat boy" or "Who did you meet John and?" or the vast, vast majority of the trillions of mathematically possible combinations of words. So when a scientist considers all the high-tech mental machinery needed to order words into everyday sentences, prescriptive rules are, at best, inconsequential decorations.

So there is no contradiction, after all, in saying that every normal person can speak grammatically (in the sense of systematically) and ungrammatically (in the sense of nonprescriptively), just as there is no contradiction in saying that a taxi obeys the laws of physics but breaks the laws of Massachusetts.

So whence the popular anxiety? This is where a less than benign explanation comes in. Someone, somewhere, must be making decisions about "correct English" for the rest of us. Who? There is no English Language Academy. The legislators of "correct English," in fact, are an informal network of copy editors, dictionary usage panelists, style manual writers, English teachers, essayists and pundits. Their authority, they claim, comes from their dedication to carrying out standards that maximize the language's clarity, logic, consistency, precision, stability and expressive range. William Safire, who writes the weekly column "On Language" for the *New York Times Magazine*, calls himself a "language maven," from the Yiddish word meaning expert, and this gives us a convenient label for the entire group.

To whom I say: Maven, shmaven! *Kibitzers* and *nudniks* is more like it. For here are the remarkable facts. Most of the prescriptive rules of the language mavens are bits of folklore that originated for screwball reasons several hundred years ago. For as long as they have existed, speakers have flouted them, spawning identical plaints about the imminent decline of the language century after century. The rules conform neither to logic nor to tradition, and if they were ever followed they would force writers into fuzzy, clumsy, incomprehensible prose, in which certain thoughts are not expressible at all. Indeed, most of the "ignorant errors" these rules are supposed to correct display an elegant logic and an acute sensitivity to the grammatical texture of the language, to which the mavens are oblivious.

The scandal of the language mavens began in the eighteenth century. The London dialect had become an important world language, and scholars began to criticize it as they would any institution, in part to question the authority of the aristocracy. Latin was considered the language of enlightenment and was offered as an ideal of precision and logic to which English should aspire. The period also saw unprecedented social mobility, and anyone who wanted to distinguish himself as cultivated had to master the best version of English. These trends created a demand for handbooks and style manuals, which were soon shaped by market forces: the manuals tried to outdo one another by including greater numbers of increasingly fastidious rules that no refined person could afford to ignore. Most of the hobgoblins of prescriptive grammar (don't split infinitives, don't end a sentence with a preposition) can be traced back to these eighteenth-century fads.

Of course, forcing modern speakers of English to not—whoops, not to split an infinitive because it isn't done in Latin makes about as much sense as forcing modern residents of England to wear laurels and togas. Julius Caesar could not have split an infinitive if he had wanted to. In Latin the infinitive is a single word such as *facere*, a syntactic atom. But in English, which prefers to build sentences around many simple words instead of a few complicated ones, the infinitive is composed of two words. Words, by definition, are rearrangeable units, and there is no conceivable reason why an adverb should not come between them:

> Space—the final frontier . . . These are the voyages of the starship *Enterprise*. Its five-year mission: to explore strange new worlds, to seek out new life and new civilizations, to boldly go where no man has gone before.

To *go boldly* where no man has gone before? Beam me up, Scotty; there's no intelligent life down here. As for outlawing sentences that end with a preposition (impossible in Latin for reasons irrelevant to English)—as Winston Churchill said, "It is a rule up with which we should not put."

But once introduced, a prescriptive rule is hard to eradicate, no matter how ridiculous. Inside the writing establishment the rules survive by the same dynamic that perpetuates ritual genital mutilations and college fraternity hazing. Anyone daring to overturn a rule by example must always worry that readers will think he or she is ignorant of the rule, rather than challenging it. Perhaps most importantly, since prescriptive rules are so psychologically unnatural that only those with access to the right schooling can abide by them, they serve as shibboleths, differentiating the elite from the rabble. Throughout the country people have spoken a dialect of English, some of whose features date to the Early Modern English period, that H. L. Mencken called The American Language. It had the misfortune of not becoming the standard of government and education, and large parts of the "grammar" curriculum in U.S. schools have been dedicated to stigmatizing it as sloppy speech.

Frequently the language mavens claim that nonstandard American English is not just different, but less sophisticated and logical. The case, they would have to admit, is hard to make for nonstandard irregular verbs such as "drag/drug" (and even more so for conversions to regularity such as "feeled" and "growed"). After all, in "correct" English, Richard Lederer noted, "Today we speak, but first we spoke; some faucets leak, but never loke. Today we write, but first we wrote; we bite our tongues, but never bote." At first glance, the mavens would seem to have a better argument when it comes to the loss of conjugational distinctions in "He don't" and "We was." But then, this has been the trend in standard English for centuries. No one gets upset that we no longer distinguish the second person singular form of verbs, as in "thou sayest." And by this criterion it is the nonstandard dialects that are superior, because they provide their speakers with second person plural pronouns like "y'all" and "youse."

At this point, defenders of the standard are likely to pull out the notorious double negative, as in "I can't get no satisfaction." Logically speaking, they teach, the two negatives cancel out each other; Mr. Jagger is actually saying that he is satisfied. The song should be titled "I Can't Get *Any* Satisfaction." But this reasoning is not satisfactory. Hundreds of languages require their speakers to use a negative element in the context of a negated verb. The so-called "double negative," far from being a corruption, was the norm in Chaucer's Middle English, and negation in standard French, as in "*Je ne sais pas*" where "*ne*" and "*pas*" are both negative, is a familiar contemporary example. Come to think of it, standard English is really no different. What do "any," "even" and "at all" mean in the following sentences?

> I didn't buy any lottery tickets.
> I didn't eat even a single french fry.
> I didn't eat junk food at all today.

Clearly, not much: you can't use them alone, as the following strange sentences show:

> I bought any lottery tickets.
> I ate even a single french fry.
> I ate junk food at all today.

What these words are doing is exactly what "no" is doing in nonstandard English, such as in the equivalent "I didn't buy no lottery tickets"—agreeing with the negated verb. The slim difference is that nonstandard English co-opted the word "no" as the agreement element, whereas standard English co-opted the word "any."

A tin ear for stress and melody along with an obliviousness to the principles of discourse and rhetoric are important tools of the trade for the language maven. Consider an alleged atrocity committed by today's youth: the expression "I could care less." The teenagers are trying to express disdain, the adults note, in which case they should be saying "I couldn't care less." If they could care less than they do, that means that they really do care, the opposite of what they are trying to say. But the argument is bogus. Listen to how the two versions are pronounced:

```
   COULDN'T care                 |     I
                   LE            |              CARE
 i                    ESS.       |                   LE
                                 |       could           ESS.
```

The melodies and stresses are completely different, and for a good reason. The second version is not illogical, it's *sarcastic*. The point of sarcasm is that by making an assertion that is manifestly false or accompanied by ostentatiously mannered intonation, one deliberately implies its opposite. A good paraphrase is, "Oh yeah, as if there were something in the world that I care less about."

Through the ages, language mavens have deplored the way English speakers convert nouns into verbs. The following verbs have all been denounced in this century: "to caveat," "to input," "to host," "to nuance," "to access," "to chair," "to dialogue," "to showcase," "to progress," "to parent," "to intrigue," "to contact," "to impact." As you can see, they range from varying degrees of awkwardness to the completely unexceptionable. In fact, easy conversion of nouns to verbs has been part of English grammar for centuries. I have estimated that about a fifth of all English verbs were originally nouns. Consider the human body: you can "head" a committee, "scalp" the missionary, "eye" a babe, "stomach" someone's complaints and so on—virtually every body part can be "verbed" (including several that cannot be printed in a family language volume).

What's the problem? The concern seems to be that fuzzy-minded speakers are eroding the distinction between nouns and verbs. But once again, the person on the street is not getting any respect. A simple quirk of everyday usage shows why the accusation is untrue. Take the baseball term "to fly out," a verb that comes from the noun "pop fly." The past form is "flied," not "flew" and "flown"; no mere mortal has ever flown out to center field. Similarly, in using the verb-from-noun "to ring the city" (form a ring around), people say "ringed," not "rang." Speakers' preference for the regular form with "-ed" shows that they tacitly keep track of the fact that the verbs came from nouns. They avoid irregular forms like "flew out" because they sense that the baseball verb "to fly" is different from the ordinary verb "to fly" (what birds do): the first is a verb based on a noun root, the second, a verb with a verb root.

The most remarkable aspect of the special status of verbs-from-nouns is that everyone feels it. I have tried out examples on hundreds of people— college students, people without college educations, children as young as 4. They all behave like good intuitive grammarians: they inflect verbs that come from nouns differently than plain old verbs. So is there anyone, any- where, who does not grasp the principle? Yes—the language mavens. Uni- formly, the style manuals bungle their explanations of "flied out" and similar lawful examples.

I am obliged to discuss one more example: the much vilified "hopefully." A sentence such as "Hopefully, the treaty will pass" is said to be a grave error. The adverb "hopefully" comes from the adjective "hopeful" meaning "in a manner full of hope." Therefore, the mavens say, it should be used only when the sentence refers to a person who is doing something in a hopeful manner. If it is the writer or reader who is hopeful, one should say, "It is hoped that the treaty will pass," or "If hopes are realized, the treaty will pass," or "I hope the treaty will pass."

Now consider the following:

(1) It is simply not true that an English adverb must indicate the manner in which the actor performs the action. Adverbs come in two kinds: "verb phrase" adverbs such as "carefully," which do refer to the actor, and "sen- tence" adverbs such as "frankly," which indicate the attitude of the speaker toward the content of the sentence. Other examples of sentence adverbs are "accordingly," "basically," "confidentially," "happily," "mercifully," "roughly," "supposedly" and "understandably." Many (such as "happily") come from verb phrase adverbs, and they are virtually never ambiguous in context. The use of "hopefully" as a sentence adverb, which has been around for at least sixty years, is a perfectly sensible example.

(2) The suggested alternatives, "It is hoped that" and "If hopes are re- alized," display four sins of bad writing: passive voice, needless words, vagueness, pomposity.

(3) The suggested alternatives do not mean the same thing as "hope- fully," so the ban would leave certain thoughts unexpressible. "Hopefully" makes a hopeful prediction, whereas "I hope that" and "It is hoped that" merely describe certain people's mental states. Thus you can say, "I hope the treaty will pass, but it isn't likely," but it would be odd to say, "Hope- fully, the treaty will pass, but it isn't likely."

(4) We are supposed to use "hopefully" only as a verb phrase adverb, as in the following:

> Hopefully, Larry hurled the ball toward the basket with one second left in the game.
>
> Hopefully, Melvin turned the record over and sat back down on the couch eleven centimeters closer to Ellen.

Call me uncouth, call me ignorant, but these sentences do not belong to any language that I speak.

I have taken these examples from generic schoolmarms, copy editors and writers of irate letters to newspaper ombudsmen. The more famous language mavens come in two temperaments: Jeremiahs and Sages.

The Jeremiahs express their bitter laments and righteous prophesies of doom. The best-known is the film and theater critic John Simon. Here is a representative opening to one of his language columns:

> The English language is being treated nowadays exactly as slave traders once handled the merchandise in their slave ships, or as the inmates of concentration camps were dealt with by their Nazi jailers.

What grammatical horror could have inspired this tasteless comparison, you might ask? It was Tip O'Neill's redundantly referring to his "fellow colleagues."

Speaking of the American Black English dialect, Simon says:

> Why should we consider some, usually poorly educated, subculture's notion of the relationship between sound and meaning? And how could a grammar—any grammar—possibly describe that relationship? . . . As for "I be," "you be," "he be," etc., which should give us all the heebie-jeebies, these may indeed be comprehensible, but they go against all accepted classical and modern grammars and are the product not of a language with roots in history but of ignorance of how language works.

This, of course, is nonsense from beginning to end (Black English is uncontroversially a language with its own systematic grammar), but there is no point in refuting this malicious know-nothing, for he is not participating in any sincere discussion. Simon has simply discovered the trick used with great effectiveness by certain comedians, talk show hosts and punk rock musicians: people of modest talent can attract attention, at least for a while, by being unrelentingly offensive.

The sages, on the other hand, typified by the late Theodore Bernstein and by William Safire himself, take a moderate, commonsense approach to matters of usage, and they tease their victims with wit rather than savaging them with invective. I enjoy reading the sages, and have nothing but awe for a pen like Safire's that can summarize the content of an anti-pornography statute as, "It isn't the teat, it's the tumidity." But the sad fact is that even Safire, the closest thing we have to an enlightened language pundit, misjudges the linguistic sophistication of the common speaker and as a result misses the target in most of his commentaries and advice. To prove this charge, I will walk you through parts of one of his columns, from the October 4, 1992, *New York Times Magazine*.

The first story was a nonpartisan analysis of supposed pronoun case errors made by the two candidates in the 1992 presidential election. George Bush had recently adopted the slogan "Who do you trust?," alienating schoolteachers across the nation who noted that "who" is a subject pronoun and the question is asking about the object of "trust." One would say "You do trust him," not "You do trust he," and so the question word should be "whom," not "who."

In reply, one might point out that the "who/whom" distinction is a relic of the English case system, abandoned by nouns centuries ago and found today only among pronouns in distinctions such as "he/him." Even among pronouns, the old distinction between subject "ye" and object "you" has vanished, leaving "you" to play both roles and "ye" as sounding archaic. Though "whom" has outlived "ye," it is clearly moribund, and already sounds pretentious in most spoken contexts. No one demands of Bush that he say, "Whom do ye trust?" If the language can bear the loss of "ye," why insist on clinging to "whom"?

Safire, with his reasonable attitude toward usage, recognizes the problem, and proposes:

> Safire's Law of Who/Whom, which forever solves the problem troubling writers and speakers caught between the pedantic and the incorrect: "When *whom* is correct, recast the sentence." Thus, instead of changing his slogan to "Whom do you trust?"—making him sound like a hypereducated Yalie stiff—Mr. Bush would win back the purist vote with "Which candidate do you trust?"

Telling people to avoid a problematic construction sounds like common sense, but in the case of object questions with "who," it demands an intolerable sacrifice. People ask questions about the objects of verbs and prepositions *a lot*. Consider the kinds of questions one might ask a child in ordinary conversation: "Who did we see on the way home?," "Who did you play with outside tonight?," "Who did you sound like?" Safire's advice is to change such questions to "Which person . . . ?" or "Which child . . . ?" But the advice would have people violate the most important maxim of good prose: omit needless words. It also subverts the supposed goal of rules of usage, which is to allow people to express their thoughts as clearly and precisely as possible. A question such as "Who did we see on the way home?" can embrace one person, many people or any combination or number of adults, babies and familiar dogs. Any specific substitution such as "Which person?" forecloses some of these possibilities. Extremism in defense of liberty is no vice. Safire should have taken his observation about "whom" to its logical conclusion and advised the president that there is no reason to change the slogan, at least no grammatical reason.

Turning to the Democrats, Safire gets on Bill Clinton's case, as he puts it, for asking voters to "give Al Gore and I a chance to bring America back." No one would say "give I a break," because the indirect object of "give" must have objective case. So it should be "give Al Gore and me a chance."

Probably no "grammatical error" has received as much scorn as the "misuse" of pronoun case inside conjunctions (phrases with two parts joined by "and" or "or"). What teenager has not been corrected for saying "Me and Jennifer are going to the mall"? The standard story is that the object pronoun "me" does not belong in the subject position—no one would say "Me is going to the mall"— so it should be "Jennifer and I." People tend to misremember the advice as, "When in doubt, say 'so-andso and I,' not 'so-and-so and me,' " so they unthinkingly overapply it, resulting in hyper-corrected solecisms like "give Al Gore and I a chance" and the even more despised "between you and I."

But if the person on the street is so good at avoiding "Me is going" and "Give I a break," and even former Rhodes Scholars and Ivy League graduates can't seem to avoid "Me and Jennifer are going" and "Give Al and I a chance," might it be the mavens that misunderstand English grammar, not the speakers? The mavens' case about case rests on one assumption: if a conjunction phrase has a grammatical feature like subject case, every word inside that phrase has to have that grammatical feature, too. But that is just false.

"Jennifer" is singular; you say "Jennifer is," not "Jennifer are." The pronoun "she" is singular; you say "She is," not "She are." But the conjunction "She and Jennifer" is not singular, it's plural; you say "She and Jennifer are," not "She and Jennifer is." So a conjunction can have a different grammatical number from the pronouns inside it. Why, then, must it have the same grammatical *case* as the pronouns inside it? The answer is that it need not. A conjunction is not grammatically equivalent to any of its parts. If John and Marsha met, it does not mean that John met and that Marsha met. If voters give Clinton and Gore a chance, they are not giving Gore his own chance, added on to the chance they are giving Clinton; they are giving the entire ticket a chance. So just because "Al Gore and I" is an object that requires object case, it does not mean that "I" is an object that requires object case. By the logic of grammar, the pronoun is free to have any case it wants.

In his third story Safire deconstructs a breathless quote from Barbra Streisand, describing tennis star Andre Agassi: "He's very, very intelligent; very, very, sensitive, very evolved; . . . He plays like a Zen master. It's very in the moment."

Safire speculates on Streisand's use of the word "evolved": "its change from the active to passive voice—from 'he *evolved from* the Missing Link' to 'He *is evolved*'—was probably influenced by the adoption of *involved* as a compliment."

These kinds of derivations have been studied intensively in linguistics, but Safire shows here that he does not appreciate how they work. He seems to think that people change words by being reminded of rhyming ones—"evolved" from "involved," a kind of malapropism. But in fact people are not that literal-minded. New usages (such as "to fly out") are based not on rhymes but on systematic rules that change the grammatical behavior of dozens of words in the same precise ways.

Thus Safire's suggestion that "very evolved" is based on "involved" does not work at all. For one thing, if you're involved, it means that something involves you (you're the object), whereas if you're evolved, it means that you have been doing some evolving (you're the subject). The problem is that the conversion of "evolved from" to "very evolved" is not a switch from the active voice of a verb to the passive voice, as in "Andre beat Boris" to "Boris was beaten by Andre." To passivize a verb you convert the direct object into a subject, so "is evolved" could only have been passivized from "Something evolved Andre"—which does not exist in contemporary English. Safire's explanation is like saying you can take "Bill bicycled from Lexington" and change it to "Bill is bicycled" and then to "Bill is very bicycled."

This breakdown is a good illustration of one of the main scandals of the language mavens: they show lapses in elementary problems of grammatical analysis, like figuring out the part-of-speech category of a word. In analyzing "very evolved," Safire refers to the active and passive voices, two forms of a verb. But the preceding adverb "very" is an unmistakable tip-off that "evolved" is not being used as a verb at all but as an adjective. Safire was misled because adjectives can look like verbs in the passive voice, and are clearly related to them, but they are not the same thing. This is the ambiguity behind the joke in the Bob Dylan lyric, "They'll stone you when you're riding in your car; They'll stone you when you're playing your guitar. . . . Everybody must get stoned."

This discovery steers us toward the real source of "evolved." There is a lively rule in English that takes the participle of certain intransitive verbs and creates a corresponding adjective:

    a leaf that has fallen → a fallen leaf
    snow that has drifted → the drifted snow
    a man who has traveled widely → a widely traveled man

Take this rule and apply it to "a tennis player who has evolved," and you get "an evolved tennis player." This solution also allows us to make sense of Streisand's meaning. When a verb is converted from the active to the passive voice, the verb's meaning is conserved: "Dog bites man" = "Man is bitten by dog." But when a verb is converted to an adjective, the adjective can acquire idiosyncratic nuances. Not every woman who has fallen is a fallen woman, and if someone stones you you are not necessarily stoned. We all evolved from a missing link, but not all of us are evolved in the sense of being more spiritually sophisticated than our contemporaries.

Safire then goes on to rebuke Streisand for "very in the moment":

> This *very* calls attention to the use of a preposition or a noun as a modifier, as in "It's very *in*," or "It's very *New York*," or the ultimate fashion compliment, "It's very *you*." To be very *in the moment* (perhaps a variation of *of the moment* or *up to the minute*) appears to be a loose translation of the French *au courant*, variously translated as "up to date, fashionable, with-it" . . .

Once again, by patronizing Streisand's language, Safire has misanalyzed its form and its meaning. He has not noticed that:

(1) The word "very" is not connected to the preposition "in"; it's connected to the entire prepositional phrase "in the moment."

(2) Streisand is not using the intransitive "in," with its special sense of "fashionable"; she is using the conventional transitive "in," with a noun phrase object "the moment."

(3) Her use of a prepositional phrase as if it were an adjective to describe some mental or emotional state follows a common pattern in English: "under the weather," "out of character," "off the wall," "in the dumps," "out to lunch," "on the ball" and "out of his mind."

(4) It's unlikely that Streisand was trying to say that Agassi is au courant or fashionable; that would be a put-down implying shallowness, not a compliment. Her reference to Zen makes her meaning clear: that Agassi is good at shutting out distractions and concentrating on the game or person he is involved with at that moment.

The foibles of the language mavens, then, can be blamed on two blind spots: a gross underestimation of the linguistic wherewithal of the common person and an ignorance of the science of language—not just technical linguistics, but basic knowledge of the constructions and idioms of English, and of how people use them.

Unlike some academics in the '60s, I am not saying that concern for grammar and composition are tools to perpetuate an oppressive status quo and that The People should be liberated to write however they please. Some aspects of how people express themselves in some settings *are* worth trying to change. What I am calling for is a more thoughtful discussion of language and how people use it, replacing *bubbe-maises* (old wives' tales) with the best scientific knowledge available. It is ironic that the jeremiads wailing about how sloppy language leads to sloppy thought are themselves hairballs of loosely associated factoids and tangled non sequiturs. All the examples of verbal behavior that the complainer takes exception to for any reason are packed together and coughed up as proof of The Decline of the Language: teenage slang, sophistry, regional variations in pronunciation and vocabulary, bureaucratic bafflegab, poor spelling and punctuation, pseudo-errors like "hopefully," government euphemism, nonstandard grammar like "ain't," misleading advertising, and so on (not to mention occasional witticisms that go over the complainer's head).

I hope to have convinced you of two things. Many prescriptive rules are just plain dumb and should be deleted from the handbooks. And most of standard English is just that, standard, in the sense of standard units of currency or household voltages. It is just common sense that people should be encouraged to learn the dialect that has become the standard in their society. But there is no need to use terms like "bad grammar," "fractured syntax" and "incorrect usage" when referring to rural, black and other nonstandard dialects (even if you dislike "politically correct" euphemism): the terms are not only insulting but scientifically inaccurate.

The aspect of language use that is most worth changing is the clarity and style of written prose. The human language faculty was not designed for putting esoteric thoughts on paper for the benefit of strangers, and this makes writing a difficult craft that must be mastered through practice, feedback and intensive exposure to good examples. There are excellent manuals of composition that discuss these skills with great wisdom—but note how their advice concentrates on important practical tips like "omit needless words" and "revise extensively," not on the trivia of split infinitives and slang.

As for slang, I'm all for it! I don't know how I ever did without "to flame," "to dis" and "to blow off," and there are thousands of now unexceptionable English words such as "clever," "fun," "sham," "banter" and "stingy" that began life as slang. It is especially hypocritical to oppose linguistic innovations reflexively and at the same time to decry the loss of distinctions like "lie" versus "lay" on the pretext of preserving expressive power. Vehicles for expressing thought are being created far more quickly than they are being abandoned.

Indeed, appreciating the linguistic genius of your ordinary Joe is the cure for the deepest fear of the mavens: that English is steadily deteriorating. Every component of every language changes over time, and at any moment a language is enduring many losses. But the richness of a language is always being replenished, because the one aspect of language that does not change is the very thing that creates it: the human mind.

2

North American Varieties of English as Byproducts of Population Contacts
Salikoko S. Mufwene

PRELIMINARIES

In the layperson's universe of knowledge, the fact that North American varieties of English are different from their British counterparts has generally been accepted without too much curiosity. The state of affairs seems as normal as the fact that there is variation within British English and within American English as national varieties. Such realities are as natural as the fact that races differ from each other physically, or that ethnic groups differ from each other culturally. He or she need not understand how such variation has developed, and the question may in fact be dismissed with the otherwise correct observation that there is beauty in diversity.

In the case of the United States, this perspective on variation has been true mostly when applied to its White-majority population. English varieties spoken especially by African Americans have attracted the attention not only of dialect experts but also of lay people, both of whom have fostered the following myths:

1. With perhaps the exception of Southern English, North American varieties of English spoken by Whites are slightly modified continuations of those brought from the British Isles. The reason for this divergence is that British English dialects have changed since the seventeenth century, and isolation by the Atlantic Ocean has prevented North American varieties from participating in the same changes. North American English is simply more conservative than British English.

2. At best, African American English varieties bear influence from the languages spoken by the Africans brought to the New World during the colonial period. The worst hypothesis, associated with Gonzales (1922),

conjectured that the Africans are intellectually too indolent and physio-
logically incapable of acquiring the English system, which they misshaped.

Contrary to this second myth, early dialectologists such as Krapp (1924), Kurath (1928), and Johnson (1930) argued that African Americans speak archaic English spoken during colonial days by the poor Whites with whom they interacted. That is, their English consists of conservative retentions from the varieties spoken by the vastly proletarian European colonists of the seventeenth and eighteenth centuries. In Krapp's own words: "The Negroes, indeed, in acquiring English have done their work so thoroughly that they have retained not a trace of any African speech. Neither have they transferred anything of importance from their native tongues to the general language" (1924, 190).

According to these early dialectologists, the underprivileged Whites from whom the Africans acquired their English have outgrown it, but African Americans have been stuck in it, so to speak, due to social isolation. This hypothesis made no allowance for influence of African languages on African American varieties of English, a state of affairs that would be unusual in any case where a language has been appropriated by a different community as a vernacular, that is, a variety for day-to-day communication within itself. Understandably, Turner (1949) disputes the position, concluding from his study, which highlights several phonological and morphosyntactic similarities between Gullah[1] and diverse African languages, that the "dialect" (as he called it) "is indebted to African sources" (254). He thereby emphasizes the importance of language contact in its development, a view that has been extended to mainland varieties of African American English now typically identified by linguists as African American Vernacular English (AAVE) (for a sample of Gullah and AAVE, see the Appendix to this chapter).

Extrapolations of Turner's hypothesis have been identified as the *substrate hypothesis*. Their proponents argue that African languages played a central role in shaping the structures of Gullah and AAVE. According to them, the systems of these language varieties and their Caribbean kin, such as Jamaican Patois and Saramaccan (spoken in Surinam), are patterned on those of the African languages spoken by the ancestors of people of African descent in the New World. Some of them also argue that AAVE started as a Gullah-like *creole* and has been changing to become more and more like the English dialects spoken by White Americans, by a process called *decreolization*.[2] This position is known as the *creole origins hypothesis*.

Although they never say so, proponents of both the dialectologist and substrate hypotheses have typically suggested that contact has little to do with why White American varieties of English are different from their British counterparts. In this respect they are alike, as they treat AAVE and Gullah as nonordinary developments from English. In this chapter, I argue that all North American varieties of English evolved out of dialect and language contact. I defend several positions both in partial support of and against the other assumptions presented above. My main theses are the following:

1. One of the reasons why African American English is different from other North American varieties of English is undoubtedly *substrate influence*, that is, influence from the languages spoken by the Africans who shifted to English and appropriated it as their vernacular. However, the nature and extent of that influence still remain to be better understood and assessed, especially since some of the features hitherto considered as African American peculiarities are also attested in nonstandard British English dialects and other nonstandard White vernaculars in the Americas, Australia, and New Zealand.[3]

2. All North American varieties of English are different from, and show only variable partial similarities to, British English dialects spoken today or during the colonial period. The variable nature of this connection reflects not only the *restructuring*[4] undergone by British English since the seventeenth century but also those changes that are germane to the appropriation of English as a vernacular by White immigrants in North America.

3. Not all Whites who immigrated to North America were native speakers of English. A large proportion of the early European immigrants, especially in the Southern colonies, were indentured servants from different nationalities, including Ireland, Germany, and France. They acquired English under conditions very similar to those of their African cohorts during the early stages of colonization.

4. Some Northern colonies were initially settled by the French (e.g., Maine) and by the Dutch (e.g., New Jersey and New York). The transfer of these territories to the English and the gradual shift of the earlier colonists to English as their vernacular entailed its acquisition as a second language, with all that is entailed by such a process, notably, substrate influence from languages previously spoken by such colonists.[5]

5. A lot in the social history of North America suggests that the language-restructuring process was similar in kind among both European and African immigrants, although the languages that came in contact with each other differ in some of their structural properties, for instance, in how they expressed possession ("John's book" or "John book"), whether or not the subject and the (auxiliary) verb must be inverted in a main-clause question ("Has Mary gone?" or "Mary has gone?"), or whether the copula is required before a nonverbal predicate ("The cow is big" or "The cow big"). Such structural variation bears on the outcome of the restructuring process, depending on the specific makeup of each contact setting and how its patterns of social interaction affect language transmission.

6. Today's British English is to some extent the result of similar processes that took place in the United Kingdom, but under somewhat different ecological conditions of language contact.

7. An important challenge for us is to understand the *ecology of language* and how it affects restructuring qua system reorganization. This notion, which is borrowed from biology, subsumes as much the social environment in which a language (variety) is used as language-internal factors that affect its evolution, in particular, the range of variants competing with each other for the same functions. The interaction of language-internal with language-external factors (e.g., social stigma associated with particular variants) can punctuate the equilibrium and trigger a change.

CONTACT AND THE EVOLUTION OF ENGLISH IN THE COLONIAL PERIOD

Much of It Began in the British Isles

It may be argued, justifiably, that the restructuring of English in North America started in the British Isles, although it took different paths, which led to divergent results on this and the other side of the Atlantic. Much of today's United Kingdom was an English colony when England undertook the colonization of North America in the seventeenth century. In Ireland, English was spoken very much as it is today in several former British colonies of Asia and Africa, that is, as a colonial language used mostly by the elite and as a second language variety by the vast majority of its speakers. The Irish still spoke dialects of Gaelic, a Celtic language, whose structures differ in several ways from Germanic languages. It was actually in the post-Cromwellian era (in the seventeenth century) that English in Ireland started spreading to rural areas, being adopted as a vernacular (Hickey 1995). The latter process has continued until recently, despite the pro-Gaelic movement.

The English colonization of North America and of other parts of the world was a response to an economic crisis at home involving widespread unemployment. This triggered many population movements in the British Isles. In part, people migrated from Scotland, from the northern part of England, and from Ireland to seek jobs in London and other southern English cities such as Bristol and Liverpool. When there were no jobs, many of the destitute indentured themselves and continued their migrations to North America to work as servants on farms and plantations. Such immigrants, many of whom spoke English as a second language variety, constituted 50–75 percent of the European colonial population in the Chesapeake (Virginia and Maryland) in the seventeenth century. In their midst were also other Europeans from Germany, France, Holland, and other nations.

These population movements led to new contacts among English speakers both in the British Isles and in North America, producing the restructuring that has resulted in present-day dialects of English in the United

Kingdom and North America. Differences in social mixes and interaction led to divergent varieties of English regionally and socially, more or less like variation in the proportions of ingredients in a recipe produces different varieties of basically the same dish or what may be considered different dishes altogether (Mufwene 1996a). As English was gradually appropriated as a vernacular in Ireland, it turned into what is known today as Irish English, that is, English with influence from Gaelic, in the same way as West African English can be described as English with influence from West African languages and Indian English as English with influence from Indic languages. Likewise, English varieties in North America bear influence of some of the languages that English came in contact with.

A Sociohistorical Ecology of the Evolution of English in North America

In North America, the Irish seldom settled in communities that were exclusively Irish, but there are some, such as in the Appalachian and Ozark mountains, where their and the Scotch-Irish presence as a founder population was very significant and a Gaelic element may be claimed in what is called Appalachian and Ozark English. This is sociologically similar to the case of Jewish communities in the nineteenth and twentieth centuries in New York, which led to the development of Yinglish, and of Italian communities, which are associated with Italian English. These examples are cited to illustrate that degree of social integration in North America accounts inversely for the extent of non-English influence in the varieties that developed on this side of the Atlantic.

According to socioeconomic historians such as Bailyn (1986), Fischer (1989), and Kulikoff (1986), there also was variation in patterns of settlements. This accounts partly for regional differences among the dialects that developed in the North American colonies (i.e., not taking into account later developments in the states that joined the Union after the Revolution).[6] The founder populations of New England consisted predominantly of Puritan family units that migrated from East Anglia and engaged in family-run subsistence farms that used little indentured or slave labor. They continued to interact among themselves in much the same way as they did in the metropole. Despite influence from speakers of other languages (e.g., French) and of other dialects (e.g., maritime English) with which they came in contact, New England's English is said to have remained the closest to British English because of those original settlement patterns of the founder colonists.

On the other hand, the Chesapeake colonies were settled from more diverse places and socioeconomic classes in the British Isles. The plantocrats, who descended largely from British aristocratic families, came in family units and mostly from southern English cities, notably the London area

(Fischer 1989). The indentured servants, who, by the mid-seventeenth century, constituted up to 75 percent of the White labor in some places (Kulikoff 1986; Fischer 1989), came not only from southern English counties but also from northern England, and many also from Ireland and Scotland. In addition, as noted earlier, some indentured servants were also from Germany, Holland, and other continental European countries. The vast majority of these proletarian colonists were male, in their prime, and single. They were joined in their ranks by African slaves, who constituted 15 percent of the total colonial population in the region by the end of the seventeenth century, according to Tate (1965), and 38 percent by the end of the eighteenth century, according to Perkins (1988).

Even if we assume that Europeans interacted mostly among themselves and that the Africans had limited contacts with them (however, cf. the sections under the headings "AAVE and Caribbean Vernaculars" and "The Development of AAVE and Gullah"), interactions between these populations of different ethnolinguistic backgrounds were bound to produce new English varieties in the Chesapeake, laying the groundwork for some of the American varieties of English spoken in the region today. The outcome of this mix alone would be consistent with, and parallel to, changes that British English underwent during the same period as a consequence of population movements that took place in the British Isles, for the same reasons that led to the English colonization of North America, Australia, and other places around the world (Bailyn 1986). That is, with or without the presence of Africans in North America, new varieties of English would have developed in this part of the world, as they did in Australia, the Falkland Islands, and other British settlement colonies (Trudgill 1986).

Noteworthy about settlements in these regions is that there was interesting discrimination among the European colonists not only by socioeconomic class but apparently also by nationality. Mostly non-English Europeans, especially among those who did not come as indentured labor, were directed to settle on the frontiers, with the Germans mostly in the swampy portions of the Chesapeake, whence the development of Pennsylvania Dutch and of German English in Virginia. The Scotch-Irish were directed to the Appalachian Mountains. In the eighteenth century, many of these settlers came in family units, having sold everything they owned at home to pay for their way. The demographic prominence of the (Scotch-) Irish in the Appalachian Mountains accounts for similarities that some linguists have posited between Appalachian English and (Scotch-)Irish English. In the latter case, common Gaelic influence—rather than (Scotch-)Irish English, which was just developing during the same time—accounts for the common element.

These observations suggest that the isolation of (descendants of) Africans by race segregation in part extended an interactional practice already in place among Europeans, in much the same way as slave labor was an ex-

treme extension of the indentured-labor practice, which is sometimes identified in historical literature as White servitude. The linguistic consequences
from these socioeconomic aspects of the American colonial societies are
likewise very similar. The less integrated a group is within the larger community speaking the target language, the more divergent the emerging dialect is likely to be.[7]

The coastal colonies of South Carolina and Georgia developed on slightly
different patterns, with a smaller proportion of European indentured labor
in the swampy settlements, which launched early into rice cultivation.[8]
There the plantocrats resorted early to African slave labor, and these became the majority within less than fifty years of the foundation of South
Carolina (Wood 1974) and within about the same time in Georgia (Coleman 1978). Racial segregation was first institutionalized in these colonies
(in 1720 in South Carolina, according to Wood 1974), and this prevented
regular interaction outside the workplace between Europeans (especially the
few native English speakers) and non-Europeans. Communication in colonial English primarily among the Africans themselves led to the development of Gullah, the African American English variety found to be the
most different from continental middle-class English and identified by linguists as a creole (as defined in note 2).

Gullah speakers' claim that they speak English is, however, justified by
the fact that Gullah has inherited about 95 percent of its vocabulary and
many of its peculiar grammatical features from English (Cassidy 1980, 7),
despite the undeniable influence of African languages. The common reason
for disfranchising it as a separate language, that it is not intelligible to
speakers of other English varieties, is not a valid one. Some British and
Australian English varieties are no more easily intelligible to Americans
than Gullah is. Despite undeniable grammatical and phonological differences, many difficulties with interpreting any nonstandard English variety
have to do with the interpreter's linguistic background and attitude to the
variety. Myths of Gullah being unintelligible to outsiders, which is often
also claimed of AAVE (to which I return below), must be interpreted taking
into account these observations.

What makes settlement patterns and types of colonization relevant to
accounts of dialect differences is the following observation. The same colonial settings in which Gullah emerged also produced what may be called
plantation English, spoken by White Americans who grew up on those
coastal plantations. This variety should not be confused with American
White Southern English and is closer to varieties of English spoken by
White Bahamians and Caribbeans. Such parallel developments between the
Caribbean, coastal South Carolina, and coastal Georgia suggest that African American and European American speech in colonial settings did not
develop independently of each other. The common elements are the English
varieties brought from England, which (descendants of) both Africans and

Europeans restructured in their respective communities, and the influences that these groups exerted on each other, despite their separate developments. I return to this question below, trying to explain how such cross-territory influences are to be interpreted.

Precursors of AAVE

Accounts of the origins of AAVE have been more controversial than those of Gullah and other North American English varieties. Here, I present some relevant sociohistorical facts that highlight its kinship to White non-standard vernaculars, to which it owes most of its structural features. I argue that even in this case one cannot deny the influence of African languages and colonial English varieties spoken by (descendants of) Africans in the Caribbean. However, such influence must be interpreted in the sense of convergence, favoring alternatives already available in the target language, rather than in the sense of import of foreign elements into the system. Moreover, even if one insists that the Caribbean slaves imported to North American colonies spoke creole varieties rather than English, many of the putative creoles' features are still traceable to colonial English itself.

These observations are not intended to suggest that some of today's descendants of English varieties spoken in the Caribbean, especially in the seventeenth century, are not creoles. Some varieties spoken today in Barbados, Jamaica, and Guyana certainly are, especially those identified as basilectal, because their structural features are the most different from those of the local standard English varieties. However, it is debatable whether the same social dialects had already developed in the seventeenth century. Evidence from individuals such as Tituba and Candy, of the Salem witch trials (1692), are not incontrovertible, despite Cassidy's (1986) claim that their speech contains "creole" features and therefore that AAVE and Gullah may have a Barbadian creole origin. When they were tried for witchcraft, Tituba, a Carib Indian woman, and Candy, a Black woman, had arrived recently from Barbados. However, it is not clear how long Candy, who is claimed by Cassidy to have had more "creole" features, had lived in Barbados before coming to Massachusetts nor how representative of other Barbadian or Caribbean slaves her competence in English was.

In her testimony, Candy refers to both Africa and Barbados: "Candy no witch in her country. Candy's mother no witch. Candy no witch, Barbados." This discourse chunk may in fact be interpreted to suggest that Candy had not lived long in Barbados, which was a slave-dispersal point. Besides, her speech contains normal English features too, like the possessive *her* and the Saxon genitive in *Candy's mother*. The absence of a locative preposition before *Barbados* is not a "creole" characteristic. Her speech may have been a normal interlanguage.[9]

Regarding the origins of AAVE, the ambivalence of the evidence from the Salem witch trials is highlighted by other colonial evidence. Advertisements about runaway slaves in the eighteenth century typically describe slaves who originated in the Caribbean or had lived long enough in North America as speaking (moderately) "good English," whereas they describe those who had just arrived from Africa as speaking no, little, or bad English (Brasch 1981). Focusing on the representation of "Black English" in the media, Brasch also observes that representations of deviations from the White norms do not start until the mid-eighteenth century, which suggests that there probably was not much that distinguished African from White nonnative English conspicuously before then. Thus Candy's speech in the Salem witch trials texts may be an isolated incident if it is not a normal case of interlanguage.

I argue below that AAVE and North American White vernaculars diverged most noticeably toward the end of the nineteenth century. The divergence must have occurred after the Jim Crow laws were passed in Southern states in 1877. Among other things, the laws fostered separate residential areas and public facilities for African and European Americans; hence they prevented the groups from interacting regularly across ethnic boundaries. Such social practices favored the divergence of ethnic dialects, even if African and European Americans met at the workplace.

When Did AAVE Develop?

A brief retrospect of the social history of the American southeastern colonies will help explain my conjecture that AAVE diverged later, rather than earlier, from other American English vernaculars. The first Africans in an English North American colony arrived in Virginia in 1619. A Dutch frigate traded twenty of them for food. Virginia aristocrats acquired them as indentured servants in more or less the same status as European indentured servants in the state. These first Africans worked mostly as domestics and were freed, or bought their freedom, at the completion of the same five-to-seven-year period of indenture. In turn, they acquired land and hired their own indentured servants (including Europeans) to cultivate it. The term *slaves* was seldom used then. When it was, it applied equally to Africans and Europeans, describing their living conditions, but not discriminating among them in status (Tate 1965). It took up to the end of the seventeenth century before the Africans were denied the same kind of entitlements as the European indentured servants, first on the basis of religion and later on the basis of race. To be sure, the Africans started losing many of these rights in the mid-seventeenth century, but the practice, including servitude for life, was codified into law in 1705.

By the beginning of the eighteenth century, the Africans represented no more than 15 percent of the Chesapeake colonial population. They worked mostly as domestics or on small farms, with higher concentrations in the coastal areas than in the hinterlands. They lived together with the European indentured laborers and there is reason to believe that even if the slaves imported from the Caribbean had brought any creolelike varieties with them, the kind of English that developed among Africans in these Chesapeake colonial settings was basically the same as the colonial English spoken by the low-class Europeans with whom they worked and sometimes had children. At least there was no reason for the slave children born in the colony in the seventeenth century to speak or develop a creole, that is, a contact-based vernacular so different from its White counterparts that it may be considered a separate language. They just spoke what the children of the European colonists spoke.

Local births, rather than slave imports, were an important factor in the slave population increase in the Chesapeake by 1670 (Thomas 1997). These creole slaves spoke colonial English, just like the White creoles they grew up with (see the following section). Gradually, their linguistic patterns became the primary models for the nonnative slaves, including those imported from the Caribbean until the early eighteenth century. By this time, as in South Carolina, the Chesapeake plantocrats found it more lucrative to invest in slaves imported directly from Africa. Their slaves grew to nearly 40 percent of the total colonial population by the end of the eighteenth century (Perkins 1988). This ethnographic shift created conditions in which more newly arriving Africans learned English not only from the creole slaves but also from other nonnative, seasoned slaves. As the proportion of noncreole slaves increased, the conditions became ripe for the gradual restructuring of colonial English into AAVE. The process was, however, not as extensive nor as rapid as in coastal South Carolina and Georgia, where the proportion of slaves often reached 90 percent of the colonial population, the death rate was high, and the population replacement was rapid in order to keep up with labor demands in the ever-growing rice fields (Mufwene 1996b).

As the proportion of native speakers got smaller and smaller, English got more and more restructured away from European American vernaculars, although the lexical and grammatical materials being rearticulated into new systems still originated from colonial English. Overall, we can conjecture that the earliest forms of AAVE and Gullah as separate vernaculars did not develop before the eighteenth century. The absence of documentation of these vernaculars during the seventeenth century (Brasch 1981) may be a reflection of the absence of such divergent varieties in those early colonial communities.

AAVE and Caribbean Vernaculars

The Virginia colony had started over a decade earlier than St. Kitts and Barbados. St. Kitts was the first English colony in the Caribbean, but Barbados became perhaps the most important slave-dispersal point for British

colonies later in the seventeenth century. In any case, Virginia started im-
porting slaves not only before these Caribbean colonies were in a position
to export slaves but even before they were founded. Although during its
rough beginnings, marked by war with the French part of the island, English St. Kitts lost a small fraction of its planters and slaves to Virginia and
other colonies, Virginia must have bought a significant proportion of its
slaves from non-English colonies and sometimes even straight from Africa,
especially before 1650. By the founder principle, that founder slave population, with its apparently large proportion of locally born children, is more
likely to have influenced AAVE's development than the slaves imported
later from the English Caribbean did.

The initial conditions in all colonies (over fifty years in the case of the
Chesapeake) generally favored the development of slaves' vernaculars structurally close to those of European colonists. This is in contrast with language evolution in the later stages, during which race segregation was in
force and the different groups influenced each other's evolving patterns only
minimally, except for the obvious fact that they all were targeting English.
As noted earlier, the Black creole children spoke like their White creole
counterparts during those early stages of colonization. All children were
generally looked after together while their parents worked together in the
fields.[10] The children's vernaculars were thus very similar, and their speech
patterns as adults would become the norm up to the early or mid-eighteenth
century. Their impact on the development of AAVE would be more determinative than any vernaculars that Caribbean slaves as newcomers brought
with them to the Chesapeake.

Things developed differently in the South Carolina colony, which was
founded in 1670 by Europeans and Africans from Barbados. The Africans
were identified as slaves from the very beginning. Within fifty years, they
constituted double the European colonial population (two-thirds of the
overall colonial population), and they maintained this ratio up to 1740. It
was only by the end of the eighteenth century that they became a minority
again in the overall population, corresponding to a little over two-thirds of
the European colonial populations (about 40 percent of the overall colonial
population). However, on the coastal plantations, they were often tenfold
the European population throughout the eighteenth century. Fears of a
racial and political takeover by the "Black majority" led to early segregation of the populations of European and African descents on the rice fields
(Wood 1974) and hence to a more merciless rule of the oppressed. These
conditions entailed that from the early stages of the colony there was little
interaction across races outside the workplace. Such living conditions favored early determinative influence of African languages on the emerging
local vernaculars and hence early divergence of English varieties spoken by
descendants of Africans and Europeans in the coastal region.

The English variety spoken by descendants of Africans on the coast of

South Carolina is known as Gullah and has been identified as a creole. Of all the vernaculars associated with African Americans, it is the one that diverges the most from (White) middle-class varieties in North America. It is more similar to Bahamian and Caribbean varieties likewise identified as creoles. Gullah is also spoken in coastal Georgia, which also developed primarily on rice agriculture. Georgia was founded in 1733 from England as a buffer and slave-free colony. However, by 1752 some planters migrated from South Carolina and brought their slaves with them. Little by little living conditions similar to those in South Carolina spread, with the vast majority of the slave population concentrated on the coastal rice fields, where no more than 10 percent of the European population lived. At least until the end of the eighteenth century, a minority of slaves lived on farms of the hinterlands, a minority within the vast majority of the European population, most of whom were yeomen. Here, the socioeconomic conditions did not favor rigid segregation if this was already in place. Such differing socioeconomic conditions between the coast and the hinterlands produced different linguistic developments: as in South Carolina, Gullah either developed or thrived along the coast, whereas what is identified today as AAVE developed in the hinterlands.

AAVE and Gullah

Despite speculations that AAVE developed from a Gullah-like variety that was widely spoken among Africans in colonial America, note first that South Carolina and Georgia were colonized, respectively, 63 and 126 years later than Virginia, and it was from the latter state that the founder slave population was imported to work on the cotton plantations of the hinterlands colonies (Kulikoff 1986). The conditions that led to the development of Gullah did not obtain in Virginia, where the slave population never exceeded 40 percent of the colonial population by the end of the eighteenth century (Perkins 1988), although it must be acknowledged that in the coastal marshes, where the Europeans were less resistant to malaria, this ratio was certainly often exceeded. However, the high proportion of Africans was relative to the overall size of the colonial population in the region. The majority of this population lived in the hinterlands, and there were mostly small farms in coastal Virginia, unlike in South Carolina and Georgia. Tobacco plantations, which thrived in the interior, generally required a smaller labor force than the rice fields (a maximum of 80 servants and slaves versus often over 200 slaves on several rice fields), and in Virginia the European indentured laborers remained the majority from the beginnings of the colony up to the end of the eighteenth century.

Although disproportional ratios may have been similar along the coast from Virginia to Georgia, the dynamics of interaction in smaller settings are not the same as in larger communities. Segregation was more motivated in communities where the "Black majority" constituted a threat than where it did not. It was easier to sustain segregation rigidly in a larger community, where those benefiting from it might interact viably among themselves, than in a smaller community, especially on the farms. In the latter settings, it is even more difficult to imagine that the Africans were prevented from sufficient exposure to the English spoken by European colonists.

These observations are not intended to deny the existence of discrimination based on race, on socioeconomic status, and on one's status as a slave or a free person. Segregation is a stronger form of discrimination that precludes usage of the same public facilities and regular casual socialization across races. In its strongest form, it entails the marginalization of the race that is discriminated against, as was evident in the first half of the twentieth century in American Southern states. Such marginalization would not have been in the interest of farm economies, especially in the seventeenth and eighteenth centuries.

We can conjecture that in Virginia and other colonies that developed on its model, socioeconomic conditions fostered developments of similar English vernaculars for descendants of Europeans and Africans. Thus the Africans developed different English vernaculars in different colonies, depending in part on the patterns of cross-race interaction that were permitted at various stages of colonization. Nothing so far justifies assuming that a Gullah-like antecedent of AAVE developed anywhere in the Chesapeake, although there were undoubtedly some isolated individuals who used Gullah-like features here and there.

AAVE, West African Pidgin English, and the Like

It has also been assumed or claimed that AAVE started from a (West African) Pidgin English spoken by the earliest African captives of the seventeenth century (Dillard 1972). Although adult Africans undoubtedly went through phases of interlanguage during their acquisition of colonial English (as is well evidenced by advertisements about runaway slaves), living conditions of the seventeenth century on mainly small farms and other homestead communities do not support the sporadic-contact and limited-interaction setting presupposed by a pidgin.[11] Some Africans may have arrived speaking a pidgin, but it is doubtful that it was widely spoken in coastal West Africa, or that every African acquired it before arriving in North America. Not all the slaves imported straight from Africa came through West Africa or on an English or American ship. So far no justification has been provided for invoking some Pidgin English as the genetic foundation of AAVE.

Perhaps a Native American Pidgin English would be worth considering as one from which either Gullah or AAVE would have started (Dillard 1995). However, so far, historians have provided little evidence of a significant presence of Native American slave or indentured labor on the largely agricultural settings in which the African American communities developed. On the other hand, there is evidence that Europeans communicated with Native Americans in contact varieties based on Native American languages, such as the Delaware and Chinook jargons. If a Native American Pidgin English contributed to the development of AAVE or Gullah, its role does not seem so critical, although this must still be investigated.

Back to the Caribbean Connection

Undoubtedly, some of the slaves who came from the anglophone Caribbean, rather than directly from Africa, spoke *Patois* (the local name for *creole*), especially among those who came in the eighteenth century. However, we cannot assume that all Caribbean slaves spoke Patois, any more than we can assume that all African Americans speak AAVE or Gullah. An important reason for rejecting the hypothesis of a Caribbean creole origins of AAVE is the lack of motivation for Patois-speaking slaves not to shift to the local vernacular and for those who preceded them in North America to shift to Caribbean varieties. This is not to deny that Caribbean slaves must have influenced the speech of some slaves coming directly from Africa, and that through the latter, they must have contributed to the post-seventeenth-century restructuring that produced AAVE and Gullah. However, this form of influence is similar to that contributed by African languages to the same restructuring process. It does not mean that AAVE or Gullah started from Caribbean Patois.

Recall that Tituba and Candy, the Caribbean slaves discussed above and assumed to have spoken a creole, had arrived recently when they were tried in Salem, and it is not clear how long Candy had lived in Barbados nor whether Tituba had come from a plantation or had been captured from her Native American community and had been speaking a pidgin that perhaps did not have much to do with the creole of some African slaves. Besides, even if Caribbean creoles have contributed to the development of AAVE, the source of several creoles' features lies in nonstandard colonial English. Even if the functions are no longer the same, the (partial) model is also attested in colonial vernaculars, whose contributing metropolitan dialects were similar in the Caribbean to those in North America.

For instance, the function of *dem* as a plural marker in *di bway dem* 'the boys' in Jamaican Patois is not identical with that of *them/dem* in *them/dem boys* 'those boys' in several nonstandard English vernaculars. However, one cannot deny the etymological connection between the two strategies of pluralization. The fact that *dem* is also used for associative plural, as in *Kate (an) dem* 'Kate and her associates/family', in Caribbean Patois, in Gullah, and in AAVE need not be interpreted as a primary influence of

Caribbean varieties on African American vernaculars. African languages, in which associative plural is a common grammatical function, are very likely to have influenced concurrently this extension of the function of *dem* in all these new English vernaculars of the African diaspora. Nigerian and Cameroon pidgins, on which Caribbean creole influence is doubtful, also have the same associative plural construction.

Thus whatever influence Caribbean creoles may have exerted on the then-emerging African American vernaculars would have been by way of convergence or reinforcement of current developments rather than otherwise (Mufwene 1998). Note also that AAVE's prosodic features (especially sentence intonation and speech tempo) are more like those of White Southern English than those of Caribbean English. It is those of Gullah, the variety that developed in socioeconomic conditions similar to Caribbean plantations, that are closer to those of its Caribbean kin. Because the proportion of Africans in the relevant colonies was generally higher than that of Europeans and because segregation was instituted in ways similar to those of coastal South Carolina, there was room for selective African substrate influence in the development of their creoles. This influence consisted either of foreign elements that clearly did not obtain in English or of features consistent with some options available in nonstandard English but not in standard English. There is still no reason for concluding that Caribbean Patois was the genetic antecedent of Gullah, although the former must have contributed to the development of the latter in more or less the same ways that African languages did in influencing the selection of particular structural alternatives from among the options available in colonial English.

The Development of AAVE and Gullah

As observed above, AAVE and Gullah must have started diverging structurally from European American English vernaculars not sooner than the eighteenth century.[12] By the end of the seventeenth century, the Virginia plantocrats found it more and more lucrative to buy African laborers, who were enslaved for life at a lower cost. European indentured labor had become too expensive. Realizing that working conditions in the colonies were harsh and the mortality rate high, fewer and fewer European destitutes considered indenture a solution to their plights. It was also at the beginning of the eighteenth century that South Carolina switched to rice as its primary agricultural industry, on which Europeans had little expertise. The labor was then imported primarily straight from Africa rather than from the Caribbean, the practice in the seventeenth century. Aside from cost considerations, the location of the rice fields in the coastal marshes predisposed the planters to prefer African laborers, who were more resistant to malaria. Still, because there was less segregation in Virginia and in colonies that were modeled on it than in coastal South Carolina and Georgia, the outcomes of linguistic restructuring in the two kinds of colonies were different, even among people of European descent, as is evidenced today by the speech of those who grew up on the plantations.

Segregation as it was known in Southern states in the twentieth century was instituted in the late nineteenth century with the Jim Crow laws, designed by white supremacists to undercut all the socioeconomic advantages that African Americans were gaining after Reconstruction. This system apparently was implemented more rigidly in urban than in rural settings, after descendants of Africans and Europeans had both shared over 200 years of close interaction with each other and apparently similar paths of restructuring English. Similarities between AAVE and vernacular White Southern English reflects that long common history of people of both races in the American Southeast.

The divergence of AAVE and vernacular White English must have intensified since the end of the nineteenth century if it started earlier.[13] Several reasons may be invoked to explain this development, the first of which is basically less and less interaction across races after the Jim Crow laws were passed. This is obvious even today, as the average African American and European American do not typically socialize together, even if they work together. Today's residential patterns in typical American cities, where the majority of African Americans now live, have fostered a sense of ethnic loyalty. Members of each group perpetuate their neighborhood norms. Although the twentieth century has seen many population movements in the United States, the patterns have not been the same. The Great Migration since the late nineteenth century through World War II brought African Americans from the rural South to urban ghettoes, even in Northern cities, in which they have continued to socialize primarily among themselves. This fact accounts for the often invoked geographical homogeneity of AAVE throughout the United States (Labov 1972), despite observations of regional variation among its native speakers.

Whites have also migrated widely, forming new communities with the development of new industries. The new pattern of residential segregation has prevented African Americans from participating in the restructuring brought about by these cross-regional population movements among Whites. The nineteenth and early twentieth centuries were also marked by continued massive immigrations from Europe, as opposed to reduced, then discontinued importation of labor from Africa and the Caribbean. Segregation must have prevented African Americans from participating in whatever form of restructuring was triggered by the European immigrants as they were absorbed into White communities. Such influence from the new immigrants must have happened despite the founder principle (Mufwene 1996b), according to which newcomers tend to adapt to established local speech ways instead of modifying them.

Besides, Europeans were not all equally integrated; some of them were less integrated than others, and several groups of immigrants also chose to live in communities where they would share nationality or culture with other immigrants or the current residents. This factor accounts for the developments of varieties identified as Italian, Jewish, or German English. One such other vernacular, developed by descendants of Scandinavians in Minnesota, has now been celebrated by the movie *Fargo*.

CONCLUSIONS: THE DEVELOPMENT OF AMERICAN ENGLISHES IN A NUTSHELL

Overall, variable patterns of interaction as made possible by variable degrees of integration into the economically and politically dominant population account for the restructuring of English in North America from its initial colonial inputs to today's different regional, class, and ethnic dialects. In some cases, race has been an important factor; in some others, it has not. Overall, race alone does not explain everything, although it contributed to the most clearly articulated system of segregation in the United States, which still persists. The basic principles of language change and divergence are the same, although the strengths of factors that regulate usage of variable features vary from one community to another.

Contact has been a common trigger of the development of all North American English varieties spoken by the descendants of both Africans and Europeans. It has brought together linguistic features that did not belong together in any one pre-seventeenth-century dialect and has set them to compete for selection into the new vernaculars. However, the composition of the elements of contact has varied from one setting to another. This state of affairs accounts in part for variation from one vernacular to another. One must realize that even if African languages did not contribute to the contact in some colonies, American English would still be different from British English, just as Australian English, for instance, differs from both.

The influence of African languages on AAVE and Gullah also cannot be denied. Without their contribution, these African American varieties would be almost the same as White vernaculars. On the other hand, because of the close typological kinship between Southern White varieties and AAVE, or between Gullah and plantation White English, the question arises of how to characterize this African influence. We should remember that AAVE is different in several ways from Caribbean English vernaculars. Moreover, AAVE, Gullah, and their Caribbean kin are all different in some ways from those English varieties spoken by Africans in Africa, especially prosodically, while the latter varieties show many cross-regional similarities. (The exceptions to this observation are Krio and Liberian Settler English, which have genetic ties with the New World varieties.)[14] The question of the nature of substrate influence remains as open as the nature of the restructuring process itself, how it proceeded, and what principles regulated it.

To date, because there has been more interest in the development of AAVE and Gullah than in any other North American English vernacular, they are the varieties about which we have gathered the most information and may form our best hypotheses. Unfortunately, given all the questions that remain unanswered or surrounded by controversies, this state of affairs highlights how little we know about the evolution of English in North America. More research on diverse varieties is definitely needed.

APPENDIX: SAMPLE GULLAH TEXT TRANSCRIBED IN EYE DIALECT

JR: *You trow way . . . trow way wha? En one day, I gone down deh . . . en talk bout something bin a bite! I bin on dat flat, en I had me line, I done ketch couple a whiting . . . I say, I ga put up da drop net . . . when I look up, duh look from yah to your car deh, I see sompin on da damn side da shoulder comin, like a damn log. I watch um, en when I see him gone down . . .*

You throw away . . . throw away what? And one day, I went/had gone down there . . . and talk[ing] about something biting! I was on that flat, and I had my line, I had caught a couple of whiting . . . I said, "I'll put up the drop net" . . . when I looked up, [I] was looking from here to your car there, I saw something on the damned side of the shoulder coming like a damned log. I watched it, and when I saw it gone down . . .

EL: *Hm hm!*

JR: *En dat tide bin a comin in . . . en dat sucker swim close, closer en closer, den I look en I see dat alligator open e damn mouth!*

And that tide was coming in . . . and that sucker swam close, closer and closer, then I looked and saw that alligator open its damned mouth! (Field Records of Salikoko S. Mufwene 1987)

SAMPLE AFRICAN AMERICAN VERNACULAR ENGLISH TEXT

Mary Walker: And uh, and here comes the yard man. And he come to mow the yard. And it wasn't like old mens today—if he see a young girl he would try to get her for himself. He says, "My wife has a son from St. Louis, Missouri." And says "He's visiting us, and would I like for you to meet him." And oh I was: flip, like most young girls. I was wanting to see what was happening. And I said "Oh sure! Well send him over."

I: MmmmHmmm

Mary Walker: And that's the man up there ((points to a large portrait)) He was curly in the front. Been like your baby.

I: MmmmHmmm

Mary Walker: And so when ah, the day he was supposed to come, I was
mopping the floor—just making strokes, you know, like that,
cleanin' up?

I: MmmmHmmm

Mary Walker: And I said to myself should I tell him the truth? I says something close to *this peckerwood walking* (laughs) (Morgan
1998, 259)

NOTES

I am grateful to Christine Corcoran and Rebecca Wheeler for feedback on a preliminary draft of this chapter. I am solely responsible for all the remaining short-
comings.

1. Gullah is the name assigned, typically by outsiders, to the English variety
spoken by African Americans on the seaboard of South Carolina and Georgia.

2. The term *creole* has been applied to vernaculars such as Gullah, Jamaican
Patois, and Saramaccan, which developed in European tropical settlement colonies
in the seventeenth and eighteenth centuries out of the contact of European and non-
European (especially African) languages. The term *decreolization* is a misnomer for
what should have been identified as *debasilectalization*, a process whereby a creole
loses its *basilect*, the variety the most different from the local standard variety of
the European language along which it developed. For recent discussions of the
debate over the creole origins hypothesis, see Winford (1997), Mufwene (1998),
and Rickford (1998). Strong arguments against it may be found in Schneider (1989)
and Poplack and Tagliamonte (1991).

3. One of the questions is whether substrate influence need be interpreted as
elements contributed by African languages that are not attested in the *lexifier*, the
model from which most of the vocabulary has been selected (in this case, nonstandard colonial English). Or can it be interpreted as the role that African languages
played in determining which of the competing alternatives in the lexifier (nonstandard varieties of colonial English in this case) would be selected into the new vernacular (Mufwene 1993)? Subscribing to the latter interpretation makes claims of
substrate influence not only more plausible but also more pervasive, consistent with
the *convergence hypothesis*, according to which structures common to most languages involved in the contact were more likely to be selected into the new vernacular.

4. *Restructuring* as defined in Mufwene (1996b) stands for "system reorganization," a process whereby, in a contact setting in which one particular language
is targeted, elements from diverse origins (different languages or dialects of the same
language) are integrated into a new system and/or some of the elements from the
same system are assigned new functions.

5. Such a shift has continued until now in Louisiana, where a Cajun Vernacular
English has attracted the attention of some linguists (e.g., Scott 1992).

6. According to the founder principle (Mufwene 1996b), the vernacular developed by the founder population bears significant influence on what later residents
in a colony will speak because every newcomer in a host community typically tries
to speak the vernacular spoken by the locals. However, this principle does not

preclude influence of the newcomers on the local vernacular under specific conditions, for instance, when they become a sudden majority or when they come to rule
the preceding population. Thus, while immigration into North America nowadays
shows negligible influence of the immigrants' nonnative speech on the extant vernaculars, changing conditions in the eighteenth and nineteenth centuries allowed
such influence. Part of New England's English reflects such later influence on the
founder population's vernacular, which is why it is not the same as the British East
Anglian dialect.

7. This is confirmed also by the development of foreign workers' varieties of
European languages in Europe, such as "Gastarbeiter Deutsch" in Germany and
"le français arabe" in France, spoken respectively and primarily (but not exclusively) by Turk and Arab immigrant manual labor. However, integration may not
be invoked so forcefully to explain the development of (Scotch-)Irish English. As in
African and Asian colonies, the colonized (Scotch-)Irish populations spoke English
more among themselves than routinely with the minority of colonizers among them.
Such conditions favored a strong substrate element in the emerging vernacular. In
North America, the (Scotch-)Irish had to interact with people from different ethnolinguistic backgrounds too, and pressures on them to shift to English were more
imperative than on those who remained at home. Their prominence in North American colonies just helped their substrate element prevail.

8. Indentured labor had then become too expensive, and the cost of buying
slaves had dropped. Both the Chesapeake and South Carolina colonies reverted to
more slave labor. The location of the rice fields in the swampy areas, where Europeans did not resist malaria well, made the South Carolina coast less attractive to
indentured laborers, who preferred the hinterlands. These factors explain why
South Carolina reached a "black majority" during the greater part of the eighteenth
century (from about 1710 to about 1780). Throughout the plantation industry,
they often constituted 90 percent of the plantation populations. Such was never the
case on the tobacco plantations of Virginia, which were mainly smaller and in the
hinterlands. Overall, the Africans never exceeded 38 percent in the latter colonies
by the end of the eighteenth century (Kulikoff 1986; Perkins 1988).

9. Cassidy provides no speech sample of Tituba's, and it is not clear whether
she originated from a plantation in Barbados.

10. This does not mean that there was no racial discrimination. It simply states
that such discrimination was not concurrent with segregation in the sense of living
in separate neighborhoods or quarters and being precluded from interacting across
race boundaries outside the workplace.

11. There is an important difference between an interlanguage and a pidgin. An
interlanguage is a transitional imperfect system through which a second-language
learner goes as he or she strives to command the target language. It is individual
based. A pidgin is a variety spoken by a group of people in a contact setting, such
as at markets or trade centers. It is relatively well established and based on insuf-
ficient exposure to the target, but it serves its purpose relatively well, for instance,
trade transactions. It is justifiably considered "broken" relative to the target language, it is used in minimum-communication contact settings, and such contacts
are typically sporadic, because the participants in the relevant speech events do not
interact with each other regularly. In the North American colonies, Europeans and
Africans interacted with each other regularly in the homesteads. On large planta-

tions, new slaves learned the local vernacular from creole or seasoned slaves, with whom they interacted regularly. In each setting, the current vernacular was targeted by the newcomers, by the founder principle.

12. It is a mistake to assume that there was/is one basilectal variety for all these new vernaculars, regardless of region or ethnicity. AAVE has its own basilect that is different from Gullah's, and Gullah's basilect is different from Bajan's or Jamaican's.

13. On the divergence hypothesis, according to which European and African American vernaculars have been growing more and more different, see especially Labov and Harris (1986), Bailey and Maynor (1987, 1989), Bailey and Thomas (1998), Butters (1989), and Fasold (1987).

14. Although several questions remain unanswered about specifics of their developments into what they are today, especially what particular varieties they developed from, Krio and Liberian Settler English are associated primarily with descendants of African former slaves who were repatriated from North America and Jamaica.

REFERENCES

Bailey, Guy, and Natalie Maynor. 1987. Decreolization? *Language in Society* 16: 449–473.

———. 1989. The divergence controversy. *American Speech* 64: 12–39.

Bailey, Guy, and Erik Thomas. 1998. Some aspects of African-American vernacular English phonology. *African-American English*, ed. by Salikoko S. Mufwene, John R. Rickford, Guy Bailey, and John Baugh, 85–109. London: Routledge.

Bailyn, Bernard. 1986. *The peopling of British North America: An introduction.* New York: Random House.

Brasch, Walter. 1981. *Black English and the mass media.* Lanham, MD: University Press of America.

Butters, Ronald. 1989. *The death of Black English: Divergence and convergence in Black and White vernaculars.* Frankfurt: Peter Lang.

Cassidy, Frederic G. 1980. The place of Gullah. *American Speech* 55: 3–16.

———. 1986. Barbadian creole: Possibility and probability. *American Speech* 61: 195–205.

Coleman, Kenneth. 1978. *Georgia history in outline.* Rev. ed. Athens: University of Georgia Press.

Dillard, J. L. 1972. *Black English: Its history and usage in the United States.* New York: Random House.

———. 1995. American English in the English diaspora. *New approaches to American English*, ed. by Zoltán Kövecses, 3–18. Budapest: Department of American Studies, Eötvös Loránd University.

Fasold, Ralph, guest ed. 1987. *Are black and white vernaculars diverging? Papers from the NWAVE-XIV Discussion Panel. American Speech* 62.1.

Fischer, David Hackett. 1989. *Albion's seed: Four British folkways in America.* New York and Oxford: Oxford University Press.

Gonzales, Ambrose. 1922. *The black border: Gullah stories of the Carolina coast (with a glossary).* Columbia, SC: State Co.

Hickey, Raymond. 1995. An assessment of language contact in the development of
    Irish English. *Linguistic change under contact conditions*, ed. by Jacek Fi-
    siak, 109–30. Berlin: Mouton de Gruyter.
Johnson, Guy. 1930. *Folk culture on St. Helena Island, South Carolina*. Chapel
    Hill: University of North Carolina Press.
Krapp, George Philip. 1924. The English of the Negro. *American Mercury* 2: 190–
    95.
Kulikoff, Allan. 1986. *Tobacco and slaves: The development of Southern cultures
    in the Chesapeake, 1680–1800*. Chapel Hill: University of North Carolina
    Press.
Kurath, Hans. 1928. The origin of dialectal differences in spoken American English.
    Modern Philology 25: 385–95.
Labov, William. 1972. *Sociolinguistic patterns*. Philadelphia: University of Penn-
    sylvania Press.
Labov, William, and Wendell A. Harris. 1986. De facto segregation of Black and
    White vernaculars. *Diversity and diachrony*, ed. by David Sankoff, 1–24.
    Amsterdam: John Benjamins.
Morgan, Marcyliena. 1998. More than a mood or an attitude: Discourse and verbal
    genres in African-American culture. *African-American English: Structure,
    history, and use*, ed. by Salikoko S. Mufwene, John R. Rickford, Guy Bailey,
    and John Baugh, 251–81. London: Routledge.
Mufwene, Salikoko S. 1993. Introduction. *Africanisms in Afro-American language
    varieties*, ed. by Salikoko S. Mufwene, 1–31. Athens: University of Georgia
    Press.
———. 1996a. The development of American Englishes: Some questions from a
    creole genesis perspective. *Varieties of English around the world: Focus on
    the USA*, ed. by Edgar W. Schneider, 231–63. Amsterdam: John Benjamins.
———. 1996b. The founder principle in creole genesis. *Diachronica* 13: 83–134.
———. 1998. Accountability in descriptions of creoles. *Creole genesis, attitudes,
    and discourse: Studies celebrating Charlene J. Sato*, ed. by John R. Rickford
    and Suzanne Romaine. Amsterdam: John Benjamins.
Perkins, Edwin J. 1988. *The economy of colonial America*. 2nd ed. New York:
    Columbia University Press.
Poplack, Shana, and Sali Tagliamonte. 1991. African American English in the di-
    aspora: Evidence from old-line Nova Scotians. *Language Variation and
    Change* 3: 301–39.
Rickford, John R. 1998. The creole origins of African-American Vernacular Eng-
    lish: Evidence from copula absence. *African-American English: Structure,
    history, and use*, ed. by Salikoko S. Mufwene, John R. Rickford, Guy Bailey,
    and John Baugh, 154–200. London: Routledge.
Schneider, Edgar W. 1989. *American earlier Black English*. University: University
    of Alabama Press.
Scott, Ann Martin, ed. 1992. *Cajun vernacular English: Informal English in French
    Louisiana*. Special issue of *Louisiana English Journal*.
Tate, Thad W. 1965. *The Negro in eighteenth-century Williamsburg*. Williamsburg,
    VA: Colonial Williamsburg Foundation.
Thomas, Hugh. 1997. *The slave trade*. New York: Simon and Schuster.
Trudgill, Peter. 1986. *Dialects in contact*. Oxford: Blackwell.

Turner, Lorenzo Dow. 1949. *Africanisms in the Gullah dialect.* Chicago: University of Chicago Press.

Winford, Donald. 1997. On the origins of African American vernacular English: A creolist perspective. *Diachronica* 14: 305–44.

Wood, Peter. 1974. *Black majority: Negroes in colonial South Carolina from 1670 through the Stono rebellion.* New York: Alfred A. Knopf.

3

African American Vernacular English Is Not Standard English with Mistakes

Geoffrey K. Pullum

It is unusual for a policy announcement at a city school-board meeting to trigger a worldwide media frenzy, but one California school-board meeting in December 1996 did exactly that. Within days of the announcement, school-board members could not leave their homes without being besieged by journalists. They were vilified, ridiculed, and attacked in newspapers and magazines around the entire world. What had happened?

The board had issued a statement to the effect that it was changing its educational policies with regard to one aspect of the local linguistic situation. They would pay more serious attention to the language spoken at home by most of the district's school students. Its status would be recognized, teachers would be trained to look at it objectively and appreciate its merits, and it would be used in the classroom as appropriate. This much was reported by the *New York Times* quite accurately and fairly. Yet opinion writers proceeded to fall upon the topic like starving dogs attacking a bone. They ridiculed, they sneered, they frothed, they flamed, they raged, they lived off the story for weeks. The talk-radio switchboards lit up, and intemperate opinions flared. What was going on?

The answer lies in the fact that the language being recognized by the school board was not Spanish or Polish or Russian or any such relatively uncontroversial language. The city was Oakland, a poor city on the east side of San Francisco Bay where half the population is African American, and the language was the one that linguists usually call African American Vernacular English (AAVE).

What makes AAVE so dramatically different as a political issue from, say, Spanish (also spoken in Oakland, by up to a quarter of the population) is its close relation to another language of much higher prestige. Most speakers of Standard English think that AAVE is just a badly spoken version of their language, marred by a lot of ignorant mistakes in grammar and pronunciation, or worse than that, an unimportant and mostly abusive repertoire of street slang used by an ignorant urban underclass. An editorial in the *New York Times* a few days after the first news report said that the Oakland school board had "declared that black slang is a distinct language."

Let me begin by getting that myth out of the way. The *Times*'s statement about slang was completely untrue, and the writers should be ashamed of themselves. So should all the newspapers and magazines that followed them. The governing board of the Oakland Unified School District never mentioned slang and never intended to imply anything approving about it.

We call an expression slang when it represents a vivid, colloquial word or phrase associated with some subculture and not yet incorporated as part of the mainstream language. No subculture's slang could constitute a separate language. The mistake is like confusing a sprinkle of hot sauce with a dinner. Slang is by definition parasitic on some larger and more encompassing host language. It has no grammar of its own; it is a small array of words and phrases used under the aegis of some ordinary language and in accordance with its grammar. The majority of slang words and phrases are in the language already and are merely assigned new slang meanings by some subpopulation.

The Oakland school board was not endorsing the nonsensical idea that black slang should be recognized as a new language. The statement it released may have been wordy, diffuse, and filled with bad bureaucratese and pompous-sounding references to "African Language Systems," but the intent was clear enough: the board wanted to acknowledge that AAVE was distinct in certain respects from Standard English, and it proposed to be responsive to the educational implications.

Buried among the jargon of the announcement was a mention of a name for AAVE, suggested by a Black scholar in 1975 but never adopted by linguists: Ebonics. That word, concocted from *ebony* (a color term from the name of a dark-colored wood) and *phonics* (the name of a method for teaching reading), was destined to attach to the board as if chiseled into a block of granite and hung round their necks. They would never hear the end of it.

One problem with the name was that it lent itself irresistibly to stupid puns and jokes. The *Economist* picked it up and printed a brief story headed "The Ebonics virus," a tasteless reference to the then-recent outbreak of the horrible Ebola fever in Zaire (the subliminal link: nasty things out of Africa). People rapidly invented other *-onics* words to mock the idea of letting African Americans have their own claim to a language. Would Jewish people propose that their way of speaking English should be designated Hebonics? Could stupid people complain that they were victims of their native language, Moronics? Cartoonists seemed to find such possibilities endlessly amusing, and the jokes kept coming for more than a year.

But I will not be primarily concerned here with analysis of the politics and the rhetoric that the "Ebonics" story provoked. I will be concerned with AAVE itself, the everyday speech of millions of people in largely segregated African American districts. The majority of English speakers think that AAVE is just English with two added factors: some special slang terms and a lot of grammatical mistakes. They are simply wrong about this.

LANGUAGES, DIALECTS, AND RULES

Let me begin by pointing out that there is obviously a difference between being an incorrect utterance of one language and being a correct utterance in another (perhaps only slightly different). This is obvious when the two languages are thoroughly different, like English and French. When a French speaker refers to the capital of the United Kingdom as *Londres*, it isn't a mistake; that's the correct French name for London. But the same is true when we are talking about two very closely related languages. There is a strong temptation, especially when one of the two has higher prestige, to take one to be the correct way to speak and the other to be incorrect. But it is not necessarily so.

I will consider a fairly subtle example involving a grammatical difference between two varieties of Standard English. Some speakers, but not all, use the word *whom* instead of *who* in some contexts. Those who do use *whom* always use it after a preposition ("a man in *whom* I have complete confidence") and may use it after a verb ("And after that you visited *whom*?"), and they may use it at the beginning of a sentence (though "*Whom* did you visit?" sounds rather stiff, and many would avoid it). But most people, even expert writers of English, will confess to scratching their heads a little about the following two cases:

(1) We are talking about a man who everyone seems to think will one day be king.

(2) We are talking about a man whom everyone seems to think will one day be king.

Which version is right? Dimly we may remember something from the grammar books about using *who* for subjects and *whom* for nonsubjects. Can't we just apply that? No, we can't. The rule "use *who* for subjects and *whom* for nonsubjects" is insufficiently explicit. These examples involve a relative clause that begins after the word *man*. The next word (*who* or *whom*) introduces the relative clause (*everyone seems to think __ will one day be king*). There are two things that "subject" might mean here: "subject of its clause," that is, subject of the clause that it logically belongs to, or "subject of the relative clause." The word *who* is logically the subject in a clause that has *will one day be king* as its predicate; if that allows it to count as a subject, then version (1) is correct. But the subject of the whole relative clause is not *who* but rather *everyone*. The word *who* is not the logical subject of that, but just of a piece of it. If that's what we mean by being a subject, then we should pick sentence (2).

Where do we turn to decide this point? We look in good manuals of English usage. And we immediately find something very interesting: there are clear examples of both types in literary works by the best authors. The *who* group—those whose writing suggests that they would plump for (1)— includes Arnold Bennett, Charles Dickens, Henry Fielding, and William Safire (the *New York Times*'s language pundit). Good company. But the *whom* group, whose usage shows they would select (2), includes early writers like William Caxton and Izaak Walton, famous novelists like Charles Kingsley and Rudyard Kipling, romantic poets like John Keats and Percy Bysshe Shelley, and at least some *New York Times* and *Publishers Weekly* writers, together with Charles Darwin and William Shakespeare. That, too, is a dream team.

What is going on? The answer is that there are two different rules involved. Some writers follow one, while others follow the other. The members of the *who* group tacitly assume that *who* has to be the subject of its clause; the members of the *whom* group tacitly assume that *who* has to be the subject of the relative clause.

What we have discovered is a division between two *syntactic dialects*— two sectors of the speech community that have very slightly different grammars. By assuming that speakers fall into these two dialect groups, you can explain both the consistencies of practice and the disagreements that occur. The disagreements do not become evident very often: only on the rare occasions when *who* occurs as the understood subject of a clause contained in a relative clause without being the subject of the relative clause as a whole.

It is crucially important to notice that people do not just flounder, as if they did not know *who* from *whom* any more. To describe either the *who* group or the *whom* group as people who are ignorant of the grammar of the language in which they are writing would be absurd. More specifically, it would predict quite falsely that you will find them blundering into sentences like the following (the asterisk prefix means that the string is not a sentence):

(3) a. *Whom wants to come and play tennis?

　　 b. *I'm the one whom loves you.

(4) a. *He is a man for who I have the highest regard.

    b. *To who do you refer?

Nobody writes things like this. So it is not true that "anything goes" regarding the use of *who* and *whom*. There are rules. But it is also not true that there is a single correct rule governing everything about *who* and *whom* and some people have failed to learn it. That does not predict the facts correctly. There is a better theory, and it is set out informally in (5):

(5) a. All English speakers use *who* when it is in subject position in a simple clause.

    b. Those speakers who use *whom* can always use it as the direct object of a transitive verb and as the object of a preposition.

    c. For *who* at the beginning of a relative clause there are two different rules, defining two bona fide syntactic dialects of the English language. They are the following:

        (i) Use *whom* when it is the subject of the clause in which it logically belongs.

        (ii) Use *who* when it is the subject of the relative clause.

Rules (i) and (ii) both agree that you should use *who* in "anyone who wants to leave" because there it is both the subject of its own clause and the subject of the relative clause (which are one and the same). But on other sentences the two rules decide things differently. The *who* group (Dickens, Safire, and company) assume (i) and thus regard example (1) as correct; the *whom* group (Shakespeare, Darwin, and company) assume rule (ii) and thus favor example (2). What this shows is that even within Standard English there is a difference between making mistakes and speaking a different variety correctly—a difference between marching out of time and marching to the beat of a different drum.

With these preliminaries out of the way, I now turn to AAVE, which turns out to be the most interestingly divergent dialect of modern English.

THE AFRICAN AMERICAN VERNACULAR DIALECT OF ENGLISH

The Oakland school board suggested that AAVE had its own rules and structure. Opinionmongers displayed anger and contempt at this. They mocked, lampooned, and attacked the very idea. But a large amount of the ink they splattered was wasted on a pointless side issue: whether AAVE was really "a separate language" from English or whether it was "just a dialect." The Oakland school board made the mistake of insisting explicitly that it was a separate language. That is another red herring (like the slang issue).

Dialects and languages are in fact the same kinds of thing. "Dialect" does not mean a marginal, archaic, rustic, or degraded mode of speech. Linguists never say things like "That is just a dialect, not a language." Rather, they refer to one language as *a dialect of* another. The claim that Tosk is a dialect of Albanian is a classificatory claim, like saying that the white-tailed deer is a kind of deer. It is not some kind of put-down of Tosk speakers.

Of course, in practice, political considerations do tend to enter decisions about when one language should be called a dialect of another. Albania is currently one country, and Tosk and Gheg are treated as dialects of one Albanian language (even though it is hard to understand one if you only know the other); but in the wrecked ex-country of Yugoslavia, the language people used to call Serbo-Croat began during the 1990s to be deliberately split up into three separate languages, Serbian, Croatian, and Bosnian, because the speakers had fallen out politically. No one would have said before that there were three languages here, even though the Croatian Yugoslavs talked a bit differently from the Serbian and Bosnian Yugoslavs. There was assumed to be one Serbo-Croat language (there is a book called *Teach Yourself Serbo-Croat*). This single language would have been described as having several different dialects—regional or ethnic variants of the same basic linguistic system. But once Serbia, Croatia, and Bosnia separated, the differences among the three trivially differing languages had to be emphasized and accentuated. The Serbs, stressing their Eastern Orthodox religious roots, revived Old Church Slavonic words and mandated use of the Cyrillic (Russian) alphabet; the Croats stressed their Catholic roots, borrowed more words from Latin, and stuck with the Roman alphabet; and the Bosnian Muslims borrowed words from Turkish to emphasize their connections with the Islamic world. Linguistic boundary lines began to emerge to reinforce the ethnic boundary lines.

Reference works on the languages of the world take different views of how many linguistic boundaries to recognize. Reasonable scholars can differ on how coarse grained or fine grained a classification is appropriate (and on how much politics should be taken into account). So it is important that in classifying AAVE there is no dispute. For example, I keep near my desk two reference books on the languages of the world: Grimes's *Ethnologue* and the Voegelins' *Classification and Index of the World's Languages*. The *Ethnologue* recognizes more than fifteen separate Romance languages in Italy, while *Classification and Index* recognizes just three (Italian, Friulian, and Ladin). But both list AAVE as a dialect of English.

This is undoubtedly the right classification. Virtually all the words used in AAVE can be clearly identified in Standard English too, and most of AAVE grammar is the same as that of Standard English. The bits that are not are mostly paralleled in certain other dialects of English that are never mistaken for other languages. As linguist John McWhorter has pointed out, there certainly are examples, in some parts of the world, of African languages that have kept their African syntax and simply replaced the words of the dictionary by English words (they are known as creole languages), and AAVE just is not like that.

This is not an insulting or demeaning thing to say about AAVE. It merely places it in a linguistic classification that unites the language of Shakespeare and the language of the Oakland ghetto very closely compared to languages in other families or in other parts of the Germanic family. It is no more insulting to call AAVE a variety (or dialect) of English than it is to say that African Americans are U.S. citizens.

It was not merely a matter of an incorrect classificatory claim when the Oakland school board made its wordy statements about how the district's black students used "African Language Systems" that did not constitute a dialect of English. It was also a major tactical error. It deflected virtually all the discussion into negative channels: journalists vied with each other to insist that AAVE should not be recognized as a language. What got lost was a much more sensible and reasonable point: AAVE as a dialect of English still deserves respect and acceptance. It has a degree of regularity and stability attributable to a set of rules of grammar and pronunciation, as with any language. It differs strikingly from Standard English, but there is no more reason for calling it bad Standard English than there is for dismissing Minnesota English as bad Virginia speech, or the reverse. Journalists did not get this; nearly everything they wrote about the purported errors that characterize AAVE was factually incorrect. It is worth devoting a little time to close analysis of some examples that demonstrate this.

MYTHS ABOUT *BE*

There is a technical term for the auxiliary verb that takes the forms *be, been, being, am, are, is, was,* and *were*. It is called the *copula*. The most popular myth about AAVE is that it involves misuse of the copula: that it is carelessly omitted or is used in incorrect forms like *be* out of ignorance. Let me try to untangle the jumble of falsehoods that are commonly bruited about.

The AAVE copula can be omitted, but there are strict rules—surprisingly detailed and specific ones—about how and where. In the following summary, AAVE examples are italicized and translations into Standard English are in double quotation marks.

(i) If the copula bears accent (stress) for any reason, it is not omitted. Example: the copula is obligatory in *There already is one!* with emphasized *is*.

(ii)   As a special case of (i), auxiliary verbs at the end of a phrase are always accented, and so the copula is always retained at the end of a phrase.
Example: the copula is obligatory in *Couldn't nobody say what color he is* (which means "Nobody could say what color he is").

(iii) Perhaps as another special case of (i), there is a special *remote present perfect tense*, completely lacking in Standard English (in fact, few Standard English speakers are aware of its presence in AAVE), expressed with an accented form of the word *been*, represented here in small capitals, and this is not omitted.
Example: *She* BEEN married means "She is married and has been for some considerable time," and the BEEN is not omissible.

(iv)   If the copula is negated, it is not omitted (the form *ain't* is never dropped).
Example: The copula is obligatory in *You ain't goin' to no heaven* ("You aren't going to any heaven") or in *I ain't no fool* ("I am not a fool").

(v)   The copula is not omitted when it is infinitival and has the base form *be*.
Example: The copula is obligatory in *You got to be strong* or in an imperative like *Be careful*.

(vi)   Perhaps as a special case of (v), the *be* that expresses *habitual aspect* is not omitted.
Example: *He be singin'* means "He usually or habitually sings" (not "He is singing"), and the *be* is obligatory.

(vii) The copula is not omitted when it is in the past tense (*was* or *were*).
Example: The copula is obligatory in *I was cool*.

(viii) The present-tense copula is not omitted when it is first-person singular (*am*).
Example: The copula is obligatory in *I'm all right*.

(ix)   The present-tense copula is not omitted when it begins a clause.
Example: The copula is obligatory in an interrogative like *Is that you?*

(x)   As a special case of (ix), when the copula occurs in a confirmatory tag on the end of a sentence, it is not omitted (because such tags have the grammar of elliptical interrogative clauses).
Example: the copula of the tag is obligatory in *I don't think you ready, are you?*

Only when none of these conditions obtains—when the copula is present tense, not first person, not accented, not negative, and not expressing the habitual or the remote present perfect—can it be omitted in AAVE speech.

Most of this can be easily confirmed from the smattering of AAVE one can pick up from popular culture—snatches of AAVE dialogue in movies, African American popular songs, and so on. Almost every American knows that the Standard English greeting *How are you doing?* can be reduced to *How you doin'?* in AAVE, but the AAVE greeting *What it is?* is never given in the form **What it?*; they know that in the line *I ain't lyin'* (in "I Put a Spell on You") you cannot leave out the *ain't*; that Otis Redding sings *I was born by a river* (in "It's Been a Long Time Coming"), and it could not be reduced to **I born by a river*; that song lines like *I'm your puppet* and *I'm a hog for you, baby* couldn't be reduced to **I your puppet* or **I a hog for you, baby*; and so on. So any general claim that AAVE speakers leave out the copula is clearly false.

Few English speakers are aware that Russian, Hungarian, Arabic, Swahili, and many other languages have rules for omitting the copula, under conditions that are of a quite similar sort though differing in details. In Arabic, for example, the copula may be omitted in the nonemphatic affirmative present tense. In Hungarian the copula *must* be omitted in the affirmative third-person-singular present tense (i.e., there is no such thing as an affirmative third-person present-tense copula form). In Russian the copula is optionally omitted in the nonemphatic affirmative present indicative when it is not expressing existence (as in *There is a god*).

Some languages, for example, Standard French, differ very clearly in that they always have a pronounced form of the copula in relevant sentence types and show no superficially verbless sentences. Standard English is a little closer to AAVE than to Standard French: it does not entirely omit the copula, but almost omits it, reducing it to a single consonant when unstressed and in the affirmative present tense (*I'm certainly interested, You're so kind, He's my brother*, and so on, but not **I certainly'm*, where *am* needs to be accented, or **He'sn't my brother*, where *is* has been negated). This is a pattern also seen in, for example, Turkish (an entirely unrelated language). These reductions are not random carelessness; they are the results of rules, and so is the omission of the copula in AAVE.

Notice that in many languages another part of the sentence is regularly omitted: languages like Russian, Swahili, Spanish, Italian, Japanese, and Chinese omit nonemphatic subject pronouns nearly all the time when the context permits the meaning to be identified without difficulty. *Te amo* in Spanish means "I love you" despite the nonoccurrence of the word for *I*. (There is such a word—it is pronounced *yo*—but it is only used emphatically.) But AAVE does not permit omission of the subject pronoun. Even in the most careful Spanish you can say *¿Dónde estás?* for "Where are you?" (omitting the word for "you") or *Llegará esta noche* for "She will arrive tonight" (omitting the word for "she"), but you cannot say **Where are?* or **Will arrive tonight* in AAVE. Subject pronouns are never omitted except in imperatives and in very casual telegraphic usages that other dialects share (we can say *'S a mystery to me* instead of *It's a mystery to me* in very informal speech, or write *Will write more soon* to save words in a telegram or on a postcard). AAVE has a grammar that determines such things, just as Standard English does, and the grammar of the two dialects agree on this point: subjects are obligatory in nearly all sentence types. AAVE speakers do not carelessly leave out subjects any more than Standard English speakers do.

NEGATIVE CONCORD: DON'T WANT NO DOUBLE NEGATION

AAVE critics talk about something called "double negation" and treat it as an illogicality. The critics generally do not know what they are talking about. AAVE negates the same way other languages do: *You ain't ugly* is true if and only if *You ugly* is false, and conversely. What does differentiate AAVE from Standard English is that negation can be multiply marked: Standard English *I am not an ugly fellow* translates into AAVE as *I ain't no ugly dude*; Standard English *I haven't ever seen anything like it* corresponds to AAVE *I ain't never seen nothin' like it*; standard English *He did not see anything* is AAVE *He di'n't see nothin'*. The critics' claim about this is that logic tells us that two negatives make a positive: if he did *not* see *nothing*, that means he *did* see *something*, and it is illogical to use that form of words to mean the opposite.

I will make only a brief detour into logic (it is a technical business, and there is much more that could be said). It is certainly true that in formal logical languages such as the propositional calculus, under classical interpretations of negation, two negatives are equivalent to an affirmative (what a logician writes as $\sim \sim P$ means "it is *not* so that it is *not* so that P," where P is any statement you like; and it is equivalent to saying P). But there is little similarity between this mechanical logical system and the grammar of any natural language. Under the classical interpretation, any even number of consecutive negations is equivalent to none, and any odd number is equivalent to one. So three negatives are equivalent to a single negative in logic, which means that the critics have some explaining to do: what is supposed to be objectionable about *I ain't never seen nothin' like it?* It has three negative words (*ain't, never, nothin'*) and a negative meaning, and that ought to be fine if all that is important is for negative sentences to have an odd number of negative words.

The truth is that many of the people who grumble about AAVE being illogical do not know enough logic even to explain what they mean by their critique. They stress something completely irrelevant (the way inference is formalized in the invented languages of logic) while missing major complications concerning the interaction of negation with quantifiers (a topic that is beyond the scope of this chapter) and failing to see the crucially relevant fact about natural languages: that the grammar of negation is not the same in all languages.

Negation in Standard English, German, or Arabic is different from negation in, for example, Spanish or Russian or Italian. In Standard Italian, the way to say "Nobody telephoned" is *Non ha telefonato nessuno*, literally "not has telephoned no one." The *non* at the beginning and the additional negativity of *nessuno* 'no one' are both required. Italian demands that a sentence like this be negated in a particular way that demands both a *non* and a *nessuno*.

To be slightly more precise about this, in those positions where indefinite words (words like *anybody*) would appear in a standard English negative clause, Italian requires their negative counterparts (words with meanings like *nobody*). This is a rule of the grammar, usually known to linguists as *negative concord*. Negative-concord languages *require* use of negative words instead of indefinite words. This is not an error; it is a demand of the grammar, rather like an agreement rule.

AAVE turns out to be like Italian with regard to negative concord, not like Standard English. The AAVE sentence *Ain't nobody called* shows exactly the same negative concord as the Italian *Non ha telefonato nessuno*: the negative element *ain't* requires that *nobody* be chosen just as the negative element *non* requires that *nessuno* be chosen. Neither AAVE nor Italian is illogical; it is just that their grammatical rules for expression of indefinites in negated clauses differ from the rules for Standard English.

AAVE is not alone as a dialect of English with negative concord. Cockney (a working-class dialect spoken in the East End of London, England) and numerous other working-class dialects in England (and America) also have it. For example, you can hear Pink Floyd sing "We don't need no education; we don't need no thought control" on their album *The Wall*; they are a white British band, and they are singing in working-class British English, not AAVE.

It is merely an accident that the negative-concord dialects of English today have a low-prestige class background. In Italy nothing of the sort is the case: people of noble birth and newspapers of the highest quality use negative concord. Pope John Paul II uses negative concord when he speaks in Italian. (Actually, he uses it when he speaks Polish, too, because Polish is like AAVE and Spanish and Italian, not like English and German and Arabic.)

NEGATIVE INVERSION

Another key feature of AAVE (not shared by Cockney or other dialects) involves repositioning a negative auxiliary verb at the beginning of the sentence when the subject is indefinite. Thus we find *Ain't nobody gonna find out*, meaning "Nobody is going to find out."

In the Standard English version, negation is expressed purely on the subject. If you want to make a sentence that is true just in those circumstances where "Somebody is going to find out" is false, you simply replace *somebody* by *nobody*, and you get "Nobody is going to find out." In AAVE the clause has to be marked as negative by its auxiliary verb, so you use *ain't*, and in addition (remember, AAVE is a negative-concord language), all words like *somebody* must be replaced by negative forms like *nobody* throughout the clause. Complying with these demands would yield *Nobody ain't gonna find out*. But that is not necessarily the most acceptable way of saying things; it is quite common for AAVE speakers to switch the order of the subject (*nobody*) and the auxiliary verb (*ain't*), yielding *Ain't nobody gonna find out*. In Standard English the auxiliary occurs before the subject in interrogatives (*Isn't anyone going to find out?*), but not in declaratives (except where, in rather formal style, a negative adverb occurs at the beginning of the sentence: *Never have I seen such a thing*). The AAVE *Ain't nobody gonna find out* is a declarative sentence (used for making a statement), not an interrogative sentence (used for asking a question), yet it has the auxiliary as the first word. This is another example of a syntactic difference between AAVE and Standard English.

There is a complication to this. Negative inversion in AAVE is not found with every type of subject noun phrase. For example, when the subject is a simple name like *Mary*, it is impossible, or at least extremely unlikely. We do not hear **Ain't Mary gonna find out*. Similarly, when the subject has the definite article *the* or a possessive article like *your*, we do not get negative inversion: **Ain't the teacher gonna find out*; **Ain't your mother gonna find out*.

So there is more to be said about the various conditions that encourage or discourage the use of negative inversion in particular sentences, but my point has been illustrated enough: negative inversion is a construction type that the standard dialect does not have. Again AAVE shows that it has certain regular syntactic principles of its own.

DROPPING CONSONANTS RIGHT AND LEF'

AAVE also has special principles of pronunciation. One fairly clear one concerns consonant clusters at the ends of words. AAVE speakers say *res'* for 'rest', *lef'* for 'left', *respec'* for 'respect', *han'* for 'hand', and so on. A superficial glance might suggest that they leave consonants off the ends of words. But it is not that simple.

We will need a small amount of phonetic terminology at this point. The *stop consonants* of English are the ones normally represented by the letters *p, t, k, b, d*, and *g*, as found on the ends of the words *up, out, oak, rob, rod*, and *log*. The *voiceless* consonants, quieter because they are pronounced with no vibration of the vocal cords, are the sounds for which *p, t*, and *k* are normally used. The other voiceless sounds in English include the ones heard at the ends of the words *off, miss*, and *fish*, which are called *fricatives*. The *voiced stops*, which are produced with vocal-cord vibration, are *b, d*, and *g*. (Some consonant letters get doubled in English spellings, but this is not relevant to the pronunciation.) Other voiced sounds in English include the consonants heard at the ends of the words *of, Oz, ridge,* and *fill.* (Standard English also has *interdental* fricatives like those in the words *breath* and *breathe,* but these are replaced by stops in several dialects, of which AAVE is one: *they* is pronounced *dey.*)

With this terminology we can describe some rather intricate restrictions concerning which consonants can be left off and which have to be retained in AAVE. The basic principle involved is the one shown in (6).

> (6) A stop consonant at the end of a word may be omitted (and usually is) if it is preceded by another consonant of the same voicing.

Note first that consonants are always pronounced when they follow a vowel. In words like *up, out, oak, rob, rod,* and *log,* no AAVE speaker leaves off the final consonant. In words like *dump, sink,* and *belt,* again all the consonants are pronounced. The consonants *p, t,* and *k* are voiceless stops, but the sounds represented by *m, n,* and *l* are voiced, so nothing gets dropped. Similarly, in words like *raps, rats,* or *racks,* the *s* is always pronounced, because although it is a consonant of the same voicing as *t,* it is not a stop, so it is retained. In words like *Dobbs, Dodds,* or *dogs,* we hear a voiced fricative *z* sound at the end, which is not dropped, because although it has a consonant of the same voicing before it, that consonant is not a stop. We therefore get consonants dropped only in cases like these:

> (7) a. *test*: voiceless stop *t* dropped after voiceless *s* *tes'*
>
> b. *desk*: voiceless stop *k* dropped after voiceless *s* *des'*
>
> c. *left*: voiceless stop *t* dropped after voiceless *f* *lef'*
>
> d. *respect*: voiceless stop *t* dropped after voiceless *k* (spelled *c*) *respec'*
>
> e. *stopped*: voiceless stop *t* (spelled *-ed*) dropped after voiceless *p* *stop'*
>
> f. *hand*: voiced stop *d* dropped after voiceless *n* *han'*
>
> g. *old*: voiced stop *d* dropped after voiced *l* *ol'*

SOMETHIN' 'BOUT NASALS

One might be tempted by the spelling to think that AAVE also leaves *g* off the end of words like *nothin', somethin',* and *singin',* but this is not true either. In Standard English these words end in the *ng* sound of *sing* (phoneticians call this sound the *velar nasal*), but today in many dialects the *-ing* ending is frequently replaced by *-in,* often represented in writing as *-in'.* Nothing has been dropped, despite that apostrophe; rather, one sound has been replaced by another.

Or, at least, nothing has been dropped in recent times. But there is an interesting little historical wrinkle to this. Further back in the history of

English a consonant was in fact dropped from words like *sing*, but the careless culprits were the speakers of what we now flatter with the term "Standard" English. Dialects in the north of England have undergone fewer changes than the standard dialect, and those dialects still have the sound *g* (as in *egg*) on the end of word roots like *sing* and in derivatives of it like *singer*. In other words, *singer* rhymes with *finger* and *linger* in northern England. Some centuries ago the southern England dialects began to lose the *g* sound after a velar nasal at the end of a word root, so now *finger* and *singer* no longer rhyme in southern England. The *g* sound is heard in *finger*, a simple word containing a *g* following a velar nasal, but not in *singer*, a complex word in which the root *sing* ends in a velar nasal and the suffix *-er* follows.

No dialects in southern Britain (or America, which was settled from there) have a *g* after a velar nasal at the end of any word anymore. So it is true that in the speech of Queen Elizabeth II, the *g* sound that used to end *sing* has been lost. But no one calls the queen sloppy or mistaken in her speech. Why? Because there is a double standard here. When Standard Southern British English introduces a simplifying change in the rules of punctuation (like "do not pronounce the *g* sound after a velar nasal except in the middle of a word"), it is respected as the standard way to speak, but when AAVE introduces such a change (like "do not pronounce a stop at the end of a word after another consonant with the same voicing"), it is unfairly regarded as sloppiness.

DIALECT SWITCHING

At this point I should make it clear that the features of AAVE I have discussed are characteristic of a rather "pure" AAVE, a version only minimally influenced by Standard English. But people are flexible, and even African Americans who have hardly any social contact with whites know an enormous amount of Standard English by the time they are adults. (It is 5-year-olds who have trouble on first confronting Standard English, perhaps in school, where they may take a while to latch onto the new way of speaking.) It is quite typical for speakers of AAVE to be able to switch back and forth between their dialect and one much closer to Standard English. The different features mentioned earlier—copula omission, negative concord, negative inversion, and others that could be cited—are options that can be called upon in one utterance and then not used in the next; a speaker can in effect switch between dialects at high speed.

This phenomenon is well known, of course. If two African Americans are chatting together privately in AAVE behind the counter in a store when a white customer enters and asks a question, the next utterance heard may have a dramatically different grammar from the last as the person who responds switches dialects.

Sometimes speakers may use both more AAVE-like and less AAVE-like ways of phrasing a sentence, for example, using *Nobody likes him* and *Don't nobody like him* interchangeably. But this happens in Standard English too. For example, although it was not mentioned in the discussion of *who* and *whom* earlier, there are writers who use either form of the pronoun in the contexts we considered (examples like *We are talking about a man who[m] everyone seems to think will one day be king*). Fine writers of English like James Boswell (the biographer of dictionary maker Samuel Johnson), Benjamin Franklin, John Galsworthy, and Oliver Goldsmith have all been found to use the when-it's-the-subject-of-its-clause rule or the when-it's-the-subject-of-the-relative-clause rule interchangeably. But they are not making mistakes; they are not blundering about confusing their *who* with their *whom*. We know that, because we know they never write *Whom are you?* or *To who was it addressed?* Languages have many rules and regularities of sentence structure, and speakers select from among the possibilities in ways that are highly complex. But that is a sign of having a sophisticated and flexible grasp of the possibilities in a rule system; it is not a sign of ignorance.

NOT ALL AFRICAN AMERICANS KNOW AAVE

The grammar of AAVE—negative concord, copula omission, dropping of final consonants, and all the rest of it—has to be learned by anyone who wants to speak AAVE and be accepted linguistically in the AAVE-speaking community. Knowing AAVE does not come free with either knowing American English or having African American ethnicity. This point is beautifully (though unintentionally) illustrated by the mocking column on Ebonics that was published in the *Washington Post* on December 26, 1996, by the distinguished African American columnist Willam Raspberry.

Raspberry's column reported a fictional conversation between an imaginary Washington, D.C., cab driver and an imaginary alter ego of Raspberry himself. The cab driver speaks in AAVE: We get a total of just thirty-two words of Raspberry's made-up AAVE dialog in the piece. But Raspberry has a problem. He just does not know AAVE. The dialog he invents has grammatical errors.

First, he has the imaginary cabbie saying, "What you be talkin' 'bout, my man?" But as we saw earlier, the uninflected *be* of AAVE marks habitual aspect. The context makes clear that the cabbie means "What are you talking about right now?" not "What do you habitually talk about?" So we can be quite sure that the normal AAVE for that would be "What you talkin' 'bout?" with the zero copula (it is present tense, unemphasized, affirmative, and not first-person singular); it would not contain the uninflected *be*. (Strike one!)

The second error is in a highly contrived interchange where the fictional cabbie, who is eating fish and chips when we come upon him, says "Sup?" meaning "What's up?" and the fictional Raspberry misunderstands this as short for "Do you wish to sup?" and replies that he has already dined (I did say it was contrived). The cabbie protests the misunderstanding and says, "I don't be offerin' you my grub." He clearly means "I am not offering you my food," so this should be *I ain't offerin' you my grub*. Again we need the present progressive, not the habitual. (Note the line from "I Put a Spell on You" mentioned earlier: we get *I ain't lyin'*, not *I don't be lyin'*, because the meaning is "I am not lying right now" rather than "I do not habitually lie.") For a more distinctively AAVE utterance Raspberry could have had the cabbie say "I ain't offerin' you no grub," with the multiple negation marking that is such a distinctive feature of AAVE, but does not occur at all in Raspberry's AAVE dialog. (Strike two!)

The third error Raspberry makes is also in the cabbie's response to the misunderstanding about his monosyllabic greeting. He explains what he meant by saying "Sup?" thus: "I be sayin' hello." He means "I am saying hello to you (right now)," not "I habitually say hello." *I be sayin'* is not the way to express this. (There is an utterance containing *they be sayin'* quoted from the speaker called Larry in William Labov's article "The Logic of Nonstandard English," and it is quite clearly habitual in meaning. But I have not encountered one in which the meaning is progressive.) Here, notice, the copula cannot be omitted: *I sayin' hello* would be ungrammatical, as we noted earlier. So the most likely form we would get for this meaning would be *I'm sayin' hello*. (Strike three!)

With three strikes against him, Raspberry is already out. But there are more errors to report. The fourth comes when the Raspberry alter ego switches into AAVE for the punchline, as he realizes that he could augment his columnist's salary by giving AAVE language lessons if the Ebonics thing catches on. Raspberry should not give up his job at the *Post*, because he does not know AAVE well enough to teach it. He says, "Maybe you be onto somethin' dere, my bruvah." But once more it is the immediate present he is referring to: he does not mean "Maybe you are habitually onto something there," but rather, "Maybe you are onto something there (right now)." The usual way of saying this in AAVE would be *Maybe you onto somethin' dere* (second person, nonemphatic, not negated, present tense, so this is another of the situations where we can get the zero copula).

There are further errors in the things Raspberry has his characters say about AAVE rather than in it. The cabbie cites his brother-in-law as claiming that in order to speak AAVE you have to "leave off final consonants." But from the cabbie's first word, *'Sup*, there isn't a single final consonant missing in any of Raspberry's AAVE dialog. (As noted earlier, words like *somethin'* are not missing a final consonant.) The dropping of consonants described earlier is not illustrated in Raspberry's dialogue at all. His imaginary cabbie's brother-in-law would have us believe that in general, or at random, the last consonant of an AAVE word is (or may be) dropped. That simply is not true, as I explained earlier.

What does Raspberry's effort at humor teach us? That a Washington columnist can sometimes come up with rather lame stuff around Christmas time. But also this: AAVE should not be thought of as the language of Black people in America. Many African Americans neither speak it nor know much about it, as Raspberry demonstrates. But those who do speak AAVE are not just blundering; they have learned a complex set of rules that happens not to be the same as the complex set of rules that defines Standard English. They know a language that the highly educated Mr. Raspberry has not learned.

WHAT OAKLAND'S CRITICS MISSED

Facts about the grammar of AAVE like the ones I have reviewed in this chapter have been known to American linguists for decades, largely because of the pioneering work of people like William Labov at the University of Pennsylvania and a significant number of AAVE specialists who originally trained with him like John Rickford of Stanford University. Knowing what they knew, the members of the American linguistics profession were dismayed at the ignorance betrayed by the media commentators' angry and offensive attacks on AAVE and the Oakland school board.

Confusing lexicon with syntax, accent with dialect, difference with deficiency, and grammar with morality, the commentators clarified little except the deep hostility and contempt whites feel for the way Blacks speak (the patois of America's meanest streets, columnist George Will called it, as if AAVE could only be spoken in slums) and the deep shame felt by Americans of African descent for speaking that way (former Black Panther party official Eldridge Cleaver published an article in the *Los Angeles Times* in which he compared acknowledging AAVE with condoning cannibalism). The saddest thing is that in their scramble to find words to evince their fury and contempt at AAVE, columnists both black and white ignored the genuine issues of educational policy that had motivated the Oakland school board.

One persistent confusion was perhaps stimulated by an ambiguity in English. The phrase "instruction in French" can be understood in two ways: it could mean instruction on how to speak French, or it could mean instruction given via the medium of French. The press never figured out the difference between these two. The Oakland board members talked about "imparting instruction to African-American students in their primary language"; but this was discussed in editorials as if the proposal had been to make AAVE a school subject. The school board's statement did not suggest to me that they even considered adding AAVE to the curriculum. The plan was to use AAVE as a medium of instruction, but not to hold classes on how to speak AAVE. (The whole point, after all, is that no such classes are necessary, since the children arrive speaking it.) In addition, it was explicitly stated that in part this was "to facilitate . . . acquisition and mastery of English Language skills."

Lost from any of the press coverage that I saw was the fact that Oakland faced an issue very similar to the dilemma of Norwegian schools in which children from rural areas arrive speaking rural dialects of Norwegian very different from the standard language of Oslo. The difference is that the Norwegians love their nonstandard dialects and treat them as valued symbols of a traditional Norwegian identity. They have experimented with both total immersion, where the child is plunged into a Standard-Norwegian-only environment from day one, and techniques more reminiscent of bilingual education, where at first the rural dialect is used in the classroom and gradually the children are taught to move toward the standard language for public and official interaction and formal writing. There is some evidence that the latter works better. Teaching children to read first in their own dialects and then gradually introducing the standard language can speed and improve the acquisition of reading skills.

There is good evidence of a similar sort pertaining to African American students in the United States. College students in Chicago who received instruction concerning the contrasts between AAVE and Standard English grammar showed improved Standard English writing skills as compared to a control group. In Oakland itself, nearly twenty-five years before the great furor, it was found that teachers who condemned AAVE pronunciations and interpreted them as reading errors got the worst results in teaching AAVE-speaking children to read, while teachers who used AAVE creatively in the classroom got the best results. These and other results in the education literature suggest that the Oakland school board's policy decision had some clear motivation and scientific support.

But instead of a sympathetic consideration of the strategy they were suggesting and the evidence that supported it, the members of the Oakland school board suffered months of unrelenting ridicule, needling, and abuse from politicians, poets, and pundits in editorials, articles, talk shows, news programs, speeches, and government statements (the U.S. Department of Education pointedly announced that no federal bilingual education funds would be spent on AAVE). It was a sad spectacle.

The horror with which Americans react to the idea of using AAVE in the classroom has something to teach us about the prejudice still targeted on America's Black citizens, whose variety of English is decried as if it were some repellent disease (recall the *Economist* with its jokey headline about the Ebonics virus). Educational conservatives often deny that prejudice is involved, dismissing linguists' objective attitude toward nonstandard dialects as if it were just left-wing propaganda. But it is not. Even conservative linguists acknowledge the facts mentioned earlier. The Linguistic Society of

America's vote on a January 1997 resolution in support of the Oakland school board was actually unanimous.

Linguists will agree, of course, that Standard English has prestige and AAVE does not, and they are not trying to suggest that *Time* and *Newsweek* should start publishing articles in AAVE. They merely note that grammar in and of itself does not establish social distinctions or justify morally tinged condemnation of nonstandard dialects. AAVE has nothing inherently wrong with it as a language; it is only an accident of history that it is not the standard language of the United States. In the United States, the standard language lacks multiple negation marking, but has syllable-final consonant clusters and interdental fricative consonants. In Italy the facts are the reverse: the standard language of that country lacks syllable-final consonant clusters and interdental fricative consonants and does exhibit multiple negation marking, exactly the same combination (coincidentally) as AAVE happens to have.

The horror among the readers who witnessed the feeding frenzy in the press over the Oakland resolution got through to the parents in the city. They were alarmed enough that, fearing linguistic ghettoization of their children, they pressed the school board to reconsider. On January 15, 1997, the board did revise its statement, dropping the reference to imparting instruction in the primary language of many of its schoolchildren (while retaining, sadly, some of its misguided references to alleged African origins of AAVE). This seemed to me to be throwing out the baby of a rather sensible change in language policy while carefully saving the bathwater of Afrocentric nonsense about AAVE going back to West Africa.

Behind the statements, however, lay more than just rhetoric for public consumption. Behind the scenes, the Oakland school system was steadfast in its intent to use AAVE wherever it could assist the learning of Standard English or other subjects by its students. The board's rhetorical backdown did not mean that the policy had changed. This should not be surprising. Several other school districts in California and elsewhere have long operated programs involving AAVE in the classroom. Of course, teachers have some discretion, and many Oakland teachers speak AAVE natively; it would be impossible in practice to police classrooms tightly enough to prevent them from using their native tongue when speaking all day to children who share it.

There is thus little doubt that African American English will continue to be heard in Oakland's classrooms. It may improve the rapport in the classroom in ways that will be beneficial to learning. It is worth a try. But whatever the success of the new policy, I hope that one thing is clear: using AAVE in the classroom does not necessarily mean lowering standards or teaching things that are wrong. AAVE speakers use a different grammar, clearly and sharply distinguished from Standard English at a number of points (though massively similar to that of Standard English overall). AAVE speakers need to learn Standard English. But anyone who thinks that AAVE users are merely speaking Standard English but making mistakes is wrong. They can try to make the case that speakers of AAVE are bad or stupid or nasty or racially inferior if they want to, but they will need arguments that do not depend on language, because linguistic study of AAVE makes one thing quite clear: AAVE is not Standard English with mistakes.

NOTES AND FURTHER READING

The *New York Times* editorial that said Oakland wanted to recognize street slang was "Linguistic confusion," 24 December 1996, A12. For the article "The Ebonics virus" see *The Economist*, January 4, 1997, 26–7. The word *Ebonics* was coined by R. L. Williams in *Ebonics: The True Language of Black Folks* (Institute of Black Studies, St Louis, 1975). The *Ethnologue* is edited by Barbara F. Grimes (Dallas, TX: Summer Institute of Linguistics, 1996). *Classification and index of the world's languages* is by C. F. and F. M. Voegelin (New York: Elsevier, 1977). John McWhorter's comments can be found in his book *The word on the street* (New York, NY: Plenum Press, 1998). Good examples of William Labov's work are "The logic of nonstandard English," reprinted in *Language and social context*, pp. 179–215, ed. by P. Giglioli (Penguin Books, 1972), and "The case of the missing copula," in *Language: An invitation to cognitive science*, 2nd ed. vol. 1, ed. by Lila R. Gleitman and Mark Y. Liberman, 25–54 (Cambridge, MA: MIT Press). For a technical study of negative inversion see Peter Sells, John Rickford, and Thomas Wasow, "An optimality-theoretic approach to variation in negative inversion in African American Vernacular English," *Natural Language and Linguistic Theory* 14 (1996) 591–627. John Rickford's work can be explored on his web site at *http://www.stanford.edu/~rickford*. George Will's reference to "the patois of America's meanest streets" was in "58 boys and the larger scheme of things," *San Francisco Chronicle*, 1 January 1997. Eldridge Cleaver compared recognizing AAVE to condoning cannibalism in a column in the *Los Angeles Times*, January 31, 1997. One study of teaching dialect speakers a standard language in Scandinavia can be found in T. Osterberg, *Bilingualism and the First School Language* (Umeå: Västerbottens Trycheri, 1961). Using AAVE in teaching black college students in Chicago was studied by Hanni Taylor in *Standard English, Black English, and bidialectalism* (Peter Lang, New York, 1989). The utility of AAVE in teaching Black first-graders in Oakland was studied by A. M. Piestrup, *Black dialect interference and accommodation of reading instruction in first grade* (Monographs of the Language Behavior Research Laboratory 4, University of California, Berkeley, 1973). William Raspberry's column "To throw in a lot of 'bes,' or not? A conversation on Ebonics" appeared in the *Washington Post* on December 26, 1996. I am deeply grateful to Barbara Scholz for extensive comments and invaluable suggestions, and to Rodney Huddleston, Bill Ladusaw, John Rickford, Rebecca Wheeler, and Arnold Zwicky for their help.

4

Home Speech as Springboard to School Speech: Oakland's Commendable Work on Ebonics

Rebecca S. Wheeler

An animation short from the late 1960s, *Bambi Meets Godzilla*, offers a twist on the familiar Disney Bambi. As the short opens, we see Bambi bouncing and frolicking amid flowers, munching grass. The sky is darkened as a vast, hairy foot encroaches. Boom. Squish. Bambi is gone.

Given public reaction to the Oakland school board's recommendation regarding the use of Ebonics in the classroom (December 18, 1996), one has the impression that America itself would like to do a Godzilla on Ebonics. From conversations over the backyard fence to writings by big-name syndicated columnists and proclamations by high-ranking federal officials, the American public has borne strong witness against Ebonics.

For example, in the *Los Angeles Times*, James Shaw served an invective smorgasbord: Ebonics, he claimed, "is nothing more than a linguistic sham, that with porcine gluttony, vacuum-sucks every verbal deformity from plantation patois to black slang, from rap to hip hop, from jive to crippled English, and serves up the resultant gumbo as 'black English.' " (Shaw 1996). "Verbal deformity?" "Crippled English?"

William Raspberry, similarly but more mundanely, diagnosed that the tongue now called Ebonics was, until recently, known as Black English, or Ghettoese. "As I recall," he continued, "it sounds rather like what our mothers used to call Bad English" (Raspberry 1996).

The Reverend Jesse Jackson initially came out like a furnace blast: "[I]n Oakland, some madness has erupted over making slang talk a second language." "You don't have to go to school to learn to talk garbage," Jackson admonished (Seligman 1996).

What is Ebonics? Is it a language or a dialect? Is it slang? Is it "bad" English? "Garbage"?

On the language/dialect question, the Linguistic Society of America (LSA), the professional society of linguists, has stated that "[t]he distinction between 'languages' and 'dialects' is usually made more on social and political grounds than on purely linguistic ones" (Linguistic Society of America 1997). Thus sociopolitical considerations, not whether speakers can understand each other, are what often lead people to say they speak different languages or dialects of the same language. For example, what used to be called one language, Serbo-Croat, is now referred to as three languages, reflecting political divisions: Serbian, Croatian, and Bosnian (Pullum 1997). Similarly, speakers of Swedish and Norwegian generally do understand each other but nonetheless see themselves as speaking different languages, reflecting national boundaries. By contrast, "different varieties of Chinese are popularly regarded as 'dialects,' though their speakers cannot understand each other" (LSA 1997). More anecdotally, Professor Charles Fillmore, a Berkeley linguist, observed that "[d]eciding whether BBC newsreaders and Lynchburg, Va., radio evangelists speak different dialects of the same language or different languages in the same language family is on the level of deciding whether Greenland is a small continent or a large island" (Fillmore 1997). Nonetheless, the case of Black English is rather clear: essentially all linguists agree that Black English is a dialect of English, just as Standard English is also a dialect of English.

Is Black English "slang"? No. Slang is a term dealing only with the style of *words* that people use. According to Geoffrey Pullum, writing in *Nature*, "Slang, in any language, consists of a finite list of words or idiomatic phrases, highly vivid and informal, in the most casual stratum of its lexicon" (1997). Thus slang is "the ephemera" of the street. Black English, on the other hand, is "a perfectly ordinary variety of English spoken by a large and diverse population of Americans of African descent, by no means all of whom are slang-users." Of course, language is made up of much more than just words; it's made up of pronunciation of those words; it's made up of word-internal structuring (e.g., word endings or beginnings that signal different meanings or functions of different sorts); and it's made up of how words are ordered into phrases, and phrases into clauses and sentences. Black English exhibits its own regular system of rules for sound, vocabulary, word structure, and ordering of words into phrases and clauses. It is much, much more than "slang."

On the matter of "bad English," "broken English," and the like, I return again to the resolution by the Linguistic Society of America.

The variety known as "Ebonics" [and] "African American Vernacular English" (AAVE) . . . is systematic and rule-governed like all natural speech varieties. In fact, all human linguistic systems—spoken, signed, and written— are fundamentally regular. The systematic and expressive nature of the grammar and pronunciation patterns of the African American vernacular has been established by numerous scientific studies over the past thirty years. Characterizations of Ebonics as "slang," "mutant," "lazy," "defective," "ungrammatical," or "broken English" are incorrect and demeaning. (Linguistic Society of America 1997)

So when James Shaw, William Raspberry, and Jesse Jackson decry Black English in the wild and degrading terms we've heard, what they're doing, among other things, is displaying a lack of familiarity with decades of scientific research on language. They have missed the point, as have many others.

During a dinner conversation in the spring of 1997, a physicist asked me, "As a linguist, what's your stand on Ebonics?" Before venturing a reply, I sought his assumptions: "What do you think Oakland has proposed to do?" I asked him. He replied, "They want to teach Black English in the schools."

No, Oakland did not suggest that schools teach Ebonics. They proposed that teachers "take Ebonics into account" in the teaching of Standard English in the classroom. They proposed that the teachers not demean students who arrived speaking a home language differing widely from the standard dialect. Now we begin to get at the real problem Oakland sought to address.

The real issue, the one to which Oakland was speaking, is that public education is failing to reach children from low-income areas. Recent evidence from the San Francisco area shows just how bad it gets. Professor John Rickford, a Stanford linguist specializing in African American English, has reported that a 1990 California study revealed that

> third grade kids in the primarily white, middle class Palo Alto School District scored on the 94th percentile in writing; by the [sixth] grade, they had topped out at the 99th percentile. By contrast, third grade kids in primarily African American working class East Palo Alto (Ravenswood School District) scored on the 21st percentile in writing, but by the sixth grade, they had fallen to the 3rd percentile, almost to the very bottom. (Rickford 1996)

Why this divergence? Why do the middle-class students soar to the top while lower-class students drop to the utter bottom? In this chapter, I will focus on a number of careful educational studies which show that language is a key culprit in minority children's failure in school. Intuitively, for the middle-class students, we see that their home speech largely matches that of the teachers and the textbooks they'll use. For lower-class students, the rift between home speech and school speech is great. Then, when teachers talk and write Standard English at children who speak something quite other than the standard, those children get lost and stay lost. If a child is unable to read successfully, that failure entrains failure in the rest of his or her school studies.

Of course, Black children falling by the school wayside is nothing new in America. More than twenty-five years ago, in the 1970s, Black families took legal action against our educational system for this very reason. William Labov of the University of Pennsylvania, who has done groundbreaking work on the language of the inner cities, reports that in the housing projects of Ann Arbor, Michigan, mothers of Black children sued the city. These mothers stated that "their children were suffering educational failure, though they were of normal intelligence and ability, because the school had failed to take into account their special cultural and linguistic background" (Labov 1995). Labov reports that the court held for the mothers, finding that "the suit had merit under Title 20, Sec. 1703(f), which stated that no child should be deprived of equal educational opportunity because of the failure of an educational agency to take appropriate action to overcome linguistic barriers" (Labov 1995).

Appropriate action to overcome linguistic barriers was precisely what psychologists Gary and Charlesetta Simpkins had in mind when they developed a series of dialect readers for Black students. It was called the *Bridge* program. Published by Houghton Mifflin in 1977, the *Bridge* program offered a "series of graded readings and cassette recordings that made use of the traditional folklore of African-American culture." These readers met the children at their linguistic home, African American English, and helped the children learn to read in their home speech vernacular. Having begun to successfully read, the children moved to the transitional reader and finally to readers in the standard dialect (Labov 1995).

The following gives you a feel for the materials *Bridge* presented fourth-grade children:

> But dig! I know where you *been*, and I know where you comin' from too. When you was jus' startin' in school, readin' got on yo' case, now didn't it, got down on you. Hurt your feelings. In the second grade, readin' jus' smacked you all upside yo' head, dared you do sump'm about it. In the third grade, hum, readin' got into your ches', knocked you down, dragged you through the *mud*, sent you home cryin' to yo' mama. Now by the time you got to the fo'th grade, you jus' about had enough of messin' around with this here readin' thing. And you said to yourself, I ain' gon' be messin' with this ol' bad boy no *more!* You jus' hung it up. But you had to keep your front so you say, I don' need no readin', it ain' nothin' I want to read nohow. . . . But dig! like I said now, this here program is kind of different. I want to hip you to that. It can help you git it together. You know, keep you from bein' pushed around by reading. And it ain't *borin'*. Cause it's about really interesting people. Matter of fact, it's about the most interesting people in the world, black people, and you know how interesting bloods can be. (Labov 1995)

And get it together the children did, that is, the children who used the *Bridge* readers. These dialect readers were tested over a 4-month period "in five areas of the United States, with 14 teachers and 27 classes from the 7th through the 12th grades, involving 540 students—all but 10 of them black" (Labov 1995). The experimental group (21 classes) used the dialect readers, whereas the control group (6 classes) did not. Instead, the control group used standard remedial English techniques.

The results were stark: When tested on the Iowa Test of Basic Skills, after 4 months of instruction, the African American students using the dialect readers showed 6.2 months of progress, while African American students using Standard English books made only 1.6 months of progress (Simpkins and Simpkins 1981, 238). Let me repeat that. Use dialect readers for 4 months and reap 6.2 months of progress. Don't use them and harvest a meager 1.6 months of progress over the same 4 months of instruction. No wonder we see the lower-income children falling to the bottom of the educational heap.

Why did the dialect readers work so well? The answer is that learning to read is a task distinct from that of learning another dialect. Conflating the two leads to student failure. Separating the tasks, reading and dialect acquisition, enables students to succeed at both.

The success of the *Bridge* readers is no isolated case, as we see from John Rickford's testimony before the Senate subcommittee hearings on Ebonics. Rickford cited six studies involving children with minority dialects learning to read: two from Europe and four from the United States. Representing Europe were Sweden and Norway, weighing in with findings paralleling those of the *Bridge* readers. Each found that "the vernacular children [taught with vernacular readers] read significantly faster and better than control subjects," those not taught with the dialect readers (Rickford 1997; Bull 1990, 78; Österberg 1961).

The same insights hold also with older students. In Chicago, one educator sought to improve the writing of inner-city university students. Hanni Taylor examined two approaches with African American students. In his experimental class, he taught writing by contrasting African American English and Standard English, thus helping students see differences between the two grammatical systems. In the control group, he used "traditional English department techniques." Rickford reported that after three months, "the experimental group showed a 59 % reduction in the use of Ebonics features in their SE [Standard English] writing, while the control group, using traditional methods, showed a slight INCREASE (8.5 %)" in the use of African American features. Taylor observed that students were often unaware of the detailed differences between African American English and Standard English. Contrasting the two systems helped students "limit AAE intrusions into their SE usage" (Rickford 1997).

Moving south, teachers in DeKalb County, Georgia, also help young speakers of minority dialects explicitly contrast their home speech with the standard. Thus when a fifth-grader answers a question with a double negative ("not no more"), the teacher prompts the student to "code-switch," to which the student replies, "not any more". The *Atlanta Constitution* reported that in this "Bidialectal Communication" program, the children learn to switch from their home speech to school speech at appropriate times and places, and that "the dialect they might use at home is valuable and 'effective' in that setting, but not for school, for work—or for American democracy" (Cumming 1997). This program has been designated a "center of excellence" by the National Council of Teachers of English. In sum, "Teaching methods which DO take vernacular dialects into account in teaching the standard work better than those which DO NOT" (Rickford 1996).

While DeKalb has received merit recognition for its bidialectal approach, not all such programs have been so well received. Where are Houghton Mifflin's hugely successful dialect readers? Canceled. Canceled by the publisher due to a storm of protest by parents, the community, and the nation against so-called bad English being taught in the schools.

Twenty years after public outcry forced the publisher to cancel the *Bridge* readers, Oakland has suffered the same firestorm. And it continues to be the case that "the longer African American inner city kids stay in school, the worse they do" (Rickford 1996; see also Labov 1995). But it doesn't have to be that way. Oakland has resolved to change this pattern.

Oakland has resolved to be aware of its audience, to take the language of its students into account in its teaching. This is just common sense. We all adjust what we say and how we say it to reflect the knowledge and circumstances of the person we're speaking with. Thus the way my lawyer-brother talks to me about his work is different from the way he discusses cases with his colleagues. Or when I'm working with a classroom of undergraduates, I adjust my vocabulary and content so they're likely to grasp my message. That's pretty basic. Speak to your audience so they can understand. Then, from a point of mutual comprehension, you can move forward. That, in large part, is what Oakland's resolution is about.

In particular, Oakland wants to recognize that its clients, the students, speak Black English. Oakland wants to use the students' knowledge of their own home speech (Black English) as a springboard to help them learn school speech (Standard English). Standard English *is* the goal. Research has shown that the students will get there if they're able to say freely and confidently, "In my dialect we say it like this."

Good has already come out of Oakland's resolution on Ebonics. I hear that the authors of the *Bridge* readers are back at work, revising the readers for new rerelease. Because of the so-called Ebonics debate, African American struggles and achievement in the schools have been front-page news. Maybe as the dust settles, we can now hear and act on Oakland's resolution. In the words of Oakland's revised resolution, "the Superintendent, in conjunction with her staff shall immediately devise and implement the best possible academic program for the combined purposes of facilitating the acquisition and mastery of English language skills, while respecting and embracing the legitimacy and richness of the language patterns" known as Ebonics, or African American English. *That* is an idea whose time has surely come.

REFERENCES

Bull, Tove. 1990. Teaching school beginners to read and write in the vernacular. *Tromsø linguistics in the 80s*. Oslo: Novus Press.

Cumming, Doug. 1997. A different approach to teaching language. *The Atlanta Constitution* (January 9): B1.

Fillmore, Charles J. 1997. A Linguist Looks at the Ebonics Debate. Center for Applied Linguistics, *http://www.cal.org*. (January 27).

Gadsden, Vivian, and Daniel Wagner, eds. 1995. *Literacy among African-American youth*. Creskill, NJ: Hampton Press.

Labov, William. 1995. Can reading failure be reversed? A linguistic approach to the question. *Literacy among African-American youth*, ed. by Vivian Gadsden and Daniel Wagner. Creskill, NJ: Hampton Press. (Citation taken from a version of this article posted on the Internet at *http://www.ling.upenn/phono__atlas/RFR.html*.)

Linguistic Society of America. 1997. Resolution on the Oakland "Ebonics" issue. Unanimously adopted at the Annual Meeting of the Linguistic Society of America, Chicago, Illinois (January 3).

Österberg, Tore. 1961. *Bilingualism and the first school language: An educational problem illustrated by results from a Swedish dialect area*. Umeå: Västerbottens Tryckeri.

Pullum, Geoffrey. 1997. Language that dare not speak its name. *Nature* 386 (March 27): 321.

Raspberry, William. 1996. To throw in a lot of "bes," or not? A conversation on Ebonics. *Washington Post* (December 26): A27.

Rickford, John R. 1996. The Oakland Ebonics decision: Commendable attack on the problem. Op-ed article. *San Jose Mercury News* (December 26).

———. 1997. Congressional testimony before the Senate Subcommittee on Labor, Health and Human Services, and Education, Senator Arlen Specter, Chairman (January 22).

Secretary of the Board of Education, Oakland, California. 1997. *Amended resolution of the Board of Education adopting the report and recommendations of the African-American Task force; A policy statement and directing the superintendent of schools to devise a program to improve the English language acquisition and application skills of African-American students*. Resolution number 9697–0063 (January 15).

Seligman, Katherine. 1996. Embattled Oakland officials hire public relations consultant, insist Black English plan is sound. *San Francisco Examiner* (December 22).

Shaw, James, E. 1996. Perspectives on 'Ebonics': Don't self-inflict another obstacle. News commentary. *Los Angeles Times* (December 27).

Simpkins, Gary, and Charletta Simpkins. 1981. Cross-cultural approach to curriculum development. *Black English and the education of Black children and youth: Proceedings of the National Invitational Symposium on the King decision*, ed. by Geneva Smitherman, 212–40. Detroit: Center for Black Studies, Wayne State University.

SOUTHERN MOUNTAIN ENGLISH: THE LANGUAGE OF THE OZARKS AND SOUTHERN APPALACHIA

Bethany K. Dumas

"I know it ain't right, but I think it's pretty good."
—Arkansas Ozarks speaker, 1974

A woman who had grown up in southeast Texas moved to Fayetteville, Arkansas, to attend graduate school at the University of Arkansas, located near the heart of the Ozark Mountains. When she did so, she left the rice fields and cattle and oil refineries of what was once called the Golden Triangle for the mountains and moonshine and barefoot hillbillies of northeast Arkansas.

There the young woman had the good fortune to become friends immediately with two folklorists, Mary Celestia Parler and Vance Randolph (later, Mr. and Mrs. Vance Randolph). Her new friends took her with them on trips into the nearby Ozark Mountains to collect folktales and folksongs. The young Texan was fascinated, both by the scenery (southeast Texas has no mountains) and by what she heard, and the Randolphs thought they had a convert.

But it was not the folklore that she found interesting; it was the hill talk—the words and expressions and the pronunciations of those words and expressions—that held her attention. It was the terms *highland fish* and *dryland fish* for *morels*, a type of mushroom (typically fried in butter, they taste something like fresh fish). It was *hit* for *it*, *bile* for *boil*, *waspers* for *wasps*, *baking powders* for *baking powder*, and *het* for *heated*.

Some of those words and expressions had been documented a few years earlier by Vance Randolph and his collaborator George P. Wilson in the 1953 book *Down in the Holler: A Gallery of Ozark Folk Speech*. That book was based primarily on a series of fifteen articles that Vance Randolph wrote between 1926 and 1936 for the American Dialect Society publications *Dialect Notes* and *American Speech*. The articles represented Randolph's attempt to write down what he had heard in the Ozarks, how he had heard it said, and what it had seemed to mean (vii). Though not trained as a linguist, Randolph had a good ear and was a careful observer, and he spent many years collecting folklore in the Ozark Mountains. He almost single-handedly preserved for us much of our Ozark folk heritage in his many publications and archives.

The book is also an entertaining and highly readable introduction to the language historically used by people who live in the Ozark Mountains, most of whom were in the 1950s the descendants of pioneers from Southern Appalachia, and by people who live in Southern Appalachia itself. It contains chapters on "Ozark Pronunciation" and "Backwoods Grammar," of course, but also "Survivals of Early English" and "Taboos and Euphemisms." This book does not deal with the folktales Randolph collected, but it does recognize the importance of "Dialect in Fiction" and contains chapters and word lists on words and expressions.

Thus was the young woman introduced to the language variety spoken in the Ozarks and, as she later discovered, also in the Southern Appalachian Mountains. I was that young woman, of course, and those expeditions in the Arkansas Ozarks in 1959 and the early 1960s changed the course of my professional life. I was studying English, and I intended to be a professor of contemporary literature. Because of my fascination with regional (and later social) dialects, I started taking courses in linguistics and the history of the English language, and I wrote a dissertation on the dialect of Newton County, Arkansas (Dumas 1971; see also Dumas 1975a). Eventually, I found myself teaching courses exclusively in linguistics, at first in Texas, then in East Tennessee in the region to which the Ozark settlers had moved from where they began their western pilgrimage. (Detailed scholarly information about Ozark and Appalachian dialects can be found in Christian, Wolfram, and Dubé 1988; Wolfram and Christian 1976; and Wolfram and Schilling-Estes 1998.)

WHAT IS A DIALECT?

By *dialect* I mean the patterns of speech that distinguish this region from others in this country. Everyone speaks a dialect; that is, everyone uses words and phrases in distinctive ways. Speakers in some parts of this country and speakers who belong to certain ethnic or other social groups are easily identified by their use of language. Speakers in the Ozarks and Southern Appalachia are a bit easier to identify in terms of their geographic origin than many other speakers, though New Yorkers and New Englanders are also quite distinctive, as are speakers from Brooklyn, the Bronx, and New

Orleans. (For an entertaining and accurate portrayal of many dialects of American English, see the film *American Tongues* from the Center for New American Media, Kolker and Alvarez, 1986.) Southern Mountaineers do not say *youse guys* or *toity-toid* (for *thirty-third*), as Brooklyn speakers do, and they do not call a *milk shake* a *cabinet*, as speakers in Rhode Island do. They do not *make groceries* or eat *jambalaya*, as speakers in New Orleans do. They *buy groceries* or *go grocery shopping* and they eat *stew*. They certainly do not *shlep about*, as Manhattanites do.

So what exactly did I hear? And how exactly was it different from what I had heard in southeast Texas and the small towns between Houston and San Antonio, where I had also spent some of my early years?

First of all, I heard very little Spanish! Many words I had heard frequently in southeast Texas disappeared. Nobody ate or talked about *frijoles* or *masa*, nobody owned a *cantina*, and of course nobody wore a *sombrero*. People ate *chittlins* and cooked *messes of greens* and carried their groceries in a *poke* and also ate *poke salit*, a green that I was not familiar with. I heard about *blinky blue-john* (*skim milk*), met *double cousins* (the product of the marriages of two brothers to two sisters; the unmodified word *cousin* may indicate distant relationship; a first cousin was always called an *own cousin*), lived through an occasional *blackberry winter* (a late spring cold spell), and learned that *laplanders* lived near the Missouri *bootheel*, not in Lapland.

I continued to hear "nonstandard" terms that I had heard all my life, of course—*ain't* and *clum* (*climbed*) and *hern* (*hers*) and *ourn* (*ours*) and *theirn* (*theirs*) and *ary* and *nary* and *they's* (*there are*) and *you all* for *you* (plural) and *go to* (*be about to*). But for the first time, I also heard *hain't* and *aim to* and *bad to* (as in "She's *bad to* make fudge," meaning that she makes it frequently, and "He was the *worst* I ever seen *to* run off," meaning that he ran off frequently) and *beal* (*gather* or *fester*) and *borned* and *bound to* and *everwhat* and *everwhen* and *everwho* and *et* (for *ate*) and *'mater* and *offen* (for *off of* 'from', as in "We bought a pony *offen* our uncle") and *twicet* (for *twice*) and *you'uns* for *you*.

And later, in Southern Appalachia itself, particularly East Tennessee, I also heard vocabulary items like *dog irons* (instead of *andirons*), *dope* (for what others call a *soft drink* or a *cold drink* or a generic *coke*), *fireboard* (for *mantel* or *mantel board*); here they also *hope how soon* certain events will happen and exchange bean recipes containing such directions as "cook 'em 'till *the bullets*'ll mash." Here *baby chicks* may be called *diddles, doodles,* or *biddies,* and *baby ducks* are *gawks* or *boomers,* depending on their age. There is some regional variation within Southern Appalachia, and there are speakers who swear that they can tell what county a speaker is from by which term she or he uses for baby chicks. (For other examples, see Dumas 1981a. Michael Montgomery is editing the *Dictionary of Smoky Mountain English*, due to be submitted for publication by the end of 1998.

His coeditor is the late Joseph Sargent Hall, on whose collections the volume is based in large part.)

All over the Ozarks and all through Southern Appalachia, I also heard pronunciation patterns different from those I encounter elsewhere. It is those pronunciation patterns that most quickly identify people as speakers of Southern Mountain English (SME), even though that variety shares characteristics with other Southern U.S. patterns, both Southern White English and African American Vernacular English.

SOUTHERN MOUNTAIN ENGLISH (SME)

African American Vernacular English (AAVE), or Ebonics, as it is sometimes called today, is clearly the most highly stigmatized social dialect in the United States, but the dialect spoken by rural inhabitants of Southern Appalachia and the Ozarks is the most highly stigmatized regional pattern. Its speakers are often referred to as "hillbillies," and their speech is often ridiculed, particularly outside the region (some features are described in their historical context in Dumas 1975b).

Most identifying characteristics of SME have been documented at least as far west as Newton County, Arkansas, and many of them have been documented as far west as West Texas. In particular, there is a settlement area in East Texas that mirrors many of the language characteristics I am discussing here. My mother, who was born in Stockdale, Texas, says *kindly* for *kind of* and knows many of the folk sayings that are found in Randolph and Wilson's book. I have heard her explain one of them, *to light a shuck for home*, meaning *to be in a hurry*, in terms of earlier artifacts. Earlier in this century, people did not own flashlights, and country roads were not lighted at night. When farm people walked home from a neighbor's at night, they carried a lighted cornstalk that had been soaked in kerosene— they literally *lit a shuck for home* when they departed, usually in a hurry.

Today, some communities celebrate their heritage of unusual things and unusual words. Cosby, Tennessee, a small town near Knoxville, holds an annual Ramp Festival in April. The festival celebrates the appearance of the *ramp*, a wild vegetable resembling a wild onion or garlic. It was traditionally the first vegetable to appear every spring. The odor of the ramp is quite strong, and Appalachian newspapers from earlier in this century contain stories about children being punished or even suspended for eating the plant on the way to school.

Stress Patterns in SME

But what of other differences? Southern dialects are distinguished partly by a pervasive stress pattern different from that heard in other varieties.

Other speakers notice that many words and phrases that elsewhere get stress only on the second syllable are stressed on the first syllable in Greater Appalachia. Representative words and phrases are *HO-tel, MO-tel, PO-lice, GI-tar* (*guitar*), and *RED light*, the invariant rural term for a *traffic signal*. Words that end in final -*ent*, particularly if they are trisyllabic words, are frequently given virtually uniform stress on the three syllables, for example, *SET-UL-MINT* for *settlement, AK-SI-DINT* for *accident*, and *CON-FI-DINT* for *confident*. Finally, in the state of Tennessee, for instance, a syllable like -*ville* (as in *Knoxville, Asheville*, and *Maryville*) receives little or no stress; the vowel in the final syllable is reduced to an unstressed *uh* sound, thus *Knox-vul, Ash-vul*, and *Mur-vul*. (What do you make of the fact that when Lamar Alexander campaigned for the vice presidency, he started saying *Ma-ry-ville?*) The pattern described here is not uniform for all speakers, of course; it is most representative of speakers in rural areas.

Vowels and Consonants in SME

Pronunciation patterns also vary with respect to how vowels and consonants are pronounced. Some differences are not particularly indicative of region, social class, or education (though they may be indicative of age). Consider, for instance, *data, almond*, and *forehead*. How do you pronounce these words? Do all family members say them alike?

Other differences, however, are diagnostic. Consider *roof, here, my, house*, and *ten*. Some vowel and consonant sounds in SME are quite different from their sounds elsewhere. The patterns are not completely uniform; some are heard widely in urban as well as rural areas, while others are heard more often in rural areas or from speakers with less formal education.

It is important to remember that many patterns are dependent on such factors as preceding and following sounds and also grammatical role. No speaker, for instance, invariably uses *hit* for *it* wherever it occurs.

Vowels in SME

The most noticeable pronunciation variation in SME is found in the pronunciation of the vowels. Three patterns are highly characteristic. First, the vowel of the personal pronoun *I* or the word *ice* or the initial syllable in a word like *island* is a long *ah* sound instead of the diphthong heard in some varieties of American English. In the state of Arkansas, a phrase like *nice white rice* will distinguish delta speakers from mountain speakers. For such speakers, *I* rhymes with *la*.

Such a pronunciation is to some extent *socially diagnostic*; that is, other speakers may make value judgments about one's intelligence and education based on hearing *ah* instead of a diphthong in words like *I*. A recent publication (Jennings 1998, 150–51) illustrates this reality, as well as the reality of pronunciation differences throughout the American South:

> My father is from east Tennessee; my mother, from piedmont North Carolina. I was raised in east Tennessee surrounded by my cousins on Daddy's side. When I was three or four—before I could read, anyway—I said something to my mother about her *arhnin'*. She looked stern and said, "Say *iron*." I said *arhn* and she said *iron*, and we went back and forth. I never did make her happy. She'd say, "Say *fire*," and I'd say *farh*, and that went on for awhile.
>
> I couldn't understand the point of it, couldn't tell the difference. To my ear we were both saying *iron* and *fire*. . . .
>
> I've puzzled over that day for years. I was 20-something before I figured out that the iron and fire struggle was a pronunciation lesson.

Second, the stressed vowel in words like *just, judge*, and *mother* is pronounced further forward in the mouth and higher, so that it is sometimes perceived as being an *eh* sound, rather than an *uh* sound. This is why comic strips like "Snuffy Smith" sometimes spell the word *just* as *jist* in the phrase *jist a minit*.

All throughout the American South, virtually all speakers pronounce pairs of words like *ten* and *tin* and *pen* and *pin* the same. There is no vowel contrast before an *n*.

Some other patterns appear to be dying out in SME. For instance, until recently, it has not been unusual to hear a glide or semivowel sound, like a *y*, after word-initial *t-, d-*, or *st-*, so that words like *Tuesday, due, new*, and *student* sound like *Tyuesday, dyue, nyew*, and *styudent*.

But other patterns are entering the dialect. One example of change in progress in SME can be seen by comparing pairs of words like *deal* and *dill* and *meal* and *mill*, which have come to be pronounced alike only in recent decades. I vividly remember the day I saw this sign on a carpet store in Knoxville, Tennessee: No Frills, Just Deals. I knew that for many speakers, the words *frill* and *deal* did not rhyme. But I also knew that retail signs rhyme just as predictably as children's nursery rhymes do. When I got to my office that day, I asked a secretary to telephone the carpet store and ask what the sign said. Sure enough, in the pronunciation of the speaker at the carpet store, the words *frill* and *deal* were pronounced *fril* and *dil*. A local realtor named Neal Hill laughed when he explained that he never knew whether people would call him *niy-ul hiy-ul* or *nil hil*.

Consonants in SME

The most striking consonant pattern in SME is the retention of the sound *r* at the ends of syllables and words. Whereas Southerners further south often lost the *r* sound, mountain speakers have kept it. They say *bear* and *care* and *fair*, not *beah* or *caeah* or *faieh*.

Sometimes a medial or final *l* is vocalized, that is, realized as a vowel-like sound, rather than as a consonantal sound, so that the pronunciation of *help*, for instance, is something like *hep*, and the pronunciation of *will* may be something like *wii* with a lengthened vowel. One sees self-service gasoline stations called HEP-UR-SEF.

Some of the most interesting consonant patterns result from the simplification of word-final clusters; words like *test, desk*, and *hand* routinely become *tes, des*, and *han*. Words like *build, cold*, and *west* sound the same as *Bill, coal*, and *Wes*. More important, the past-tense forms of verbs like *missed, messed*, and *dressed* may be heard as identical with their present-tense forms.

Final nasal consonants, spelled *m, n*, or *ng*, are sometimes lost. When this happens, a vowel occurring earlier in the word may be lengthened and even given a nasal sound. When this pattern is combined with other simplification patterns, such phrases as *I am going to* or its contracted equivalent *I'm going to* become something like a simple *I'ma*, again often with an accompanying nasal sound. Thus a sentence like *I'm going to go to town* may be realized as *I'ma go to town*. Such patterns sometimes may lead well-meaning people to talk about the "laziness" of Southern speech. The pattern is actually a reflection of the complexity of pronunciation rules in Southern speech.

Verb Phrases in SME

A similar complexity is seen in some sentence patterns, particularly verb-phrase patterns, that continue to exist in SME, though they have changed elsewhere. Some Ozark and Southern Appalachian grammatical patterns that arouse a lot of comment outside the Southern Mountains are so clearly related to earlier forms of English that people occasionally say that speakers in the hills speak "pure Elizabethan English" or "pure Shakespearean English." Those statements are not true, of course. But SME does preserve some patterns that have died out in English spoken elsewhere in the United States. For instance, Ozark and Appalachian speakers still use *double modals* and *a-prefixing*.

Double Modals in SME

Modal verbs are those auxiliary verbs (sometimes used alone) or helping verbs that are used together with main verbs. A complete list includes *can, could, may, might, shall, should, will*, and *would*. In addition, the words and phrases *must, have to*, and *ought to*, sometimes called quasi-modals, behave somewhat like true modals. These verbs have in common the fact that, with two exceptions, they suggest possibility or probability rather than surety. The exceptions are *shall* and *will*, which often indicate simple future time.

The "rule" about modal auxiliaries in Standard English and most English dialects is that they cannot combine with each other. Speakers can say "I *might* go" or "He *could* fix it," but not "I *might can* go" or "He *might should* go early today." But the "rule" in the Southern Mountain region is that these combinations are quite ordinary and usual. Even triple combinations occur, particularly with *ought to* (often pronounced *oughta*), as in "She *might should ought to* leave well enough alone."

A- Prefixing in SME

The *a*-prefixing pattern is one that involves preceding an *-ing* form of the verb with the syllable *a-* (always pronounced *uh*). Here are some representative sentences:

1. I hadn't been *a-foolin'* 'round with her in the first place.
2. They wouldn't, hadn't believed him—thought he's *a-lyin'*.
3. And I always, when I was *a-raisin'* my family, tried to raise from three to five hundred bushel o' corn a year.
4. I've worked them up 'n' down for the blacksmith, when he'd be *a-heatin'* iron to fix up shoes.
5. Listen you get out of this yard, or you're gonna be findin' yourself *a-layin'* right where you're at, woman!

Don't Care to in SME

Occasionally, an ordinary phrase has a dialect meaning quite different from its meaning elsewhere. For most speakers, the phrase *don't care to* means *don't want to*, as in "I *don't care to* go to the Mall on the weekend." But in Southern Appalachia and the Ozarks, the phrase almost always means *don't mind* or even *want to*, as in "I *don't care to* go to the movies," meaning "Yes, I want to go to the movies." Occasionally, students in my dialects class at the University of Tennessee will say, when I talk about this pattern, "Oh, you mean that when my roommate said last week that she didn't care to do such-and-such, she wasn't refusing to do it?!?" The light dawns as they understand that they completely misunderstood what was being said!

SME AND EDITED AMERICAN ENGLISH

We have seen that SME differs from other dialects in its choice of words, its pronunciation of words, its meanings of words and phrases, and its use of grammatical structures. Some of the patterns are quite different from those that are used in what we might call edited American English, the kind of written English that appears in textbooks, major newspapers like the *New York Times* and the *Washington Post*, and most books that appear on best-seller lists. The question arises: Are these patterns in some way "wrong"? That raises an even larger question, "Does it make sense to talk about *right* and *wrong* when we are talking about dialect differences?"

English teachers seem to think that the answer to both those questions is "yes." In school, students spend a lot of time filling in blanks and getting grammar questions "right." My own experience in school was that I could always fill in the blank with the right noun plural or past-tense verb and that I knew how to spell. I knew in some sense that many of the words and phrases I mentioned earlier in this chapter were "ungrammatical." I also knew, though, that what was "right" in the English classroom did not always match what was usual and ordinary in the world outside the English classroom, and I had no trouble leaving behind the somewhat artificial norms of the classroom when I left school for the day.

DIALECTS AND LINGUISTIC PREJUDICE

I was in graduate school, though, before I began to understand the nature and force of the linguistic prejudice that can result from prescriptivist attitudes coupled with ignorance about the history of our language and the nature of language change and variation. What do I mean by prescriptivist attitudes? I mean those attitudes that give credence to some language myths that are in fact not true.

One myth says that there is a uniform spoken and written Standard English used by educated speakers everywhere in this country. The reality, as we have seen, is that speakers vary widely with respect to the words they use, how they pronounce those words, and how they combine those words into phrases, clauses, sentences, and even, as we shall see, longer texts. Another myth is that dialects other than Standard English are deficient for communication purposes. The reality, as most of us intuitively know, is quite otherwise.

CHANGE IS INEVITABLE

The single most important fact about language is that it is always changing. There is no more reason for us to speak and write like William Shakespeare or Alexander Pope did than there was for Shakespeare or Pope to speak and write like the author of *Beowulf* did. And if you have looked at the original language of *Beowulf*, you are probably very glad that they did not! And there is no reason to assume that speakers in the year 2050 will sound like we do today. Prescriptivists in our classrooms sometimes devote much energy to telling students how they ought to use language, ignoring the reality that we need to use language differently in different social situations. (A recent book with more about this is Lippi-Green 1997.)

To recognize that fact is not to say that there is no reason for us to ignore the usefulness of being able to function in edited American English. There is every reason to think that such an ability is crucial to personal and professional success for many of us. But rather than taking a right-wrong approach to matters of language variation, we can take an approach that recognizes and even celebrates our diversity and heritage, rather than one that denies its validity and usefulness.

Many scholars today worry about "dialect levelling." Largely because of television, they say, we are all beginning to sound alike around the country. My experience is that this is not so. We do tend to use standard terms for objects today, but that has been true since the first Sears, Roebuck catalogues were mailed out! But other differences continue to exist. One of the functions of the differences seems to be the preservation of our heritage. Through our language, we announce who we are and what our relationship to others is.

LANGUAGE AND IDENTITY: PERSONAL NARRATIVES IN SME

Another way we use language to announce our identity is through the stories that we tell about ourselves and our communities. In fact, long after vocabulary differences have disappeared, and maybe even after speakers of American English sound more alike in our pronunciation and grammar, we will probably encounter differences in personal narratives.

We tell stories in order to establish who we are and what our values are. In other words, we construct and announce our identity by telling stories from our past. Some people worry about the fact that family or community stories have a tendency to change over time. It may be that our stories change as we change our notions of who we are and what our relationship to our community is.

Earlier, I presented some examples of *a-* prefixing. All my examples were taken from Ozark or Appalachian speakers telling their stories. The forms of such stories vary. Because speakers often tell narratives in order to explain who they are, they tend to be quite relaxed about their grammar and to tell narratives that contain a high percentage of regional speech patterns. In other words, they relax their linguistic behavior. For this reason, they are often prized by sociolinguists.

SOME EXAMPLES OF OZARK NARRATIVES

In one interview with an Ozark speaker, an interviewer (the speaker's granddaughter) asked this question: "Were there any people around Smithville [the name of the community has been changed] that didn't talk to each other for awhile, you know they got mad at each other?" In response she obtained four different narratives, all with a common theme, and all fairly long. See if you can identify dialect features in the extracts from the two narratives that follow, each one told in response to the question above. Then, see if you can identify the values of the speaker and her community that are implicit in the narrative. You may want to ask members of your family to tell you such stories from their past.

In the examples that follow, the spelling has been modified (as I have done earlier) so that I can indicate approximate pronunciation patterns without having to use a special phonetic alphabet such as the one professional linguists use in their scholarly publications. Such respellings present some problems. Correct spelling is highly prized in our society (remember that we have national spelling bees and we award large prizes to those who win). Therefore, when a speaker is presented through what appear to be "misspelled" words, that speaker may appear to be unintelligent or uneducated. Also, many dialect spellings (in comic strips, for instance) are really only indications of the ways in which all speakers of American English pronounce certain words. So, in the examples that follow, keep in mind that the respellings are not misspellings, but are modifications of standard spelling used to represent approximate pronunciation.

Also, the examples that follow are punctuated more or less as they would be in written English. But most of us do not talk exactly the way we write, so punctuation marks have to be approximate. We do not talk in sentences in the same way that we write in sentences. But the statements that follow are punctuated as though they had been written, since they are designed for you as readers to use.

Ozark Narrative 1

There was a terrible woman lived in Smithville. She, you, it was hard for anybody to live by 'er, and if you didn't do what she wanted to she'd get mad at cha an'. . . . So she got mad at me once but I, I just didn't fool around with her, I hadn't been a-foolin' 'round with her in the first place, just somehow she managed to get mad at me. I scared her old hen, or I guess it was her hen—she said it was—off my back porch. It was a—I had a big old stalk of pepper there, you know, and he got on the back porch and—just scratchin' in this tub of pepper, and, uh, I like pepper sauce, you know, I wanted some pepper, and I scared that hen off and made her mad. And she came over there and went to fussing about it. It wasn't her hen. So Jack and Joe Harper told me. It was their chicken. . . . I thought it was Joe Harvey's an' Mr. Harvey's. I wouldn'ta hurt it. He lived right, he lived right there by me. I wouldn'ta hurt nobody's chicken. I just didn't want it in my pepper, and I thought if I'd scare it off a few times it'd stay out of it, but I didn't have nothin' to say to her. I just told her to go on back home.

Ozark Narrative 2

But now later I, I got a gun to that woman. . . . And uh, so she come out there. I mean she was just a-raisin' Cain, just as loud as she could talk around 'ere, and all the neighbors a-hearin'. Jim had a gun—he was a night-watchman then—and he had a gun hangin' up on the wall. And I reached up 'ere and got that gun, and I walked out there, and I said, "Listen you get out of this yard, or you're gonna be findin' yourself a-layin' right where you're at, woman! You get out of this yard, and right now! You get out of it!" And I had that gun pointed at her. I's gonna shoot her! . . . Well, she didn't never come back in that yard again.

CONCLUSION

Today, most of us grow up with a sharp awareness that we do not all use language the same way. We encounter the differences on television, if not next door. That was not always true. Generally, individuals who lived in rural and relatively isolated areas spoke most differently from Americans who lived in large cities and who had easy access to formal education. Even today, some speakers in the Ozarks and the Southern Appalachian Mountains retain dialect features from earlier periods of English. The differences do not mean that those speakers are either smarter or less intelligent than the rest of us. It does give us a glimpse of some of the ways in which the English language of the past was different from the English we speak today. If we value ourselves, we will value our history. We will also value those cultural differences that give us a glimpse of who we used to be. Southern Mountain English is sometimes called "hillbilly" and "uneducated." It may be more accurate to speak of it, as Cratis Williams did (1961; see also Williams 1992), as "the language of our contemporary ancestors." It is some evidence of who we collectively used to be.

REFERENCES

Bradley, M. Z. 1997. *Exile's Song: A Novel of Darkover*. New York: DAW Books.

Christian, Donna, Walt Wolfram, and Nanjo Dubé. 1988. *Variation and change in geographically isolated communities: Appalachian English and Ozark English*. Publication of the American Dialect Society no. 74. Tuscaloosa: University of Alabama Press.

Dumas, Bethany K. 1971. A study of the dialect of Newton County, Arkansas. Ph.D. dissertation, University of Arkansas, Fayetteville.

———. 1975a. The morphology of Newton County, Arkansas: An exercise in studying Ozark dialect. *Mid-South Folklore* 3: 115–25.

———. 1975b. Smoky Mountain speech. *Pioneer Spirit '76*, ed. by Dolly Berthelot. 24–29. Knoxville, TN: Dolly Berthelot.

———. 1981a. Appalachian glossary. *An Encyclopedia of East Tennessee*, ed. by J. Stokely and J. Johnson, 16–18. Oak Ridge, TN: Children's Museum.

————. 1981b. East Tennessee Talk. *An Encyclopedia of East Tennessee*, ed. by J. Stokely and J. Johnson, 170–76. Oak Ridge, TN: Children's Museum.

Jennings, Kathy. 1998. White like me: A confession on race, region, and class. *Appalachian Journal* 25.2 (Winter): 150–74.

Kolker, Andrew, and Louis Alvarez. 1986. *American Tongues* [videotape]. New York, NY: The Center for New American Media.

Lippi-Green, Rosina. 1997. *English with an accent: Language, ideology, and discrimination in the United States*. London and New York: Routledge.

Montgomery, Michael B., ed. In progress. "Dictionary of Smoky Mountain English" (with Joseph Sargent Hall, on whose collections the volumes are based in large part).

Randolph, Vance, and George P. Wilson. 1953. *Down in the holler: A gallery of Ozark folk speech*. Norman: University of Oklahoma Press.

Williams, Cratis D. 1961. The Southerner Mountaineer in fact and fiction. Ph.D. dissertation, New York University.

————. 1992. *Southern Mountain speech*. [Berea, KY:] Berea College Press.

Wolfram, Walt, and Donna Christian. 1976. *Appalachian speech*. Arlington, VA: Center for Applied Linguistics.

Wolfram, Walt, and Natalie Schilling-Estes. 1998. *American English: Dialects and variation*. Oxford and Malden, MA: Blackwell.

On the Other Hand: American Sign Language, Signed Englishes, and Other Visual Language Systems

Lynn S. Messing

This chapter will provide answers to some common questions about signed languages and other visual language systems. It will discuss many different types of signing and will argue that American Sign Language is indeed a language.

ISN'T SIGNING JUST A BUNCH OF GESTURING, SORT OF LIKE MIME?

American Sign Language (ASL) is not merely gesturing; it is actually a real language, just like English or Chinese. There are lots of ways to differentiate real languages from other types of communication systems, and for all of them, ASL falls into the language group. Languages can be used to discuss a wide variety of topics; there are strict rules about how languages are used; languages build larger units (e.g., words, sentences) out of smaller ones (e.g., sounds, words). Three examples of nonlanguage communication systems are mime, gestures, and, of course, bees' dances.[1] The gestures I just referred to are the "hand waving" that accompanies speech, as opposed to the small lexicon of stock gestures—such as the thumbs-up gesture or "the finger"—which can stand in place of speech and which convey a specific, culturally determined meaning. (The extent to which any gestures are linguistic is a subject for debate, but some researchers consider the stock gestures as being more language-like than the hand-waving variety.)

Languages can be used to discuss not only things that are right in the room with you, but also abstract ideas like freedom, or things that are very far away in place or time, such as the South Pole or the first-ever production of a Shakespeare play, or even things that never existed at all, such as unicorns. One can easily discuss all these things in ASL, too; but one could not discuss such a broad range of topics in nonlanguage communication systems. For instance, it would be hard to convey to someone else the meaning in the sentence "My parents were poor but honest" by gesturing, and bees could never make such a statement with their dances.

Language is conventionalized in a way that many nonlanguage systems are not. People who use a given language will reject as not being part of that language any utterances that break these conventions. I'm not talking here about whether it is okay to use *ain't* or to end a sentence with a preposition; I mean something much more basic to understanding what someone is saying, or even to considering whether or not what is being said is part of a given language. For example, people who know English also know that although *fip* isn't an English word, it could be; in contrast, *ngip* could not be an English word. Not all possible groups of speech sounds can be words in a given spoken language. Similarly, ASL only uses a small number of possible handshapes, movements, or places in its signs. If someone tried to invent a sign for ASL in which the ring and pinkie fingers were extended and the rest of the fingers were closed, that sign would be as unacceptable to ASL users as *ngip* would be to English speakers. Many nonlanguage communication systems, such as gestures, don't have such rigid boundaries between what is acceptable in them and what is not.

All languages also have rules about how sentences are assembled. In English, for example, you can't say, "I have three book blue." ASL also has rules about how to put together a sentence, although ASL sentence structures are very different from those in English. Not only are things ordered differently in the two languages (the sign BLUE[2] can follow BOOK), ASL even uses facial expressions to distinguish different types of sentences. ASL translations of the following three English sentences would all look the same on the hands; their meanings would be distinguished by differences in the head and face:

1. Your name is John.
2. Your name isn't John.
3. Is your name John?

The head nods during the signing of the first sentence and shakes during the signing of the second. During the last sentence, the head is tilted forward, the eyebrows are raised, and the signer looks directly at the addressee. This expression is used for questions that can be answered with a simple "yes" or "no." Questions such as "What is your name?" that require a different answer have a similar head tilt and eye gaze, but the brows are lowered instead of raised.

Languages also build meaningful units out of smaller building blocks that do not have any meaning in themselves. The English word *cat*, of course, has a meaning, but its three sounds, corresponding to the three letters in the word, do not. But if we substitute the sound *b*, also meaningless by itself, for the first sound in *cat*, we have *bat*—a whole new word with a different meaning. Meaningful ASL signs can also be broken down into smaller meaningless units. A sign is made with a particular handshape placed in a particular location and having a particular movement.[3] For example, for a right-hander, the sign SUMMER begins with the right hand having only the index finger extended, palm down, just in front of the left temple. As the hand moves to the front of the right temple, the index finger bends to form a crook. Lowering the sign so that it is made in front of the nose changes the sign to UGLY. Lowering it still further to be in front of the chin makes it DRY. If the hand moves at temple height but the index finger does not bend, the sign is BLACK.

So we've seen that ASL, like other languages, can form meaningful units from meaningless ones. It has rules for assembling words/signs and sentences. If you don't follow these rules, the result will be something which will not be recognized as being in the language. ASL can be used to discuss both concrete and abstract concepts and to describe situations distanced by both time and place. Nonlanguage systems might have some of these properties, but only real languages have all of them.

WHY ARE YOU CALLING IT *AMERICAN* SIGN LANGUAGE? ISN'T SIGNING THE SAME THE WORLD OVER?

No. A more accurate, although somewhat oversimplified, description is that each country has its own signed language. A country's natural signed language is completely different from its spoken one(s). It is not even possible to guess from two countries' spoken languages how similar their signed languages are. For example, the spoken language in the United States is much closer to that of Great Britain (both use forms of English) than it is to the French used in France. One might think that the English-speaking countries would therefore have similar signed languages. However, ASL is actually more like French Sign Language than it is like British Sign Language. One need only look at the fingerspelling in these signed languages to see this.

Fingerspelling is how signed languages represent words from spoken languages. Each letter of the Roman alphabet has its own sign. Fingerspelling is used to convey things such as proper names or technical terms which either don't have their own individual signs or which have signs that the viewer would not be expected to know. American Sign Language and French Sign Language have very similar fingerspelling alphabets. Both represent each letter on one hand, and most of the letters are identical between the two fingerspelling alphabets. In contrast, signers must use both hands to form the letters of the British fingerspelling alphabet.

Not only are there different signed languages throughout the world, but any given signed language can have the same kinds of variation that spoken languages have. There are dialects in ASL. On the east coast, one sign for "ask" involves the index finger changing shape from being completely open to being crooked; on the west coast, the comparable sign has the finger start out crooked and end open. (There are also other, somewhat more subtle, differences between the way this sign is made on the two coasts.) A more dramatic example of a vocabulary difference is that a sign which means "shoes" in many parts of the United States has the meaning "homosexual" in New York City, which has, of course, a different sign for "shoes." People sign differently when they are among friends than they do in more formal situations, such as in a classroom or on stage. In everyday signing, the sign ME is made with a hand with only the index finger extended and pointing at the signer. The more theatrical or elegant sign uses a flattened-O handshape. Older people sign differently than younger people, and there are also some gender differences in signing. Political correctness has resulted in many new signs being adopted into ASL. The old signs for different countries are being replaced by new signs based on the signs those countries' signed languages use to refer to themselves.

As an aside, it is actually possible to have an accent in sign. For example, both Chinese and American sign languages have handshapes that look like a fist with the thumb pointing up. However, the Chinese handshape is made with the fist closed more tightly and with the thumb placed in a slightly different position. If people who know Chinese Sign Language try to imitate ASL signs, they will typically use the Chinese Sign Language version of this fist handshape rather than the ASL one.

HOW SIMILAR ARE ASL AND ENGLISH?

ASL and English are quite different. They have different vocabularies and different ways to put words/signs and sentences together. In fact, the sign order of ASL is more like the word order of Chinese than it is of English! In English, word order is SUBJECT-VERB-OBJECT; this means that typically sentences start with who/what is doing an action, then what is being done, and finally, what is being acted upon. In the sentence "Students read books," *students* is the subject, *read* the verb, and *books* the object. In contrast, Chinese and ASL are topic-comment languages. In both of these languages, the word/sign order would be different depending on what the main thing being discussed in the sentence is. For instance, consider an ASL equivalent of "Students read books." If someone were to sign this as the start of a conversation about what students do, the sign STUDENTS would come first; but if the sentence were to begin a discussion of what happens to books, then BOOKS would begin the sentence. A special facial expression is also used when the topic of a sentence is signed. The precise rules of sign ordering are complex, but even this brief discussion is enough to show that the rules in ASL are clearly different from those of English.

The vocabularies of ASL and English are also quite different, and not just because they are presented in different modes. Consider the English word *run*, for instance. It seems a simple, everyday word, and yet it has many different meanings which would have to be translated by different signs. For example, the signs used to correspond to the word *run* would be different in the translations of each of these sentences:

1. Alex will run a marathon next week.
2. Did you run for office?
3. Sue has a run in her stocking.
4. I thought I was getting over my cold, but then my nose started to run.
5. Before we knew it, we had run up a huge bill.
6. Did the cars run into each other head on?
7. If you run into Bob, be sure to tell him I said, "Hello."

Several other differences between the languages are mentioned throughout this chapter.

YOU'VE SAID ASL IS A VERY DIFFERENT LANGUAGE THAN ENGLISH, BUT I'VE SEEN PEOPLE SIGNING AND SPEAKING AT THE SAME TIME. ARE THEY REALLY USING TWO DIFFERENT LANGUAGES AT ONCE?

When people speak and sign at the same time, they are probably not using ASL. Because the two languages present information in very different orderings, and because it is impossible to speak while making some ASL facial expressions (such as the puffed-cheeks facial expression which is used to indicate that something is large), it is extremely difficult to use ASL and English at the same time for any but the simplest utterances. These people are far more likely to be using either a MANUALLY CODED ENGLISH (MCE) system or a type of contact signing. MCEs, or SIGNED ENGLISH systems, are artificially created systems designed to make English visible on the hands. They draw upon ASL for much of their vocabulary, and they have additional signs created for them. Every unit of meaning in English is given its own sign. So in an MCE, two signs would be used to represent the word *cats*; one sign would be used for the concept "feline" and another for plural. The signs are presented in the same order as they would be in spoken English. MCEs put together both words and sentences in the way English does, rather than the way ASL does.

In practice, one rarely sees a "pure" MCE. It takes about the same amount of time on average to present an idea in any natural language, whether signed or spoken. This is true even though it takes two to three times as long to make a sign as it does to say a word. This seeming paradox is explained by the fact that natural signed languages can present a great deal of information simultaneously. For example, there is a basic ASL sign WEEK. If you make this sign with the handshape for the number *two*, the sign becomes TWO-WEEKS. If you then change the movement, the sign becomes TWO-WEEKS-AGO. Because MCEs try to present information in the same way as English, a pure MCE would need four different signs to convey the same meaning as the single sign TWO-WEEKS-AGO: one sign each for "two," "week," "s," and "ago." Having to make so many signs can become quite cumbersome and time-consuming, so people trying to use an MCE often leave out a lot of signs and wind up using a type of signing called a CONTACT SIGN (known until recently as PIDGIN SIGNED ENGLISH). Contact signing typically occurs between a user of ASL and someone who is less than fluent in that language. Contact signing is neither real English nor real ASL. It varies from person to person, and even the same individual can convey a given sentence in very different ways at different times.

CAN ASL BE WRITTEN?

Several attempts have been made to develop writing systems for ASL, but no single system has become widely accepted. Different linguists have developed elaborate systems which are useful for describing the appearance of short passages of signing, but these systems are too unwieldy for use with anything longer than a few signs. Signs have also been referred to in writing by glosses, fully capitalized written versions of their closest English counterparts. We've seen glosses of individual signs throughout this chapter. Glosses can include superscripts to indicate grammatically relevant facial expressions and subscripts to show how a particular instance of a sign differs from its dictionary form. But glosses have a lot of drawbacks: They can be somewhat awkward; they require that the reader and writer be fluent in both English and ASL; they can be ambiguous when one English word can be translated by more than one sign within a given context; and they give the impression to the uninformed that ASL is merely a "broken" form of English.

The writing system which seems most likely to become popular with nonlinguists is Valerie Sutton's and the Deaf Action Committee's Sign Writing®. This is a fairly iconic system which is relatively easy to learn and use, can readily be adapted to different signed languages, and is currently being taught in a school in Nicaragua, as well as being used by small groups of individuals throughout the world. Although it is not yet widely employed, it is gaining in popularity.

SUMMARY

ASL is but one of the world's numerous natural signed languages. Signed languages are true languages in their own right and are distinct from spoken languages. They are rule governed and contain as much variation as spoken languages. They are not to be confused with artificial systems, such as Manually Coded English systems, which are designed to make visible the structure of spoken languages.

NOTES

This chapter was made possible by funding from Interdisciplinary Research Training in Rehabilitation Technology Grant Number H133P30003–96 from the National Institute on Disability and Rehabilitation Research of the U.S. Department of Education, and the Nemours Foundation.

1. Honeybees that have found a food source return to the nest and "tell" other bees the location and richness of the source by the shape, orientation, speed, and vigor of the dance.

2. ASL signs will be represented here by versions in full capitals of their English "glosses," or nearest single-word translations.

3. This discussion is based on Stokoe's seminal analysis of ASL; more complex and more explanatory analyses have since superseded Stokoe's, but his is the most intuitive one and the easiest to describe in a chapter of this scope.

REFERENCE

Stokoe, William C. 1960. *Sign language structure*. Studies in linguistics: Occasional papers, 8. Buffalo, NY: Department of Anthropology and Linguistics, University of Buffalo.

FURTHER READING

Bellugi, Ursula, and Susan Fischer. 1972. A comparison of sign language and spoken language: Rate and grammatical mechanisms. *Cognition* 1: 173–200.

Klima, Edward, and Ursula Bellugi. 1979. *The signs of language*. Cambridge, MA: Harvard University Press.

Lucas, Ceil, and Clayton Valli. 1989. Language contact in the American Deaf community. *The sociolinguistics of the Deaf community*, ed. by Ceil Lucas, 11–40. San Diego: Academic Press.

Stokoe, William C., Dorothy C. Casterline, and Carl G. Croneberg. 1965. *A dictionary of American Sign Language on linguistic principles*. Washington, DC: Galladuet Press.

II

ENGLISHES, ENGLISH-ONLY, AND LANGUAGES IN DANGER OF EXTINCTION

"From Out in Left Field? That's Not Cricket": Finding a Focus for the Language Curriculum

David Crystal

AN ANECDOTAL INTRODUCTION

Some time ago, I was attending an international seminar at a European university. Around the table were representatives of some twenty countries. There were two people from the United Kingdom, two from the United States, and one from Australia, with the others all from countries where English was either a second (official) language or a foreign language. The lingua franca of the meeting was English, and everyone seemed to be using the language competently, even the native speakers.

We were well into the discussion period following a paper which had generated a lively buzz of comment and countercomment. Someone then made a telling remark. There was a silence round the table, which was broken by one of the U.S. delegates observing, "That came from out in left field." There was another silence, and I could see some of the delegates turning to their neighbors in a surreptitious way, as one does when one does not understand what on earth is going on, and wants to check that one is not alone. But they were not pondering the telling remark. They were asking each other what "from out in left field" meant. My neighbor asked me; as a native speaker, he felt confident that I would know. I did not know. Baseball at that time was a closed book to me—and still is, very largely.

One of the braver of the delegates spoke up: "Out where?" he asked. It took the U.S. delegate by surprise, as plainly he'd never had that idiom questioned before; but he managed to explain that it was a figure of speech from baseball, a ball coming from an unusual direction, and what he had meant was that the remark was surprising, unexpected. There were nods

of relief from around the table. Then one of the UK delegates chipped in,
"You played that with a straight bat." he said. "Huh?" said the American.
"Oh, I say, that's not cricket," I added, parodically. "Isn't it?" asked a
delegate from Asia, now totally confused.

The next few minutes of the meeting were somewhat chaotic. The original theme was quite forgotten as people energetically debated the meaning
of cricket and baseball idioms with their neighbors. Those who could added
their own local version of how they said things like that in their part of
the world—the sports metaphors they lived by. Eventually, the chairman
called everyone back to order, and the discussion of the paper continued.
But my attention was blown, and I spent the remainder of the session
listening not to what delegates were saying, but to how they were saying
it.

What was immediately noticeable was that the native speakers seemed
to become much less colloquial. In particular, I didn't sense any further use
of national idioms. Indeed, the speakers seemed to be going out of their
way to avoid them. I made a small contribution towards the end, and I
remember thinking while I was doing it—"don't use any cricket terms."
Afterwards, in the bar, others admitted to doing the same. My British colleague said he'd consciously avoided using the word *fortnight*, replacing it
by *two weeks*, as he'd "had trouble with that one before." And as the
evening wore on, people began apologizing facetiously when they noticed
themselves using a national idiom, or when somebody else used one. It
became something of a game—the kind that linguists love to play.

There was one nice moment, I recall, when the U.S., U.K., and Australian
delegates were all reduced to incoherence when they found that they had
disbarred themselves from using any of their natural expressions for "the
safe walking route at the side of a road"—*pavement* (U.K.), *sidewalk*
(U.S.), and *footpath* (Australian). In the absence of a regionally neutral
term, all they were left with was circumlocution (such as the one just given).
I also remember "engine cover" being proposed as a neutral term for *bon-
net* and *hood*. Somebody made a joke about the need for a linguistic United
Nations. The rest is a blur.

AN INTERPRETATION

In the cold, sober light of later days, it seemed to me that what I had
observed taking place at that seminar was of some significance as far as
the future of the English language was concerned—and probably was taking place regularly at international gatherings all over the world. I was
seeing a new kind of English being born—a variety which was intended
for international spoken usage and which was thus avoiding the idiosyncrasies associated with national varieties of expression. Such a variety is

not yet with us as a living entity with standardized usage, but it still needs a name. Let us call it World Standard Spoken English (WSSE).

Although WSSE does not exist as an institutionalized variety, its written equivalent does, traditionally called Standard English, but in the present context perhaps better called World Standard Printed English (WSPE). It is sometimes forgotten that what we call Standard English is essentially a written—and primarily a printed—variety of language (Quirk and Stein 1990, chap. 9), and moreover one which has developed as a standard precisely because it guarantees mutual written intelligibility, first within individual countries, then internationally. An examination of the textbooks, documents, and newspapers published around the world (for the latter, see Crystal 1995, 300–305) shows very little linguistic differentiation: the range of grammatical constructions is virtually identical, as are most of the pragmatic conventions and most of the vocabulary. Only in spelling and punctuation are there noticeable national differences, reflecting British versus American points of origin, and it is a moot point whether these can any longer be called "national," given the way these two standards have come to be used erratically throughout the world, even appearing in "mixed" versions in several countries, such as in Canada and Australia (where there may be variation even between provinces or states) and in Britain (where the influence of U.S. spelling is widespread). On the whole, WSPE is the same wherever it is encountered. It would not be able to fulfill its role as an international (written) lingua franca if it were riddled with regional idiosyncrasies.

What the seminar example seems to be suggesting is the emergence of a spoken equivalent to WSPE in international settings where educated people come to talk to each other and choose to use English as their (spoken) lingua franca. It is not surprising that such a variety should be growing, given the way in which English developed as a genuine global language in the second half of the twentieth century (Crystal 1997). At present, the linguistic characteristics of this variety are unclear: it is not yet obvious which features of vocabulary, grammar, and pronunciation will come to identify it. But, based on what we know about language in general, one of the first things we would expect to see in the development of an international variety would be uncertainties about usage. Chief amongst these would be intelligibility difficulties over national regional norms (as in the case of the baseball idiom) as people using English from one part of the world come into contact with those using English from another. Because most regional dialect differentiation is a matter of vocabulary, this is the domain where usage problems will be most immediately and noticeably encountered. Close behind will be differences in grammar, insofar as national variations exist at all (see the index to the grammar by Quirk, Greenbaum, Leech, and Svartvik 1985 for a checklist, specifically the index entries at "British English" and "American English"). And the domain of pronunciation will provide a third kind of close encounter—already observable in the "midatlantic" accents which emerge when people speaking different regional Englishes accommodate to each other, or in the unique amalgam of ex-European accents which characterizes the corridors of power in the European Union.

This is an exciting time for linguist observers of the world scene. No language has ever had such global exposure as English has, so there are no precedents for what is currently taking place. We do not know what happens to a language when it becomes a genuinely world language—recognized as a prestige language in all countries and used in the aggregate by more people (especially as a second or foreign language) for more purposes than any other language. The WSSE scenario suggests that during the twenty-first century, people with an international presence who speak English as a first language will find themselves adding a third variety to their repertoire. They already have a national formal variety, or dialect ("I speak British/U.S./Australian . . . English") and an intranational informal variety, which is often regionally biased ("I speak the colloquial English of Liverpool, Glasgow, Boston, New Orleans . . ."). Those who are bidialectal in this way slip into each of these varieties without thinking about it. In the future, the earlier examples suggest, they will become tridialectal, with the international variety offering them a further option of an English in which national usages have been replaced by regionally neutral forms—to be used, of course, only when circumstances are right.

VARIETY AND CHANGE

Several things are currently happening to English as people increasingly engage with it globally. In addition to the emergence of possible new international standards as part of the concern to preserve intelligibility, there is the growth of new national standards—the so-called new Englishes in such countries as India, Singapore, and Ghana—whose role is to preserve national identity (Schneider 1997; Bamgbose, Banjo, and Thomas 1995). To be a happy language-using individual (or community), both dimensions are essential: one needs to be able to talk to others outside one's community and to understand them; at the same time, one needs to be able to demonstrate, through one's speech, that one is not the same as them. The demands appear to be contradictory, and when people do see them as contradictory, there is always trouble in the form of acrimonious debates about standards in the school curriculum or in society at large, widespread anxiety about the survival of a local language or dialect, and—in the extreme cases—language marches, rioting, and deaths. Wise language planning can avoid the contradiction: it is possible to have your linguistic cake and eat it, as can be seen in such countries as Switzerland and Finland, where policies of sensitive multilingualism recognize the strengths of individual languages and the different purposes for which they are used, and real support is given to developing a bilingual way of life. Bidialectism can likewise be sensitively promoted. However, such situations are often not easy to implement: they are bedeviled by complications arising out of individual national histories, whereby the political aspirations of minority groups come into conflict with national government policies. A bilingual or bidialectal policy can also be extremely expensive. But it is the only way in which the otherwise competing demands of intelligibility and identity can be reconciled.

These are important issues for anyone interested in language, at any age, to address; and certainly any language curriculum should give its students the opportunity to do so. The issues are important because everyone is affected by them. No one can avoid being part of the current of linguistic change or—to extend the metaphor—can avoid bathing in the sea of linguistic variety. Nor can anyone escape the variations of attitude which people express in reaction to what is happening as some try to swim against the current while others blithely let it carry them along. Everyone, at some time or other, will have their usage challenged by someone else, whether it be a parent, teacher, peer-group member, neighbor, editor, colleague, or boss. The contexts might be local, national, or global. To cope with such challenges or to respond to them coherently, people need confidence, and confidence comes from knowledge, an awareness of what is happening to language and what the issues are. A linguistically informed curriculum can provide the foundation on which such confidence can be built, because it gives people insight into principles which can make sense of the multifaceted and potentially confusing linguistic world which surrounds them.

Central to any curriculum should be the recognition of language variety and language change—topics which have traditionally been seen as separate, but which are now known to be intimately related. In 1989 appeared the first issue of a journal, *Language Variation and Change*, whose title neatly captured the desired emphasis. The "variation" referred to all kinds of linguistic variability within the speech community, whether as a result of age, sex, social class, region, occupation, or whatever. And "change" referred to any linguistic change, in any period, of any language. The underlying philosophy is that these processes are interconnected. Change does not just happen. There has to be a reason why people change their speech habits from one way of talking to another. Some of these reasons are bound up with the developmental physiology of the individual (changes in voice quality from childhood to old age, for example), but for the most part the reasons are to be found within the network of social relationships which underlie a speech community. These relationships are ever changing because society is ever changing: people are continually finding themselves subjected to new influences and pressures, and their language alters accordingly as they (consciously or unconsciously) strive to identify themselves with or distinguish themselves from others. A cross-section of society at any point in time will bring to light relatively stable clusters of distinctive linguistic features which provide the basis of what we call dialects or varieties. But no variety ever stands still. All are subject to change, though some (e.g., teenage street dialects) change more rapidly than others (e.g., the genres of institutionalized religion).

The fundamental axiom of linguistic enquiry is—or should be—that language changes; and language change, accordingly, should be at the core of any curriculum. Everything else derives from this axiom—the existence of different languages, the endangerment and death of languages, the emergence of new usages, and the promotion of stylistic idiosyncrasy. Anything which is of linguistic interest, whether in the individual or the group, comes about as a result of recent or ancient language change. And within linguistics, this notion has become increasingly centre-stage during the 1990s, with more attention being paid to ways of capturing the effects of change, modeling them, and quantifying them (see, for example, Hughes 1988; Milroy 1992; Baker and Syea 1996; Dixon 1997). The originally purely structural and textual investigation of language change, at first in the form of philology, then within historical linguistics, has come to be supplemented by an account of the dynamic psychological, social, and cultural processes involved. As a consequence, fresh kinds of explanation have emerged in such areas as comparative linguistics, pidgin and creole languages, child language acquisition, and the investigation of usage.

The topic of disputed grammatical usage is a good instance of the way traditional static accounts of language have been replaced by explanations of a dynamic kind, in which variety and change are central. The early concern, from the mid-eighteenth century, was solely to identify "incorrect" sentences, such as whether a sentence should or should not end with a preposition. Within the prescriptive tradition, sentences of the type "That is the doctor to whom I was talking" would be recommended, as opposed to those of the type "That is the doctor I was talking to." The former would be considered "right" and the latter "wrong." The judgments were fixed, immutable, absolute. The view of language was a monodialectal one in which the role of language education was to eliminate (through the use of sanctions) variant forms, thus maintaining the language's imagined purity, and to impose norms of perceived linguistic excellence, thus safeguarding its future. Linguistic change of any kind was widely perceived to be deterioration. New pronunciations were castigated as careless or ugly; changes in vocabulary were regretted, because they involved the loss of essential distinctions in meaning; and changes in grammar were condemned as unnecessary and sloppy (see further Milroy and Milroy 1991).

The descriptive tradition introduced by linguistics in the mid-twentieth century attempted to replace this static and decontextualized account by a dynamic, interactional one. Its approach to such sentence pairs as the one in the preceding paragraph emphasized the value of having both versions available in the language and the perversity of disbarring people from using one of them. The existence of the alternatives gave people the choice of expressing themselves in English in a formal or informal way, an option which added "power" to their linguistic repertoire. In much the same way as the acquisition of a foreign language opens up fresh contacts and experiences, so the mastery of both formal and informal varieties within a language was seen as giving individuals an increased range of opportunities for personal growth and progress. One of the main functions of the school curriculum, it was argued, was to give children the chance to develop bidialectally in this way—obtaining a confident command of formal varieties of English, but without losing the ability to operate informally. If you can control both Standard English and a local dialect, this approach concluded, you are in the best of both worlds: the former gives you the intelligibility you need to communicate with the world at large; the latter gives you the identity you need to show that you belong with your workmates, family, and friends. It is the same scenario as the one working itself out at the macro level of world English, but now encountered in the micro world of the classroom.

Linguists have spent a great deal of time and effort during the past fifty years trying to introduce this philosophy into educational thinking around the world—and with some success, as can be seen by the linguistic perspectives which are now a routine part of the British National Curriculum in English, introduced during the 1990s, or those which have been influencing curricular thinking in some states of Australia. This is not to say that the purist attitudes which have been attacked are no longer about. On the contrary, they are still powerful and pervasive in society, surfacing at regular intervals in newspaper usage columns and in items on radio and television stations. It will doubtless never be possible to eliminate them completely. Indeed, it can be argued that purism may well have an essential role to play within the network of language attitudes which constitute a modern society. But it needs to be kept in its place, for uncontrolled purism has unfortunate consequences in the many manifestations of linguistic intolerance. The linguist's frame of reference has a crucial balancing role to play, in this respect, placing at its foundation a broader conception of individual worth, identity, and self-respect than the purist tradition is capable of recognizing.

A DYNAMIC PERSPECTIVE IN THE CURRICULUM

This chapter began by focusing on some of the things that are happening to English at a global level, but it has since broadened the scope of its enquiry. This is as it should be. The phenomenon of an emerging world

English is not just something which is taking place "out there," in parts of the world that most students will never have an opportunity to visit. Students encounter the varieties of world English daily on radio and television, in the cinema, through pop music, and via the Internet. In some towns and cities, they may find themselves working alongside others, from a range of ethnic backgrounds, who speak a very different kind of English to the one(s) they use themselves. Those who are learning English as a foreign language will be faced with the question of which model to use as a target—both American and British English are available in some of the commercially published programs—and all teachers of English as a foreign language have at some point to make a decision about which variety of English is acceptable within their classrooms. World English also has an impact on everyday usage: one of the commonest complaints by purist commentators in the United Kingdom, Canada, Australia, and New Zealand is to do with the growing influence of American usage on their local speech. Nor is it entirely a one-way street: British English, for example, forces its way into U.S. consciousness from time to time, as when a British film does well in the Academy Awards. And the Internet is introducing a greater multidialectal democracy into linguistic interchange than ever before.

From a curricular point of view, what is important is the recognition that, whatever the settings and circumstances, the events which affect a language in its international or global manifestation result from the same principles and processes as those which affect it intranationally or locally. One language may manifest more change than another or respond to change very differently from another (the differences between the ways in which English and French react to loan words is a contemporary case in point; see Hausmann 1986; Schiffman 1996, chap. 4), but there are only so many ways in which languages can and do change, and even though the study of linguistic change has received but limited empirical treatment, the theoretical frame of reference which we need in order to explain the phenomenon is now fairly well established. Even if not all the relevant factors are known, enough of an explanation is in place to provide a language curriculum with more than enough content and motivation. And there is certainly no shortage of relevant technology, in the form of the various kinds of equipment for recording and analysis, to help students get to grips with the issues.

Giving students a solid grasp of the nature of language variation and change has all kinds of beneficial outcomes. To begin with, the subject has an intrinsic interest which is valued in society at large—people are always ready to talk about such matters as regional accents, dialect variations, new words and meanings, where words come from, and the similarities between languages. The subject also has a role which may be of value to society at large in that it can replace protectionist notions of "eternal vigilance" by

empowering notions of "eternal tolerance." The more people come to realize the inevitability of language change and the reasons why languages
change, the more they are likely to react to it positively. The sooner this
new mood is established, the better. All over the world, at the end of the
twentieth century, people are slowly extricating themselves from 250 years
of prescriptive linguistic history. It will take two generations, at least, for
the extrication to be complete, because it takes that long for those young
people who did not experience the prescriptive tradition in school to grow
up into positions of influential seniority. At present, young people with an
informed awareness of language variation are still likely to encounter, in
their first jobs, senior people who know no other language philosophy than
one of prescriptive control. When I presented the series *English Now* on
BBC Radio 4 during the 1980s, I would regularly receive letters from junior
people in this awkward position. One person, I recall, complained to me
that he had been severely criticized by his boss for splitting an infinitive
when he did not even know what an infinitive was, let alone how to split
one, or why it was wrong to do so. There are serious cases on record of
people who have found themselves unable to cope with irrational linguistic
pressure from above, and who have left their jobs as a consequence. Faced
with the linguistic intolerance of a prescriptively brainwashed society, some
have even committed suicide (Crystal 1995, 298). Only a systematic approach to language awareness can successfully begin to combat such feelings of personal inferiority and insecurity. A language-aware curriculum,
centered on a dynamic, variationist perspective, is the only way I know to
enable students to face up to the linguistically intransigent elements in the
world with greater confidence. The curriculum doesn't make the problems
go away, but it does give students a means of coming to terms with them.

An appreciation of the principles of variation and change, as stimulated
by reflecting on the world English situation, can have other beneficial outcomes. In particular, it forces people to think in some depth about what
happens when languages come to be used globally. The major linguistic
issue for the new millennium is not the emergence of English as a global
language, or whether it will continue to hold this position (speculations
reviewed in Graddol 1997), but what impact a global language will have
on the other languages of the world. The statistics of several surveys conducted in the 1990s leave us in no doubt that during the twenty-first century a significant proportion, probably of the order of 50 percent, of the
world's languages will die out (Grenoble and Whaley 1998; Crystal 2000).
The process of endangerment is of course a historical one, reaching back
to the early days of Western colonialism and extending well beyond English. For example, the savage reduction in the Indian languages spoken in
Amazonia in recent times has been the result of economic and cultural
factors that are nothing to do with the growth of English as a world language. On the other hand, the pressures which have caused Amazonian

peoples to drop their mother tongue in favor of Portuguese are not dissimilar to those seen in North America, where Amerindian languages have long been threatened by English, or in Russia and China, where the national languages have displaced the languages of many minority ethnic communities.

Here too, a linguistically informed curriculum has a valuable role to play. No amount of coaching in linguistic sensitivities is going to turn the clock back and save those languages which are most seriously endangered. On the other hand, an enlightened awareness of the values of linguistic diversity to the world community is something which can and should become part of everyone's consciousness. At present any such "green linguistics" is lacking. Only a tiny percentage of the world population is aware that so many languages are endangered, and probably only a small proportion of them care about it. A massive exercise in consciousness raising is essential if anything is to be done to save those languages which are capable of having their fortunes reversed. The founding of international organizations with the primary aim of focusing attention on the problem is an essential first step, and several of these organizations were created during the 1990s, notably the UNESCO-sponsored International Clearing House for Endangered Languages, based at Tokyo University. But if these organizations are to succeed in their aims, they need to be able to rely on a grass-roots body of sympathy among the general population—on voters, in short. And it would be no bad thing if a language curriculum were able to inspire the next generations of voters with a proper sense of linguistic responsibility towards the languages of the world. This, as Chomsky (1957) might have said, is one of those colourful, green ideas which needs to start waking, furiously.

There is a third topic, long at the centre of the English curriculum, which can benefit from a dynamic variationist focus and a world English perspective: the study of (the language of) literature. A global perspective will increasingly make itself felt in this domain in the twenty-first century. For the first time in English linguistic history, there are now more people speaking English as a second or foreign language than speak it as a first language (Crystal 1997). Already, in many of the countries where these "new Englishes" are found, a strong and vibrant body of literature has been emerging. The process has not been without controversy, for the question of whether one should write in English or in the language of one's ethnic origins is a matter of some consequence; and during the 1960s, when most of these new Englishes took a major step forward as a result of the many successful independence movements, there was considerable debate when authors took different stands on the matter. At the heart of the debate was the question of identity: how could one be true to one's ethnicity if one used the language of former oppressors? On the other hand, how could one get one's message across to the world at large if one used a language which few others understood? Forty years on, these new Englishes, now very different in character from Standard British or American English, have given authors a fresh set of options, enabling them to communicate with a huge global audience in a language which they and their community have made their own. Novelist Salman Rushdie (1991) put it this way:

> I don't think it is always necessary to take up the anti-colonial—or is it post-colonial—cudgels against English. What seems to me to be happening is that those people who were once colonized by the language are now rapidly re-making it, domesticating it, becoming more and more relaxed about the way they use it. Assisted by the English language's enormous flexibility and size, they are carving out large territories for themselves within its front. To take the case of India, only because it's the one in which I'm most familiar. The debate about the appropriateness of English in post-British India has been raging ever since 1947; but today, I find, it is a debate which has meaning only for the older generation. The children of independent India seem not to think of English as being irredeemably tainted by its colonial provenance. They use it as an Indian language, as one of the tools they have to hand.

If Rushdie is right—and I think he is—then the amount of quality literature in varieties of English other than traditional Standard British and American is going to significantly increase as a result of the vastly increased numbers of new writers. This in itself will necessitate a greater focus on the characteristics of the varieties of world English for students of literature. African and Caribbean literature in English have already provided many examples. In the typical case, a novel will contain an admixture of varieties. A narrative voice might use Standard British or American English, but characters are likely to use different kinds of regional English—an educated local standard, perhaps, or a creolized or pidginized variety. Their choices of words and grammatical constructions belong to the different localized varieties and carry nuances reflecting their social backgrounds in much the same way as British or American novelists, such as Charles Dickens and Mark Twain, made use of regional speech patterns in their characterizations. Whole texts might be written in the local variety, as is often seen in the poetry coming out of the Caribbean. And the longer-established national Englishes, other than British and American, are also developing increasingly confident voices, as is demonstrated by much contemporary Irish, Australian, and Canadian writing.

Although literature is a domain in which individualism is highly valued, from a linguistic point of view authors are as constrained by the principles of variation and change as much as anyone else. They may take more risks in their use of language, they may bend and break more rules, but if the end product is to be intelligible to a readership, they must keep control of the extent to which their language is idiosyncratic. As in other domains, it is the need to preserve a balance between intelligibility and identity which gives distinctive shape to a variety. Authors are no exception when they make decisions about which language to use. However perceptive they may be about the human condition, when it comes to communicating their insights, they have to live within the same currents of language variation and change as do the rest of us. There is enormous overlap between the linguistic intuitions of the members of a speech community. This is one of the basic truths about language which linguists have convincingly demonstrated in recent decades.

In terms of the curriculum, this commonalty of intuition can be put to immediate and effective use. It denies, once and for all, the existence of any fundamental qualitative barrier between the language of literature and the language of everything else. I have always found it difficult to understand how, other than in terms of pedagogical convenience, such a divide ever came to be. If literature is mimetic of all human experience, we must expect to encounter, within its domain, the whole gamut of possibilities of linguistic variation and change in society. Authors have to work with "the language of the age" as much as linguists do (Crystal 1987). And even if authors choose not to reflect the language of the age in their work, but try to cultivate a distinctive or esoteric language, any new variety which they create will inevitably be judged as a departure from previously existing norms and be interpreted in relation to those norms. Creative writers are continually and unavoidably being brought back into a relationship with a community's linguistic norms, and with the processes of variation and change which are the driving forces behind those norms. It is unavoidable, because each of us has only the one set of linguistic intuitions (per language) to invoke in the production and comprehension of everything we speak, listen to, read, and write. Some uses of language—such as comedy, advertising, literature—make more demands on our intuitions than others, but we do not switch from one set of intuitions to another as we go from one situation to another in our daily lives.

Students, therefore, have a unique advantage over other areas of the curriculum when it comes to the study of the literature written in their own language. Faced with a curriculum in history or geography or chemistry, they may have little or no prior knowledge—other than a generalized common sense—of what it is they are being expected to learn. But with literature it is different; for they already know a great deal (about the language) that the author knows. They already have an intuitive sense of what is possible (acceptable) and what is not, and what is in between (problems of usage). If they have followed a language course, they will already have developed some degree of ability to articulate that knowledge to others. All of this is an immense potential advantage, but it is an advantage only if the curriculum gives them the opportunity to make use of this knowledge. If the lang/lit divide is unyielding, such cross-fertilization cannot happen. If students are banned from making linguistic observations about nonliterary usage in their literature class or are not motivated to take into account literary texts in their linguistic work, they are being treated as if they had two types of linguistic intuition. So much is lost when this happens.

A curriculum based on the principles of variation and change would never allow such a separation to take place. Literary uses of language would be seen as a community's most highly valued varieties, partly because of their aesthetic properties, partly because of their role as expressions of special insight into the human condition. At the same time, such a curriculum would draw attention to the way in which these varieties depend for their effect on the norms of the language as a whole. Illuminating contrasts could then be drawn. The critic who first said that playwright Harold Pinter had a tape recorder for an ear was making a rhetorical point; but a lot can be learned about Pinter's dramatic art by comparing his tightly controlled dialogue with the loosely structured clause sequences which form much of everyday conversational interaction (Crystal 1995, 413; Burton 1980, chap. 1). It is just such an integrated view of language which was assumed by Robert Graves when he once remarked in a letter to a newspaper that "a poet should master the rules of grammar before he attempts to bend or break them"—a point which applies equally to all who encounter literature, whether literary critics or just plain readers (*The Times*, 21 October 1961). And it is the same spirit of integration which must have moved Dylan Thomas to once observe in a review: "Traditional criticism has regarded the aesthetic approach towards literature as apart from the functional approach towards the way of words; languages themselves intensify the differences which appear in literature, but languages and literatures are not two different phenomena, but the same phenomenon" (Thomas 1935).

CONCLUSION

A curriculum needs an underlying philosophy, if it is to be coherent, realistic, and viable. In the case of the English language, this philosophy can be driven by any number of principles. Some might see a philological principle to be appropriate, because their concern is to enable students to engage in the historical study of texts. Some might prefer an observational principle, thus facilitating analyses of a sociological or anthropological kind. Some might support a regional principle, allowing them to focus just on the usage of their own speech community. There are clearly many possibilities. The argument of this chapter, however, is that the most meaningful English-language curricula for the twenty-first century will need to be all-inclusive, recognizing first and foremost the existence of global trends as a perspective for understanding regional or national realities and then using the principles of language variation and change to incorporate accounts of a historical, social, psychological, literary, or other kind. It would be a shame if, as we enter the new millennium, university departments would still think of these arguments as coming from out in left field.

REFERENCES

Baker, Philip, and Anand Syea. 1996. *Changing meanings, changing functions*. London: University of Westminster Press.

Bamgbose, Ayo, Ayo Banjo, and Andrew Thomas eds. 1995. *New Englishes: A West African perspective*. Ibadan: Mosuro and the British Council.

Burton, Deirdre. 1980. *Dialogue and discourse*. London and Boston: Routledge and Kegan Paul.

Chomsky, Noam. 1957. *Syntactic structures*. The Hague: Mouton.

Crystal, David. 1987. Literature of the future: Language of the past (and present). *Proceedings from the Third Nordic Conference for English Studies*, ed. by Ishrat Lindblad and Magnus Ljung, 41–52. Stockholm: Almqvist & Wiksell.

———. 1995. *The Cambridge encyclopedia of the English language*. Cambridge and New York: Cambridge University Press.

———. 1997. *English as a global language*. Cambridge and New York: Cambridge University Press.

———. 2000. *Language death*. Cambridge and New York: Cambridge University Press.

Dixon, R. M. W. 1997. *The rise and fall of languages*. Cambridge and New York: Cambridge University Press.

Graddol, David. 1997. *The future of English*. London: British Council.

Graves, Robert. Letter to the editor. *The Times*. 21 October 1961.

Grenoble, Lenore A., and Lindsay J. Whaley, eds. 1998. *Endangered languages: Language loss and community response*. Cambridge and New York: Cambridge University Press.

Hausmann, Franz Jozef. 1986. The influence of the English language on French. *English in contact with other languages*, ed. by Wolfgang Viereck and Wolf-Dietrich Bald, 79–105. Budapest: Akademiai Kiado.

Hughes, Geoffrey. 1988. *Words in time*. Oxford: Blackwell.

Milroy, James. 1992. *Linguistic variation and change*. Oxford: Blackwell.

Milroy, James, and Lesley Milroy. 1991. *Authority in language*. 2nd ed. London and New York: Routledge.

Quirk, Randolph, Sidney Greenbaum, Geoffrey Leech, and Jan Svartvik. 1985. *A comprehensive grammar of the English language*. London: Longman.

Quirk, Randolph, and Gabriele Stein. 1990. *English in use*. London: Longman.

Rushdie, Salman. 1996. "Commonwealth literature" does not exist. *Imaginary Homelands*, by Salman Rushdie. New York: Viking and Granta.

Schiffman, Harold F. 1996. *Linguistic culture and language policy*. London and New York: Routledge.

Schneider, Edgar W. ed. 1997. *Englishes around the world*. Amsterdam and Philadelphia: John Benjamins.

Thomas, Dylan. 1935. Review of *A comparison of literatures*, by R. D. Jameson. *Adelphi* 11.1: 58–59.

FURTHER READING

Burchfield, Robert, ed. 1994. *The Cambridge history of the English language*. Vol. 5, *English in Britain and overseas*. Cambridge and New York: Cambridge University Press.

Cheshire, Jenny, ed. 1991. *English around the world: Sociolinguistic perspectives*. Cambridge and New York: Cambridge University Press.

Crystal, David. 1995. *The Cambridge encyclopedia of the English language*, Parts 1 and 5. Cambridge and New York: Cambridge University Press.

————. 1997. *English as a global language*. Cambridge and New York: Cambridge University Press.

Graddol, David. 1997. *The future of English*. London: British Council.

Platt, John, Heidi Weber, and Ho Mian Lian. 1984. *The new Englishes*. London and Boston: Routledge and Kegan Paul.

Todd, Loreto. 1984. *Modern Englishes: Pidgins and creoles*. Oxford: Blackwell.

SYLLABUS SUGGESTION

The series produced by the Open University in the United Kingdom, supported by radio and television material, consists in its published form of four books, all published by Routledge (London and New York) in 1996.

Goodman, Sharon, and David Graddol, eds. *Redesigning English: New texts, new identities*.

Graddol, David, Dick Leith, and Joan Swann, eds. *English: History, diversity, and change*.

Maybin, Janet, and Neil Mercer, eds. *Using English: From conversation to canon*.

Mercer, Neil, and Joan Swann, eds. *Learning English: Development and diversity*.

INVESTIGATING ENGLISH AROUND THE WORLD: THE INTERNATIONAL CORPUS OF ENGLISH

Gerald Nelson and Bas Aarts

The spread of English around the world has been one of the greatest linguistic developments of the twentieth century. The figures are impressive: an estimated 350 million people speak English as a first language, with about four times this number using it as a second language. The status of English is such that it has been adopted as the world's lingua franca for communication in Olympic sport, international trade, and air-traffic control. Unlike any other language, past or present, English has spread to all five continents and has become a truly global language.

Because English has spread so widely, it has been impossible for linguists to keep track of developments in it around the world. Until now. In this chapter we introduce an ongoing research project, the International Corpus of English (ICE), which was set up to provide data for the study of English worldwide. Before we describe ICE, however, we need to look a little more closely at how English has become a world language.

THE SPREAD OF ENGLISH

One of the leading scholars of world English, Braj Kachru, has described the spread of English in terms of three concentric circles (Kachru 1985). The *inner circle* consists of countries where English has traditionally been spoken as a first language. Countries in the inner circle include Great Britain, the United States, Canada, and Australia, and they account for approximately 350 million speakers. Moving out from the center, we have the *outer circle*. This comprises countries, such as India and Singapore, where English has become institutionalized as a second language and plays an important role in public administration. The English-speaking population of the outer circle is estimated to be at least 130 million. Finally, the *expanding circle* comprises countries in which English does not have any official status, but where it is recognized as an important international language. In countries of the expanding circle, such as Japan, Israel, and China, English is given prominence among foreign languages, and it has an important place in school curricula. Precisely because this circle is expanding, it is difficult to give a population count for it. Kachru puts the figure at somewhere between 100 million and 1 billion English speakers.

Apart from giving us some useful terminology, Kachru's model quantifies the importance of English today in terms of both geographical coverage and numbers of speakers. The phenomenon of world English raises many issues that are of interest to linguists and nonlinguists alike. Most fundamentally, is it still meaningful to speak of English as a single language, or should we simply speak of British English, American English, Indian English, and so on? In other words, is English fragmenting as it spreads across the globe, or does it retain a core of vocabulary and grammar wherever it goes? Do the countries of the inner circle still exert the same linguistic influence that they did in the past? Traditionally, British and American English have been the dominant models for both the outer circle and the expanding circle, but is this still the case? To what extent is the Australian variety, for instance, now beginning to exert its influence on the English spoken in Asia and the Pacific?

These are fairly theoretical issues, but the spread of English also has important practical implications, especially for countries in the expanding circle. For example, language teachers in, say, Japan and China need to know which variety of English they should teach in their schools. Should they teach British English or American English? Or perhaps Australian English? Which variety will be most useful to their students in, say, twenty years' time for international trade and communication?

INVESTIGATING ENGLISH

At present, we can offer little more than speculative answers to these questions. To remedy this situation, linguists are increasingly turning to computer technology for help. Linguists now compile large computerized databases or "corpora" of naturally occurring samples of English, which they then subject to a range of systematic analyses. This area of study is known as corpus linguistics, and it began in the early 1960s. The Brown Corpus sampled written American English produced in 1961, and the Survey of English Usage corpus sampled spoken and written British English from the 1960s to the early 1980s. These were pioneering corpora and set the standards for subsequent work. A great many corpora are now available, some on CD-ROM and some on the Internet. However, like their predecessors, the major modern corpora still tend to focus on the two dom-

Figure 8.1
Countries and Regions Participating in the ICE Project

Australia	Kenya
Cameroon	Malawi
Canada	New Zealand
Fiji	Nigeria
Ghana	Philippines
Great Britain	Sierra Leone
Hong Kong	Singapore
India	Tanzania
Ireland	South Africa
Jamaica	United States

inant varieties, British English and American English. Notable exceptions include the Kolhapur Corpus of Indian English (Shastri 1985) and the Macquarie Corpus of Australian English (Collins and Peters 1988). This still leaves a great many varieties of English that have never been collected or analyzed in a systematic way.

THE INTERNATIONAL CORPUS OF ENGLISH

In an attempt to gain systematic knowledge of the many varieties of English, Sidney Greenbaum initiated the International Corpus of English (ICE). In an article published in *World Englishes* in 1988, Greenbaum proposed that teams of researchers should collect samples of English in countries where English is used as a first language or as a second official language. The samples should be collected, computerized, and analyzed in parallel with each other in order to provide data for comparative studies of English around the world (Greenbaum 1988).

The proposal was greeted with much enthusiasm. ICE now involves research teams in twenty countries or regions. These are listed in figure 8.1. Each team is compiling a corpus of 1 million words of its own national or regional variety of English. In many cases, ICE represents the first systematic study of the variety.

As figure 8.1 shows, ICE includes countries of the inner circle (e.g., Great Britain, the United States, Australia, New Zealand) and of the outer circle (e.g., India, Singapore, Nigeria, Kenya). The expanding circle is catered for in a related project known as the International Corpus of Learner English (ICLE). ICLE is a corpus of writing by advanced learners of English from different mother-tongue backgrounds, including French, Spanish, German, Dutch, Swedish, Czech, Japanese, and Chinese (Granger 1996).

Figure 8.2
Written Text Categories

NONPRINTED (50)

    Nonprofessional writing (20)
        student untimed essays (10)
        student examination essays (10)

    Correspondence (30)
        social letters (15)
        business letters (15)

PRINTED (150)

    Informational (academic) (40)
        humanities (10)
        social sciences (10)
        natural sciences (10)
        technology (10)

    Informational (nonacademic) (40)
        humanities (10)
        social sciences (10)
        natural sciences (10)
        technology (10)

    Informational (reportage) (20)
        press news reports (20)

    Instructional (20)
        administrative/regulatory (10)
        skills/hobbies (10)

    Persuasive (10)
        press editorials (10)

    Creative (20)
        novels/stories (20)

The collection of samples for ICE began in 1990, and in most participating countries this stage is still in progress. At the time of writing, only the British corpus (ICE-GB) has been completed and is available for research. For practical reasons, each corpus is limited in size to 500 samples or "texts," each containing approximately 2,000 words (a total of 1 million words). The texts are distributed among many text categories, shown in figures 8.2 and 8.3. The number of 2,000-word samples in each category is shown in parentheses. These text categories have been selected to give a representative sample of current English usage in each country (Nelson 1996).

As well as the texts themselves, ICE researchers are recording a wide

Figure 8.3
Spoken Text Categories

DIALOGUE (180)

    Private (100)
      face-to-face conversations (90)
      telephone calls (10)

    Public (80)
      class lessons (20)
      broadcast discussions (20)
      broadcast interviews (10)
      parliamentary debates (10)
      legal cross-examinations (10)
      business transactions (10)

MONOLOGUE (120)

    Unscripted (70)
      spontaneous commentaries (20)
      unscripted speeches (30)
      demonstrations (10)
      legal presentations (10)

    Scripted (50)
      broadcast news (20)
      broadcast talks (20)
      nonbroadcast speeches (10)

range of sociolinguistic variables about each text. We record the age and educational level of each speaker and writer, as well as his or her ethnic background, occupation, and any other languages spoken.

ANNOTATING THE CORPORA

The ICE corpora are not simply collections of raw text. They have been designed to allow researchers to compare varieties of English specifically at the grammatical level, so each corpus is analyzed grammatically in two stages. The first stage concentrates on individual words and involves labeling each word for its word class. We refer to this as "tagging" the corpus, and the repertoire of word class tags is known as the ICE Tagset. Each tag consists of a main word class label, for example, N for noun and V for verb. This is followed by one or more features in parentheses. Here are some examples of grammatical tags, with an explanation of their meaning:

	Tag	*Key*
Coastal	ADJ(ge)	General adjective
shipping	N(com, sing)	Common, singular noun
gave	V(ditr, past)	Ditransitive verb, past tense
England	N(prop, sing)	Proper, singular noun
an	ART(indef)	Indefinite article
industrial	ADJ(ge)	General adjective
lead	N(com, sing)	Common, singular noun

The ICE Tagset was devised by researchers at the Survey of English Usage, University College London, in collaboration with the TOSCA (Tools for Syntactic Corpus Analysis) group at the University of Nijmegen (Greenbaum 1993). Its approach and terminology are largely traditional, and it relies heavily on the descriptions of English given by Quirk et al. (1985). The terminology in this grammar is likely to be familiar to most potential users of the corpus, so the annotation scheme we have used will be generally comprehensible to most linguists.

The tagged corpus forms the basis of the second annotation stage, syntactic parsing. During this stage, we concentrate on syntactic structures, rather than on the individual words. With the help of computer programs, we draw a labeled tree diagram for every sentence in the corpus. An example is shown in figure 8.4. Each node is labeled first for function (subject, object, and so on) and then for category (noun phrase, clause, and so on). In this example, the topmost node carries the function label PU (parsing unit) and the category label CL (clause). Additional features are added below these labels.

Again, our syntactic analyses are broadly traditional, and the terminology we use will be familiar to anyone with a basic knowledge of grammar. In some cases, however, we have had to devise new terms for structures that are not described in traditional grammar. Informal conversations, in particular, threw up many structures that had never been systematically described before. This is because traditional grammars tend to consider only "textbook" examples—ones that are grammatically very clear, without the repetitions, false starts, hesitations, and the like that are characteristic of real speech. Traditional grammars, for instance, do not generally attempt to analyze examples like "Very nice certainly yes," which is from a conversation in the British corpus. This type of utterance presents many problems for the grammarian. Not least among these is what to call it: is it a sentence, a clause, or even a phrase? We call it a *nonclause* (NONCL), since it has no clausal elements at all—no subject, no verb, and so on. Nonclauses are far more common in English than the grammar books would lead us to believe. In fact, they account for almost a quarter of all the utterances in the British corpus.

Figure 8.4
Example of a Tree Diagram from the IGE-GB Corpus

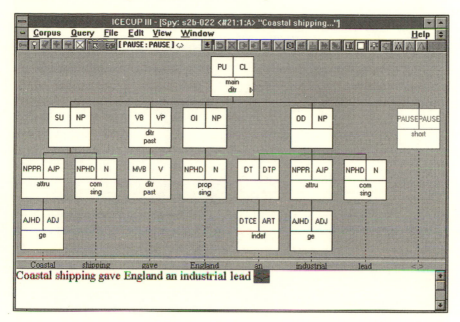

APPLICATIONS

From the examples given here, it is clear that the ICE corpora contain a great deal of useful information, and when they are completed, they will afford us many new insights into English as it is really used. The British corpus alone contains about 83,000 text units, each of which has been syntactically analyzed. To exploit this information fully, we have developed dedicated software, the ICE Corpus Utility Program (ICECUP). ICECUP will be distributed with each of the component corpora and will allow end users to search the corpora in a variety of ways. It supports lexical searches, searches for word class tags, and combinations of the two, as well as complex searches for syntactic patterns. The result of a search in ICE-GB for coordinated noun phrases is shown in figure 8.5.

ICECUP also allows researchers to refine their searches using the biographical data that are recorded with each text. This permits searches to be confined to, say, utterances by speakers from selected countries or regions, or speakers in selected age groups.

We anticipate that the availability of ICE data and software will stimulate research into the less well known varieties of English. In the early part of the next century, we can reasonably expect to see a series of grammars of varieties of English from Africa, Asia, and the Caribbean. These efforts

Figure 8.5
Result of a Search for Coordinated Noun Phrases Using ICECUP

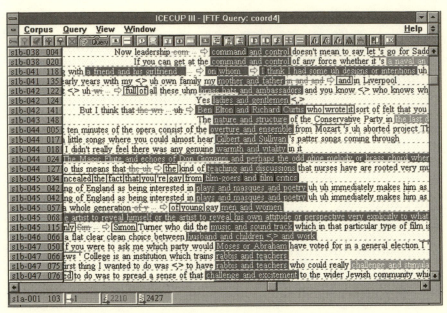

will inevitably lead to a more balanced description of English than the one presented in traditional grammars, which are largely based on varieties from the inner circle. The corpora from India and Singapore will allow us to compare inner- and outer-circle varieties to determine how far these Englishes have moved away from their original parent languages. Using computer software, it will be possible to compare syntactic trees from the different varieties simply by superimposing them on each other. This will reveal at a glance the structures that are common to every variety, thereby revealing the grammatical "core" of English. This will obviously be of great benefit to teachers of English as a foreign language, since the core will indicate those structures that they must teach their students for effective international communication.

The same computational procedure will also reveal structures that are unique to any one variety and those that are shared by particular varieties, for example, Australian English and New Zealand English. We will be able to group varieties according to their common lexical and grammatical properties and thereby produce the first-ever linguistic map of world English. At present, we can only guess what this map will look like. We can be confident, however, that it will offer a comprehensive picture of English around the world.

Further information about ICE may be obtained from the Survey of English Usage Web site at *http://www.ucl.ac.uk/english-usage/*. The ICE project is being coordinated by Professor Charles F. Meyer, University of Massachusetts at Boston (*http://www.cs.umb/edu/~meyer/*). The International Corpus of Learner English (ICLE) is being coordinated by Professor Sylviane Granger, Université Catholique de Louvain, Belgium (*http://www.fltr. ucl.ac.be/FLTR/GERM/ETAN/CECL/cecl.html*).

REFERENCES

Collins, P. C., and P. Peters. 1988. The Australian corpus project. *Corpus linguistics hard and soft*, ed. by M. Kyto, O. Ihalainen, and M. Rissanen, 103–21. Amsterdam: Rodopi.

Granger, Sylviane. 1996. Learner English around the world. *Comparing English worldwide: The International Corpus of English*, ed. by Sidney Greenbaum, 13–24. Oxford: Clarendon Press.

Greenbaum, Sidney. 1988. A proposal for an international computerized corpus of English. *World Englishes* 7: 315.

———. 1993. The Tagset for the International Corpus of English. *Corpus-based computational linguistics*, ed. by Clive Souter and Eric Atwell, 11–24. Amsterdam: Rodopi.

Kachru, Braj. 1985. Standards, codification, and sociolinguistic realism: The English language in the outer circle. *English in the world*, ed. by Randolph Quirk and H. G. Widdowson, 11–30. Cambridge: Cambridge University Press.

Nelson, Gerald. 1996. The design of the corpus. *Comparing English worldwide: The International Corpus of English*, ed. by Sidney Greenbaum, 27–35. Oxford: Clarendon Press.

Quirk, Randolph, Sidney Greenbaum, Geoffrey Leech, and Jan Svartvik. 1985. *A comprehensive grammar of the English language*. London: Longman.

Shastri, S. V. 1985. Towards a description of Indian English: A standard corpus in machine-readable form. *English World-Wide* 6: 275–78.

SPEAKING OF AMERICA: WHY ENGLISH-ONLY IS A BAD IDEA

Geoffrey Nunberg

The story told by the English-only movement is nonsense from begin-ning to end. No language was ever less in need of official protection.

Since Slovakia became an independent state on January 1, 1993, the Slovak majority has been imposing increasingly stringent language restrictions on the ethnic Hungarian minority, whom they suspect of irredentist leanings. Hungarian place-names must be changed to accord with Slovak spellings, all official business must be transacted in Slovak even in districts that are almost entirely Hungarian-speaking, and so forth. It's a familiar enough pattern in that part of the world, where antique ethnic antagonisms are routinely fought out on the field of language, except that in this case, the Slovakians have insisted that their policies are in fact thoroughly modern— even American. By way of demonstrating this, the Slovak State Language Law of 1995 cites the example of American official-English bills, and the drafters of the law made a point of entertaining a delegation from the U.S. English organization. In American eyes, though, the similarities might lead to another, more disquieting conclusion: What if it's we who are becoming more like them?

For most of our history, language has not been a major theme in Amer-ican political life. The chief reason for that, to be sure, is that God in his wisdom has given us a single dominant language, with few real dialects or patois of the sort that European nations have had to deal with in the course of their nation building. (One notable exception is the post-Creole variety spoken by many African Americans.) It's true that America has always had substantial communities of speakers of non-English languages: indigenous peoples; groups absorbed in the course of colonial expansion, like the Francophones of Louisiana and the Hispanics of the Southwest; and the great flows of immigrants from 1880 to 1920 and during the past 30 years. And since the eighteenth century there have been recurrent efforts to discourage or suppress the use of other languages by various minorities, particularly at the time of the nativist movement of the turn of the century. But the focus on language has always been opportunistic, a convenient way of underscoring the difference between us and them; the issue has always subsided as minorities have become anglicized, leaving little symbolic residue in its wake. Unlike the Slovakians, the Italians, the Germans, or those paragons of official orality, the French, we have not until now made how we speak an essential element of what we are.

Given the minor role that language has played in our historical self-conception, it isn't surprising that the current English-only movement began in the political margins, the brainchild of slightly flaky figures like Senator S. I. Hayakawa and John Tanton, a Michigan ophthalmologist who co-founded the U.S. English organization as an outgrowth of his involvement in zero population growth and immigration restriction. (The term "English-only" was originally introduced by supporters of a 1984 California initiative opposing bilingual ballots, a stalking horse for other official-language measures. Leaders of the movement have since rejected the label, pointing out that they have no objection to the use of foreign languages in the home. But the phrase is a fair characterization of the goals of the movement so far as public life is concerned.)

Until recently, English-only was not a high priority for the establishment right. President Bush was opposed to the movement, and Barbara Bush once went so far as to describe it as "racist." And while a number of figures in the Republican leadership have been among the sponsors of official-language bills, most did not become vocal enthusiasts of the policy until the successes of English-only measures and of anti-immigrant initiatives like California's Proposition 187 persuaded them that anti-immigrant politics might have broad voter appeal. Senator Dole endorsed English-only in the 1996 presidential campaign, and Newt Gingrich recently described bilingualism as a menace to American civilization.

The successes of English-only are undeniably impressive. Polls show between 65 percent and 86 percent of Americans favoring making English the official language, and the U.S. English organization currently claims more than 650,000 members. Largely owing to its efforts, 18 states have adopted official-language measures via either referenda or legislative action, with legislation pending in 13 more (four other states have official-language statutes that date from earlier periods). The majority of these laws are largely symbolic, like the 1987 Arkansas law—which President Clinton now says it was "a mistake" to sign—that states merely, "The English language shall be the official language of the state of Arkansas." But a few are more restrictive, notably the measure adopted by Arizona voters in

1988, which bars the state or its employees from conducting business in any language other than English, apart from some narrow exceptions for purposes like health and public safety. In 1996 the House passed H.R. 123, which is similar in most respects to the Arizona law. (Its title is the "English Language Empowerment Act," which as the writer James Crawford has observed is a small assault on the language in its own right.) While the Senate did not act on that bill, subsequent versions have been regularly reintroduced. Indeed the English Language Empowerment Act of 1999 is up for House consideration as this volume goes to press. The House and Senate have seen somewhat differently on these matters, with some Senate Republicans preferring a watered-down version as they are apprehensive about offending Hispanic constituents. In that form, as little more than a symbolic affirmation of the official status of English, the bill would likely win the support of some Democrats, and might prove difficult for President Clinton to veto.

In any case, to the extent that the bill is symbolic, its adoption is more or less facultative; the movement achieves most of its goals simply by raising the issue. At the local level, the public discussion of English-only has encouraged numerous private acts of discrimination. In recent years, for example, dozens of firms and institutions have adopted English-only workplace rules that bar employees from using foreign languages even when speaking among themselves or when on breaks. More generally, the mere fact that politicians and the press are willing to take the proposals of English-only seriously tends to establish the basic premise of the movement: that there is a question about the continued status of English as the common language of American public discourse. In the end, the success of the movement should be measured not by the number of official-language statutes passed, but by its success in persuading people—including many who are unsympathetic to the English-only approach—to accept large parts of the English-only account of the situation of language in America.

IS ENGLISH REALLY ENDANGERED?

In rough outline, the English-only story goes like this: The result of recent immigration has been a huge influx of non-English speakers, who now constitute a substantial proportion of the population. Advocates of English-only often claim that there are 32 million Americans who are not proficient in English, a figure that will rise to 40 million by the year 2000. Moreover, these recent arrivals, particularly the Hispanics, are not learning English as earlier generations of immigrants did. According to Senator Hayakawa, "large populations of Mexican Americans, Cubans, and Puerto Ricans do not speak English and have no intention of learning."

The alleged failure to learn English is laid to several causes. There are the ethnic leaders accused of advocating a multiculturalist doctrine that asserts, as Peter Salins describes it, that "ethnic Americans [have] the right to function in their 'native' language—not just at home but in the public realm." Government is charged with impeding linguistic assimilation by providing a full range of services in other languages, even as bilingual education enables immigrant children to complete their schooling without ever making the transition to English. Moreover, it is claimed, the peculiar geographic situation of Hispanics creates communities in which linguistic or cultural assimilation is unnecessary. For example, Paul Kennedy (himself no supporter of English-only) writes of an impending "Hispanicization of the American Southwest," where

> Mexican-Americans will have sufficient coherence and critical mass in a defined region so that, if they choose, they can preserve their distinctive culture indefinitely. They could also undertake to do what no previous immigrant group could ever have dreamed of doing: challenge the existing cultural, political, legal, commercial, and educational systems to change fundamentally not only the language but also the very institutions in which they do business.

Once you accept all this, it is not hard to conclude, as Congressman Norman Shumway puts it, that "the primacy of English is being threatened, and we are moving to a bilingual society," with all the prospects of disorder and disunity that bilingualism seems to imply. As Senator Hayakawa wrote:

> For the first time in our history, our nation is faced with the possibility of the kind of linguistic division that has torn apart Canada in recent years; that has been a major feature of the unhappy history of Belgium, split into speakers of French and Flemish; that is at this very moment a bloody division between the Sinhalese and Tamil populations of Sri Lanka.

A U.S. English ad makes the point more graphically: A knife bearing the legend "official bilingualism" slashes through a map of the United States.

But the English-only story is nonsense from beginning to end. Take, for starters, the claim that there are 32 million Americans who are not proficient in English. To see how wild that figure is, consider that the total number of foreign-born residents over five years old is only 18 million, some of them immigrants from other English-speaking countries and most of the rest speaking English well. The actual Census figure for residents over five who speak no English is only 1.9 million—proportionately only a quarter as high as it was in 1890, at the peak of the last great wave of immigration. And even if we include people who report speaking English "not well," the number of residents with limited English proficiency stands at around six million people in all. This is not a huge figure when you consider the extent of recent immigration and the difficulty that adults have in acquiring a new language, particularly when they are working in menial jobs that involve little regular contact with English speakers. (Or to put it another way: More than 97 percent of Americans speak English well, a level of linguistic homogeneity unsurpassed by any other large nation in history.)

What is more, recent immigrants are in fact learning English at a faster rate than any earlier generations of immigrants did—and by all the evidence, with at least as much enthusiasm. Whatever "multiculturalism" may mean to its proponents, it most assuredly does not involve a rejection of English as the national lingua franca. No ethnic leaders have been crazy enough to suggest that immigrants can get along without learning English, nor would any immigrants pay the slightest attention to such a suggestion if it were made. According to a recent Florida poll, 98 percent of Hispanics want their children to speak English well. And the wish is father to the deed: Immigrants of all nationalities are moving to English at a faster rate than ever before in our history. The demographer Calvin Veltman has observed that the traditional three-generation period for a complete shift to English is being shortened to two generations. A recent RAND Corporation study showed that more than 90 percent of first-generation Hispanics born in California have native fluency in English, and that only about 50 percent of the second generation still speak Spanish.

That latter figure suggests that for recent Hispanic arrivals, as for many groups of immigrants that preceded them, becoming American entails not just mastering English but also rejecting the language and culture of one's parents. It is a regrettable attitude (and the very one that English-only has battened on), but the process seems inevitable: Relatively few Hispanics display the fierce religious or patriotic loyalty to their mother tongue that the Germans did a hundred years ago. The only exception is the Cubans, who have a special political motivation for wanting to hang on to Spanish, but even here the preference for English is increasingly marked—a survey of first- and second-generation Cuban college students in Miami found that 86 percent preferred to use English in speaking among themselves. It is only the assimilated third- and fourth-generation descendants of immigrants who feel the loss of languages keenly, and by then it is almost always too late. (For a linguist, there is no more poignant experience than to watch a class of American college freshmen struggling to master the basic grammar of the language that their grandparents spoke with indifferent fluency.)

A number of factors contribute to the accelerated pace of language shift among immigrants: the increased mobility, both social and geographical, of modern life; the ubiquity of English-language media; universal schooling; and the demands of the urban work-place. In the nineteenth century, by contrast, many immigrants could hold on to their native language for several generations at no great cost: some because they lived in isolated farming communities and required very little contact with English speakers, others because they lived in one of the many states or cities that provided public schooling in their native tongues. At the turn of the century, in fact, more than 6 percent of American schoolchildren were receiving most or all of their primary education in the German language alone—programs that were eliminated only around the time of the First World War.

All of this underscores the irony of the frequent claims that unlike earlier generations, modern immigrants are refusing to learn English—or that modern bilingual education is an "unprecedented" concession to immigrants who insist on maintaining their own language. In point of fact, there's a good chance that great-grandpa didn't work very hard to learn English, and a fair probability that his kids didn't, either. Today, by contrast, all publicly supported bilingual education programs are aimed at facilitating the transition to English. The programs are unevenly implemented, it's true, owing to limited funding, to the resistance of school administrators, and to the shortage of trained teachers. (An early study found that 50 percent of teachers hired in "bilingual" programs lacked proficiency in their students' native languages.) And in any case such programs are available right now for only about 25 percent of limited-English students. Still, the method clearly works better than any of the alternatives. An extensive 1992 study sponsored by the National Academy of Sciences found that, compared with various types of "immersion" programs, bilingual education reduces the time to reach full English fluency by between two and three years.

What of the other government programs that critics describe as opening the door to "official bilingualism"? Measured against the numerous social and economic motivations that limited-English immigrants have for learning English, the availability of official information in their own language is a negligible disincentive, and there are strong arguments for providing these services. To take an example that the English-only people are fond of raising, why in the world would we want to keep immigrants with limited English from taking their driver's license tests in their native languages? Do we want to keep them from driving to work until they have learned the English word *pedestrian*? Or to be more realistic about it—since many of them will have no choice but to drive anyway—do we want to drive to work on roads full of drivers who are ignorant of the traffic laws?

In any event, these programs are extremely, even excessively, limited. Federal law mandates provision of foreign-language services only in a handful of special cases—interpreters must be provided for migrant worker health care centers and for certain Immigration and Naturalization Service procedures, for example—and a recent General Accounting Office survey found that the total number of federal documents printed in languages other than English over the past five years amounted to less than one-tenth of 1 percent of the total number of titles, hardly a sign of any massive shift to multilingualism in the public realm.

LANGUAGE AS SYMBOLISM

Considered strictly in the light of the actualities, then, English-only is an irrelevant provocation. It is a bad cure for an imaginary disease, and moreover, one that encourages an unseemly hypochondria about the health of the dominant language and culture. But it is probably a mistake to try to engage the issue primarily at this level, as opponents of these measures have tried to do with little success. Despite the insistence of English-only advocates that they have launched their campaign "for the immigrants' own good," it's hard to avoid the conclusion that the needs of non-English speakers are a pretext, not a rationale, for the movement. At every stage, the success of the movement has depended on its capacity to provoke widespread indignation over allegations that government bilingual programs are promoting a dangerous drift toward a multilingual society. The movement's supporters seem to have little interest in modifying that story to take the actual situation of immigrants into account. To take just one example, there are currently long waiting lists in most cities for English-language adult classes—around 50,000 people in Los Angeles County alone—but none of the English-only bills that have been introduced in the Congress make any direct provision for funding of such programs. Who, after all, would care about that?

One indication of just how broadly the movement transcends any immediate, practical concerns about immigrants is the success it has had in regions where issues like immigration and multiculturalism ought by rights to be fairly remote concerns. Of the states that have passed official-English laws in recent years, only four (California, Florida, Arizona, and Colorado) have large immigrant populations. The remainder consist of western states like Montana, North and South Dakota, and Wyoming; Indiana and New Hampshire; and all of the southern and border states except Louisiana (apart from Florida, the only state in the region with substantial numbers of non-English speakers). The breadth of support for these measures seems to increase as its local relevance diminishes, as witness the 89 percent majority that the measure won in an Alabama referendum and the unanimous or near-unanimous legislative votes for English-only measures in states like Arkansas, Georgia, Tennessee, Kentucky, and Virginia. These are not the sorts of places where voters could feel any imminent threat to English from the babel of alien tongues, or indeed, where we would expect to see voters or legislators giving much attention to immigration at all.

At the national level, then, English-only is not strictly comparable to explicit antiimmigrant measures like Proposition 187, which raise genuine substantive issues. The English-only movement has been successful because it provides a symbolic means of registering dissatisfaction with a range of disquieting social phenomena—immigration, yes, but also multiculturalism, affirmative action, and even public assistance. (Not missing a trick, U.S. English advocates like to describe bilingual programs as "linguistic welfare.") By way of response, the movement offers an apparently minimal conception of American identity: We are at the very least a people who speak English.

It seems an unexceptionable stipulation. Even Horace Kallen, who introduced the notion of "cultural pluralism" 70 years ago as a counter to the ideology of the melting pot, readily acknowledged that all Americans must accept English as "the common language of [our] great tradition." But the decision to invest a language with official status is almost never based on merely practical considerations. Language always trails symbolic baggage in its wake and frames the notion of national identity in a particular way. That is why the designation of a national language is controversial wherever the matter arises.

However, the actual significance varies enormously from one nation to the next. Sometimes language is made the embodiment of a liturgical tradition, as in various Balkan countries, and sometimes of a narrowly ethnic conception of nationality, as in Slovakia or the Baltic states. In the recent French debates over the status of the language and the use of English words, the language is standing in more than anything else for the cultural authority of traditional republican institutions—a recent constitutional amendment declared French not the national language, but *la langue de la Republique.*

Even in the American context, the case for English has been made in very different ways over the course of the century. For the nativists of Kallen's time, language was charged with a specifically ideological burden. The imposition of English was the cornerstone of an aggressive program of Americanization, aimed at sanitizing immigrant groups of the undemocratic doctrines they were thought to harbor. The laws passed in this period undid almost all the extensive public bilingualism of the late nineteenth century, particularly in the civic and political domains. The ability to speak English was made a condition for citizenship in 1906, and in 1915 an English-literacy requirement was added, over President Wilson's veto. A 1919 Nebraska statute stipulated that all public meetings be conducted in English; Oregon required that foreign-language periodicals provide an English translation of their entire contents. More than 30 states passed laws prohibiting or restricting foreign-language instruction in primary schools.

The justification provided for these measures was a peculiar doctrine about the connection between language and political thought, which held that speaking a foreign language was inimical to grasping the fundamental concepts of democratic society. The Nebraska supreme court, for example, warned against the "baneful effects" of educating children in foreign languages, which must "naturally inculcate in them the ideas and sentiments foreign to the best interests of their country." English was viewed as a kind of "chosen language," the consecrated bearer of "Anglo-Saxon" political ideals and institutions. A New York official told immigrants in 1916: "You have got to learn our language because that is the vehicle of the thought that has been handed down from the men in whose breasts first burned the fire of freedom." (Like many other defenders of this doctrine, he dated the tradition from the Magna Carta, a text written, as it happens, in Latin.)

Taken literally, the chosen-language doctrine does not stand up under scrutiny, either linguistically or philosophically. Nothing could be more alien to the Enlightenment universalism of the Founders than the notion that the truths they held to be "self-evident" were ineffable in other languages. But it is almost always a mistake to take talk of language literally. It was not our democratic ideals that seemed to require expression in English, but the patriotic rituals that were charged with mediating the sense of national identity in the period, such as the obligatory school-room declamations of the sacred texts of American democracy; and more broadly, the Anglo culture in which those rituals were embedded. Theodore Roosevelt made the connection clear when he said: "We must . . . have but one language. That must be the language of the Declaration of Independence, of Washington's Farewell Address, of Lincoln's Gettysburg speech and second inaugural." The list is significant in its omissions. English might also be the language of Shakespeare, Emerson, and Melville, but its claim to merit official recognition had to be made on political grounds, as the only cloth from which our defining ideals could be woven.

In this regard, the "new nativism" is greatly different from the old. The modern English-only movement makes the case for a national language in what seem to be apolitical (or at least, nonideological) terms. English is important solely as a lingua franca, the "social glue" or "common bond" that unites all Americans. Indeed, advocates are careful to avoid suggesting that English has any unique virtues that make it appropriate in this role. A U.S. English publication explains: "We hold no special brief for English. If Dutch (or French, or Spanish, or German) had become our national language, we would now be enthusiastically defending Dutch." (It is hard to imagine Theodore Roosevelt passing over the special genius of English so lightly.)

On the face of things, the contemporary English-only movement seems a less coercive point of view. Indeed, the movement often seems eager to discharge English of any cultural or ideological responsibility whatsoever. Its advocates cast their arguments with due homage to the sanctity of pluralism. As former Kentucky Senator Walter Huddleston puts it, Americans are "a generous people, appreciative of cultural diversity," and the existence of a common language has enabled us "to develop a stable and cohesive society that is the envy of many fractured ones, without imposing any strict standards of homogeneity." At the limit, advocates seem to suggest that Americans need have nothing at all in common, so long as we have the resources for talking about it.

That is misleading, though. Language is as much a proxy for culture now as it was at the turn of the century, except that now neither English nor Anglo culture needs any doctrinal justification. This explains why English-only advocates are so drawn to comparisons with polities like Canada, Belgium, and Sri Lanka. Turn-of-the-century nativists rarely invoked the cases of Austria-Hungary or the Turkish empire in making the case against multilingualism, not because such scenarios were implausible—after all, the nativists had no qualms about invoking equally implausible scenarios of immigrant hordes inciting revolution—but because they were irrelevant: What could Americans learn about their national identity from comparisons with places like those? And the fact that Americans are now disposed to find these specters plausible is an indication of how far the sense of national identity has moved from its doctrinal base. The ethnic divisions in Canada and Belgium are generally and rightly perceived as having no ideological significance, and the moral seems to be that cultural differences alone are sufficient to fragment a state, even this one.

There are a number of reasons for the shift in emphasis. One, certainly, is a generally diminished role for our particular political ideology in an age in which it seems to lack serious doctrinal rivals. Over the long term, though, the new sense of the role of a common language also reflects the emergence of new mechanisms for mediating the sense of national community—radio, film, television—which require no direct institutional intervention. And the effects of the new media are complemented by the techniques of mass merchandising, which ensure that apart from "colorful" local differences, the material setting of American life will look the same from one place to another. ("To be American is to learn to shop," Newt Gingrich observed not long ago, without apparent irony.)

As Raymond Williams noted, the broadcast media aren't direct replacements for traditional institutions: They do not inculcate an ideology so much as presuppose one. In this sense they are capable of imposing a high degree of cultural and ideological uniformity without explicit indoctrination, or indeed, without seeming to "impose" at all. This may help to explain why the English-only movement appears indifferent to the schools or the courses in citizenship that played such an important part in the program of the turn-of-the-century Americanization movement, as well as to the theories about the special mission of English that were so prominent then. It's hard to imagine anyone making the case for English as the language of Washington's farewell speech or Lincoln's second inaugural, when students are no longer required to memorize or even read those texts anymore. Of all our sacred texts, only the Pledge of Allegiance and the national anthem are still capable of rousing strong feelings. But these are, notably, the most linguistically empty of all the American liturgy (schoolchildren say the first as if it were four long words, and I have never encountered anybody who is capable of parsing the second), which derive their significance chiefly from their association with the non-linguistic symbol of the flag.

CHERISHED CONFORMITY

It is inevitable, then, that modern formulations of the basis of national identity should come to focus increasingly on the importance of common experience and common knowledge, in place of (or at least, on an equal footing with) common political ideals. Michael Lind, for example, has argued that American identity ought to be officially vested in a national culture, which has native competence in American English as its primary index but is also based on American "folkways" that include

> particular ways of acting and dressing; conventions of masculinity and femininity; ways of celebrating major events like births, marriages, and funerals; particular kinds of sports and recreations; and conceptions of the proper boundaries between the secular and religious spheres. And there is also a body of material—ranging from historical events that everyone is expected to know about to widely shared but ephemeral knowledge of sports and cinema and music—that might be called common knowledge.

Once we begin to insist on these cultural commonalities as necessary ingredients of national identity, it is inevitable that the insistence on English will become more categorical and sweeping. Where turn-of-the-century Americanizationists emphasized the explicitly civic uses of language, English-only casts its net a lot wider. It's true that the movement has tended to focus its criticism on the government bilingual programs, but only because these are the most accessible to direct political action; and within this domain, it has paid as much attention to wholly apolitical texts like driver's license tests and tax forms as to bilingual ballots. Where convenient, moreover, English-only advocates have also opposed the wholly apolitical private-sector uses of foreign languages. They have urged the California Public Utilities Commission to prohibit Pac Tel from publishing the Hispanic Yellow Pages; they have opposed the FCC licensing of foreign-language television and radio stations; they have proposed boycotts of Philip Morris for advertising in Spanish and of Burger King for furnishing bilingual menus in some localities. For all their talk of "cherished diversity," English-only advocates are in their way more intolerant of difference than their nativist predecessors. "This is America; speak English," English-only supporters like to say, and they mean 24 hours a day.

The irony of all this is that there was never a culture or a language so little in need of official support. Indeed, for someone whose first allegiance is to the English language and its culture, what is most distressing about the movement is not so much the insult it offers to immigrants as its evident lack of faith in the ability of English-language culture to make its way in the open market—and this at the very moment of the triumph of English as a world language of unprecedented currency. (A Frenchman I know described the English-only measures as akin to declaring crabgrass an endangered species.) The entire movement comes to seem tainted with the defensive character we associate with linguistic nationalism in other nations. I don't mean to say that English will ever acquire the particular significance that national languages have in places like Slovakia or France. But it's getting harder to tell the difference.

Language Loss, Our Loss

Mari Rhydwen

When the Beings first arrived here, we were completely seduced by their urbane charm, their gentleness, and their peculiarly animated way of talking. We watched them on television, meeting formally with world leaders or being relaxed and witty on chat shows. I don't think we realised quite how much our lives were going to change. They promised us a better life, and certainly the material benefits they offered exceeded the wildest fantasies of fairytale or science fiction. Once we were hooked, they educated us in Beingtalk so that we could communicate with all the Others and trade with them. At first we were taught by Beings in English, but later we were not allowed to speak our own languages in school or for business. Eventually our languages were forbidden anywhere in public and we stopped speaking them, even amongst ourselves. As the years passed, we lost our concepts of kinship, nation, memory, and ritual. We no longer had words for ideas or for feelings that were to do with attachment to family, since the Beings never live in family groups and do not even have a word that translates as mother. Similarly now, in English, I cannot find words to describe the efficient and calm but rather dry and colourless ways that living groups are organised now.[1] I can hardly understand why, but we did not seem troubled that our children could not talk to their grandparents, our parents, who were stuck in their dreams reminiscing about our lands and notions of family relations, our days of celebrating birthdays, or funerals. To be honest, we were happy to speak Beingtalk. We liked the sounds and the accompanying hand movements that were so much more accurately able to convey the ambiguous physiologics of Being connection but oddly inadequate when it came to talking about the links between bodies and feelings. We negotiated business deals across the galaxies with ease, but were unable to speak of the ties of

*mother to suckling baby, let alone the bonds to the earth we first knew
in reality, later metaphorically, as mother.*

*English, Chinese, Spanish, Hindi, the big languages we thought could
never grow quiet are kept alive by small groups of us who meet at
night in bleak, draughty education halls. Our group has been reading
the plays of Shakespeare, which are never performed in Beingtalk, for
in that language the tragedy becomes comedy, stories of love translate
as trivial superstition, and death is merely embarrassing. But I know
we are being nostalgic, hanging onto the idea that English has any
relevance in the Beingworld, and selfish too, wanting our children to
put effort into learning a language that is no longer useful. Even as I
write, I know that only a handful of people could understand these
words and share my love of their ability to express my sorrow. Not
that I can use them like the poets did, the talkers and singers. Skill
now lies in using hand and finger with the words to convey what only
mathematical symbols once did, and the world cannot be spoken, it
cannot be thought, in the language of our ancestors.*

For those of us who speak one of the big ten languages currently used by
over half the world's population,[2] the idea that our particular language
could disappear is almost unimaginable. It is necessary to construct fictions
to accommodate the idea. Yet over the past few hundred years and increasingly now, thousands of the world's languages have been and are disappearing, replaced by those of the politically powerful. For the speakers of
those languages that have already gone or are endangered, the idea that
their language could vanish would, until quite recently, have seemed as far-
fetched as the idea that English or Chinese could disappear seems to us
now. When the first Europeans settled Australia just over two hundred
years ago, the Aboriginal people would have found inconceivable the idea
that their languages would be almost eradicated.[3] Not only do languages
die, but with them much of the knowledge they expressed, the social systems, rituals, laws, and the names and healing properties of plants and
minerals, as well as intimate stories of place that connect people with their
homeland. Imagining alien invasion is a way to try to understand what it
means to lose not just a language but a way of life.

There are around 6,500 languages in the world, but estimates indicate
that as many as 90 percent will disappear over the next century (Krauss
1992, 70). They are being replaced by widely spoken standard languages.
The apparent advantages of national monolingualism are well known, well
documented, and commonsensical. They range from the facilitation of com-
mercial growth and bureaucratic efficiency to access to social justice. It is
argued that mass education and literacy in one national language are ways
of ensuring equality of access to knowledge, justice, and all the other basic
rights of a citizen. Monolingualism has often been associated with educational achievement, efficient administration, and economic growth. It was

no doubt for such reasons that my grandfather, raised in Wales by Welsh-speaking parents, was humiliated by being forced to wear a wooden board hung from a rope around his neck displaying the words "Welsh not" when he spoke Welsh at school. Yet the punishment of children for speaking their own language is not an historical curiosity. Children around the world continue to be forced to speak a language that is not their mother tongue at school. Although in many cases the methods of coercion are more subtle, the systematic humiliation of children who refuse to conform to the demands that they speak an alien language continues. The notorious "Welsh not" is surely the model for the metal board emblazoned with the words "I am stupid" hung around the necks of Gikuyu-speaking children in Kenya who, like Welsh children a century ago, dared to speak their mother tongue instead of English (Ngugi 1985, 112).

Currently the most economically dominant nations are monolingual, so many people have assumed that the correlation is evidence of a causal relationship. Studies of more than a hundred states have shown this to be untrue. There is also a widely held belief that monolingualism leads to national unity. The example of Bosnians who share a language with Serbs and Croats is one of many that disprove this belief. Beliefs that multilingualism is a cause of both poverty and conflict have been revealed as myths by linguists investigating language policy (Phillipson, Rannut, and Skutnabb-Kangas 1995, 4). Yet despite the fact that monolingualism does not guarantee prosperity, social justice, or peace, there is a worldwide movement toward linguistic homogeneity. This shift is all the more worrying in view of international agreement that minority groups and indigenous people have the fundamental right to speak their own languages.[4] Why are so many languages disappearing so fast when there is evidence that this does not lead to the anticipated economic or social benefits and, in many cases, alienates a basic human right?

In the cosmopolitan cities of the world, those with financial resources can enjoy the products of a range of different cultures. People can eat spaghetti, curry, tacos, and stir-fry. They can listen to flamenco, play Mah Jong, wear sarongs at the beach, and go home to sleep on futons. Tourists pick destinations where they can experience the exotic for themselves: ancient temples in Greece, Aboriginal coroborees in Australia, Zen gardens in Japan, and pyramids in Egypt. We desire difference, excitement, and novelty, but we often seek something that is also ancient. The surfeit of books that recycle ancient wisdom is testimony to a desire to learn from other long-standing human traditions.

Yet whilst in the industrialized Western nations our appetite for traditional exotica is unabated, we are simultaneously destroying the environments in which people with different cultures and traditions thrive. In 1997 The Stolen Children Report was released in Australia (National Inquiry 1997). Until as recently as 1970, very large numbers of Aboriginal children had been taken from their parents and placed in institutions. One of the findings of the inquiry was that, under international law, the forcible separation of children from their parents amounted to genocide. It is not necessary for a people to be physically killed; they can be erased by killing their way of being, their culture. Central to culture is language.

Without language, the stories, laws, and history in which the wisdom and knowledge of a people are embedded disappear. Although people can and do maintain a cultural identity when they no longer speak their former language,[5] it is undeniable that, just as countless unknown and unnamed species of plants and animals vanish when forests are destroyed, so too do undocumented ways of knowing vanish when a language is lost. The loss of cultural and linguistic diversity has often been compared to the loss of biological diversity, for the two are closely intertwined. Just as one of the arguments against the wholesale destruction of tropical rainforests is that plant species with potential curative properties may be permanently eradicated before their value is ever discovered, so too it is argued that traditional medical wisdom is lost when people's cultures are erased. In Western Australia, the uses of varieties of smokebush have long been known to the coastal Aboriginal people, and this has led to current work by a major pharmaceutical company on developing an anti-AIDS drug. Without the traditional wisdom about the plant's therapeutic value, it is extremely unlikely that anyone would have discovered its anti-AIDS properties. Around the world, bioethnographers are racing against time to gather the disappearing wisdom about flora and fauna of endangered traditions.

Yet there is a danger in reducing the arguments for preservation of biological or of cultural and linguistic diversity to one of resource management and in regarding cultures as commodities that we judge in terms of their monetary value. Again, there are analogies with biological diversity. People get upset about the disappearance of giant pandas because they are attractive to human beings because they are cute and cuddly. Presumably this is why the World Wild Fund for Nature (WWF) uses a panda in its logo and not a venomous snake or crop-eating insect. There is a similar danger that people may be encouraged to lobby for the preservation of cultural groups that are metaphorically "cute and cuddly" whereas, as with biological species, it is whole interdependent ecological systems which are at risk. When some part of an ecosystem is destroyed, the system itself is changed, and the consequences are often both unforeseen and irrevocable. We do not know what the world will be like if the thousands of different cultures which have, until recently, comprised the population of the world are reduced. It is because we do not know the implications that we need to take care of what is happening right now. We need to take action to maintain languages immediately. For some languages, one generation's delay will be too late.

People often find talking and thinking about these matters too uncomfortable, and I am aware of the danger of sounding like a prophet of the apocalypse. The history of humankind is the history of the rise and fall of the groupings and regroupings of people we call nations and cultures. Languages and cultures die, but new languages and cultures arise. Surely this is the way of the world. This is true, but what has changed is the extraordinary rapidity with which languages are disappearing at a rate unprecedented in human history. Studies of language change over time have shown that if a group of speakers of a language were to be isolated, it would take around a thousand years for that language to become a different language from the original one. This means that the 6,500 existing languages have taken tens of thousands of years to evolve. Since they can die out in little more than a generation, it is clear that they are disappearing far more quickly than the rate at which they could be replaced.

Ironically, at a time when because of the burgeoning electronic media we can learn about the existence of other lives and other worlds as never before and enjoy and celebrate the diversity of which humanity is capable, this same technology is contributing to the loss of this diversity. These days, it is not only deliberate policy to eradicate the use of minority languages that is leading to their decline,[6] but the introduction of television, video, and computers. When I was teaching literacy workers from remote areas of the Northern Territory of Australia, students asked for classes to be stopped in the middle of the day so they could watch *Days of Our Lives*. People whose first language is not English are exposed, through television and film, not only to English but to another way of life. While the primary aim of makers of television soaps is not the homogenization of world culture, it is a potent side effect. Soapies are, after all, not called soapies for nothing. Their original purpose was to sell soap powder to bored housewives,[7] and no one cares whether those women previously washed their undies in copper tubs in rural Ohio or on the banks of the Ganges.

The Internet is more complex than other mass media in that it has been hailed as a tool of democracy, as a means to challenge "the existing political hierarchy's monopoly on powerful communications media, and perhaps thus revitalize citizen-based democracy" (Rheingold 1994, 14). Yet access to the Internet depends upon having access to appropriate technology, access to a service provider, and the ability to use English (Gupta 1997). Thus people in the world's poorest nations such as Chad, Zaire, Burma, and Cambodia do not have Internet access. While global communications technology had the potential to foster diversity, in reality it contributes powerfully to the spread of English as a global lingua franca.

There are many so-called killer languages. Everywhere that a major political power has dominated, the domination has spread to linguistic domination, as can be seen in China and the former Soviet Union. This is a widespread phenomenon and has been so throughout history, accounting for the spread of Latin in much of Europe. Colonisation and imperialism have always depended upon colonising through education. As Kenyan writer Ngugi wa Thiong'o wrote, "The night of the sword and the bullet was followed by the morning of chalk and the blackboard" (1986, 9). Yet right now it is the dominance of English in the mass media, on the Internet, and in other channels of global communication such as business and academic publications that is posing one of the biggest threats to smaller languages.

The loss of the world's languages has thus been interpreted in various ways. Some people regard the increasing use of major languages, promoted through mass education programs, as evidence of increasing equality and justice. Others see such programs as yet another form of colonisation. Some commentators regard the effects of education programs as insignificant compared to those of the global saturation by electronic media, the consequence of rampant global capitalism in which monolingualism facilitates more efficient advertising and consumerism. Whether the causes of language loss are altruism, greed, or accident does not alter the fact that there is now more rapid linguistic and cultural homogenization than has ever occurred in the history of humankind.

This loss of linguistic diversity has troubled people who have been aware of the rapid decline in the number of world languages over the past decades. It is a cause for concern not only for those people whose languages are endangered, but for all of us. Peter Mühlhäusler has spoken of the loss of linguistic diversity as "a grave danger to our species," arguing that the "extent of diversity is a direct indicator of the well being of an ecology."[8] Such rhetoric is compelling, yet it can sometimes be difficult to convey why so many linguists regard language loss so gravely. There has been a long-standing controversy in linguistics about the extent to which our languages shape our worldviews. This debate started with Whorf (1956), who was the first linguist to argue that our reality is constructed by the language in which we fashion it and that destroying a language is destroying a way of being in the world. Increasingly, postmodern and critical theories tend to support the argument that our reality is socially constructed. As with biological diversity, linguistic and cultural diversity are important to us all for a number of reasons. First, when languages are lost, wisdom and knowledge that can be of wide benefit to humanity is also lost. Second, the right to speak and maintain one's language and culture is a fundamental human right, and we have a responsibility to ensure that all human rights are recognised, not just those of dominant peoples or those whose cultures we like and admire. Third, diversity of all kinds is pleasurable and valuable in itself. We may not be able to prove that this yellow flower or that blue butterfly is valuable in itself, but they have value just by being part of the complexity of life on earth. Different languages which have developed over thousands of years, their songs and poetry, and their unique words that may express an idea undreamed in any other tongue are precious traces of our complex and varied creativity.

We may be convinced that the loss of diversity is "a grave danger to our species," but we may feel helpless to do anything about it. Yet we can contribute in small ways. Many of us, even if we live in English-speaking nations, can trace our ancestry back to non-English-speaking roots, and if we cannot, a quick survey of our friends will often reveal unimagined diversity of linguistic connections. Just hearing the stories of our families and friends can make a difference because one of the reasons people in predominantly monolingual countries stop speaking their ancestral languages, or even revealing their cultural backgrounds, is that they feel stigmatised. Fortunately, we are not restricted to monolingualism. Whilst nations may embrace one national language, for individuals, bilingualism and even multilingualism are not only possible but desirable, being beneficial both intellectually and emotionally. We do not need to despair that we are moving inexorably toward monoculturalism. Rather, we can each, in our own ways, start to foster diversity by being aware of it, valuing it, and encouraging it whenever we have the opportunity.

NOTES

1. Whether it is always possible to adequately translate concepts from one language into another continues to be a matter of debate both in linguistics and in literary theory.

2. According to *Ethnologue (www.sil.org/ethnologue)* the ten languages with the most mother-tongue speakers are (in millions): Mandarin Chinese, 885; English, 322; Spanish, 266; Bengali, 187; Hindi, 182; Portuguese, 175; Russian, 170; Japanese, 125; German, 98; and Wu Chinese, 77.

3. Two-thirds of the original 250 Aboriginal languages are extinct or nearly so, and the remainder are severely threatened; see Schmidt 1990.

4. See the draft United Nations declaration on the rights of indigenous people and the United Nations declaration on the rights of persons belonging to national or ethnic, religious, and linguistic minorities (Varennes 1996).

5. There is much introspection about the relationship between language and cultural identity. For example, see Lloyd 1994 on Irish nationalism.

6. The Unz initiative, Proposition 227, in which people voted to end bilingual education in California, is an example of such a policy. As the American Civil Liberties Union argues, the initiative was predicated on "the notion that multiple language services provided by the government constitute a threat to the stability of the American society" (*ACLU News*). The full ACLU text, and others relating to the Proposition 227, can be accessed from the Web site of the University of Southern California Center for Multilingual, Multicultural Research *http://www.usc.edu/dept/education/CMMR/policy*.

7. I use the word *housewife* deliberately and ironically here. As Michele Mattelart (1986, 64) shows, the genre of soap opera was designed to fulfill "a twofold

function that is in fact unified: to promote the sale of household products, and to integrate the housewife into her function and task by offering her romantic gratification."

8. Peter Mühlhäusler, Inaugural Lecture at the University of Adelaide, 1993.

REFERENCES

Gupta, Anthea Frazer. 1997. The Internet and the English language. Paper submitted for the First Online Conference on Postcolonial Theory. This paper was available online for participants at the online conference at the time it was running.

Krauss, Michael. 1992. The world's languages in crisis. *Language* 68.1: 4–10.

Lloyd, David. 1994. Adulteration and the nation: Monologic nationalism and the colonial hybrid. *An other tongue: Nation and ethnicity in the linguistic borderlands*, ed. by Alfred Arteaga, 53–93. Durham, NC: Duke University Press.

Mattelart, Michele. 1986. Women and the cultural industries. *Media, culture, and society: A critical reader*, ed. by Richard Collins et al., 63–82. London: Sage.

National Inquiry into the Separation of Aboriginal and Torres Strait Islander Children from Their Families (Australia). 1997. *Bringing them home: Report of the National Inquiry into the Separation of Aboriginal and Torres Strait Islander Children from their Families*. Commissioner: Ronald Wilson. Sydney: Human Rights and Equal Opportunity Commission. This report is commonly known as the Stolen Children Report or Stolen Generations Report. It is also available via the Internet: *http://www.austlii.edu.au/au/special/rsjproject/rsjlibrary/hreoc/stolen/*.

Ngugi wa Thiong'o. 1985. The language of African literature. *New Left Review* (April–June): 109–27.

———. 1986. *Decolonising the mind: The politics of language in African literature*. London: James Currey.

Phillipson, Robert, Mart Rannut, and Tove Skutnabb-Kangas. 1995. Introduction. *Linguistic human rights*, ed. by Tove Skutnabb-Kangas and Robert Phillipson, 1–22. Berlin: Mouton de Gruyter.

Rheingold, Howard. 1994. *The virtual community: Finding connection in a computerized world*. London: Secker and Warburg.

Schmidt, Annette. 1990. *The loss of Australia's aboriginal language heritage*. Canberra: Aboriginal Studies Press.

Varennes, Fernand de. 1996. *Language, minorities, and human rights*. The Hague: Martinus Nijhoff.

Whorf, Benjamin Lee. 1956. *Language, thought, and reality*. Cambridge, MA: M.I.T. Press.

III

LANGUAGE AND POLITICS, PREJUDICE, THE MEDIA, CREATIVITY, HUMOR, AND GENDER

METAPHOR, MORALITY, AND POLITICS: OR, WHY CONSERVATIVES HAVE LEFT LIBERALS IN THE DUST

George Lakoff

We may not always know it, but we think in metaphor.[1] A large proportion of our most commonplace thoughts make use of an extensive, but unconscious, system of metaphorical concepts, that is, concepts from a typically concrete realm of thought that are used to comprehend another, completely different domain. Such concepts are often reflected in everyday language, but their most dramatic effect comes in ordinary reasoning. Because so much of our social and political reasoning makes use of this system of metaphorical concepts, any adequate appreciation of even the most mundane social and political thought requires an understanding of this system. But unless one knows that the system exists, one may miss it altogether and be mystified by its effects.

For me, one of the most poignant effects of the ignorance of metaphorical thought is the mystification of liberals concerning the recent electoral successes of conservatives. Conservatives regularly chide liberals for not understanding them, and they are right. Liberals don't understand how antiabortion "right-to-life" activists can favor the death penalty and oppose reducing infant mortality through prenatal care programs. They don't understand why budget-cutting conservatives spare no public expense to build prison after prison to house even nonviolent offenders, or why they are willing to spend extra money to take children away from their mothers and put them in orphanages—in the name of family values. They don't understand why conservatives attack violence in the media while promoting the right to own machine guns. Liberals tend not to understand the logic of conservatism; they don't understand what form of morality makes conservative positions moral or what conservative family values have to do with the rest of conservative politics. The reason at bottom is that liberals do not understand the form of metaphorical thought that unifies and makes sense of the full range of conservative values.

CONSERVATIVE MORALITY

Of the roughly two dozen conceptual metaphors for morality in our conceptual systems, most are used by both conservatives and liberals alike. But conservatives and liberals give different priorities to these metaphors, and the same moral metaphors with differences in priority result in radically different moral systems. The metaphor with the highest priority in the conservative moral system is moral strength. This is a complex metaphor with a number of parts, beginning with the following:

- Being Good is Being Upright.
- Being Bad is Being Low.

Examples include sentences like the following:

He's an *upstanding* citizen.

He's on the *up and up*.

That was a *low* thing to do.

He's *underhanded*.

He's a *snake* in the grass.

Doing evil is therefore moving from a position of morality (uprightness) to a position of immorality (being low). Hence:

- Doing Evil is Falling.

The most famous example, of course, is the *fall* from grace.

A major part of the moral-strength metaphor has to do with the conception of immorality, or evil. Evil is reified as a force, either internal or external, that can make you fall, that is, commit immoral acts.

- Evil is a Force (either Internal or External).

Thus, to remain upright, one must be strong enough to "stand up to evil." Hence morality is conceptualized as strength, as having the "moral fibre" or "backbone" to resist evil.

- Morality is Strength.

But people are not simply born strong. Moral strength must be built. Just as in building physical strength, where self-discipline and self-denial ("no pain, no gain") are crucial, so moral strength is also built through self-discipline and self-denial, in two ways:

1. Through sufficient self-discipline to meet one's responsibilities and face existing hardships
2. Actively through self-denial and further self-discipline

To summarize, the metaphor of Moral Strength is a set of correspondences between the moral and physical domains:

- Being Good is Being Upright.
- Being Bad is Being Low.
- Doing Evil is Falling.
- Evil is a Force (either Internal or External).
- Morality is Strength.

One consequence of this metaphor is that punishment can be good for you, since going through hardships builds moral strength. Hence the homily "Spare the rod and spoil the child." By the logic of this metaphor, moral weakness is in itself a form of immorality. The reasoning goes like this: A morally weak person is likely to fall, to give in to evil, to perform immoral acts, and thus to become part of the forces of evil. Moral weakness is thus nascent immorality—immorality waiting to happen.

There are two forms of moral strength, depending on whether the evil to be faced is external or internal. *Courage* is the strength to stand up to *external* evils and to overcome fear and hardship.

Much of the metaphor of Moral Strength is concerned with *internal* evils, cases where the issue of "self-control" arises. What has to be strengthened is one's will. One must develop willpower in order to exercise control over the body, which is seen as the seat of passion and desire. Desires—typically for money, sex, food, comfort, glory, and things other people have—are seen in this metaphor as "temptations," evils that threaten to overcome one's self-control. Anger is seen as another internal evil to be overcome, since it too is a threat to self-control. The opposite of self-control is "self-indulgence," a concept that only makes sense if one accepts the metaphor of moral strength. Self-indulgence is seen in this metaphor as a vice, while frugality and self-denial are virtues. The seven deadly sins constitute a catalogue of internal evils to be overcome: greed, lust, gluttony, sloth, pride, envy, and anger. It is the metaphor of moral strength that makes them "sins." The corresponding virtues are charity, sexual restraint, temperance, industry, modesty, satisfaction with one's lot, and calmness. It is the metaphor of Moral Strength that makes these "virtues."

This metaphor has an important set of entailments:

- The world is divided into good and evil.
- To remain good in the face of evil (to "stand up to" evil), one must be morally strong.
- One becomes morally strong through self-discipline and self-denial.
- Someone who is morally weak cannot stand up to evil and so will eventually commit evil.
- Therefore, moral weakness is a form of immorality.
- Lack of self-control (the lack of self-discipline) and self-indulgence (the refusal to engage in self-denial) are therefore forms of immorality.

Moral strength thus has two very different aspects. First, it is required if one is to stand up to some externally defined evil. Second, it itself defines a form of evil, namely, the lack of self-discipline and the refusal to engage in self-denial. That is, it defines forms of internal evil.

Those who give a very high priority to Moral Strength, of course, see it as a form of idealism. The metaphor of Moral Strength sees the world in terms of a war of good against the forces of evil, which must be fought ruthlessly. Ruthless behavior in the name of the good fight is thus seen as justified. Moreover, the metaphor entails that one cannot respect the views of one's adversary. Evil does not deserve respect; it deserves to be attacked.

The metaphor of Moral Strength imposes a strict us-them moral dichotomy. The metaphor that morality is strength induces a view of evil as the force that moral strength is needed to counter. Evil must be fought. You do not empathize with evil, nor do you accord evil some truth of its own. You just fight it.

Moral Strength, importantly, imposes a form of asceticism. To be morally strong, you must be self-disciplined and self-denying. Otherwise you are self-indulgent, and such moral flabbiness ultimately helps the forces of evil.

In the conservative mind, the metaphor of Moral Strength has the highest priority. Though it clusters with other metaphors that we will consider shortly, it is the one that matters most. It determines much of conservative thought and language, as well as social policy. It is behind the view that social programs are immoral and promote evil because they are seen as working against self-discipline and self-reliance. Given the priority of Moral Strength, welfare and affirmative action are immoral because they work against self-reliance. The priority of Moral Strength underlies conservative opposition to providing condoms to high-school students and clean needles to drug addicts in the fight against teen pregnancy and AIDS. These are seen as promoting the evil of self-indulgence; the morally strong should be able to "just say no." The morally weak are evil and deserve what they get. Orphanages are seen as imposing discipline, which serves morality. They may cost more than AFDC payments to mothers, but the issue for conservatives is morality, not just money. Conservative opposition to student aid also follows from this metaphor; morally strong students should be self-reliant and pay for the full cost of their own education. Similarly, the opposition to prenatal care programs to lower infant mortality stems from the view that moral mothers should be able to provide their own prenatal care, and if they cannot, they should abstain from sex and not have babies.

An important consequence of giving highest priority to the metaphor of Moral Strength is that it rules out any explanations in terms of social forces or social class. If it is always possible to muster the discipline to just say no to drugs or sex and to support yourself in this land of opportunity, then failure to do so is laziness, and social class and social forces cannot explain your poverty or your drug habit or your illegitimate children. If you lack such discipline, then by the metaphor of Moral Strength, you are immoral and deserve any punishment you get.

The metaphor of Moral Strength does not occur in isolation. It defines a cluster of other common metaphors for morality that are important in the conservative worldview. Here is a list of the others:

Moral Bounds: Here action is seen as motion, and moral action is seen as motion within prescribed bounds or on a prescribed path. Immoral people are those who transgress the bounds or deviate from the path. The logic of this metaphor is that transgressors and deviants are dangerous to society not only because they can lead others astray, but because they create new paths to traverse, thus blurring the clear, prescribed, socially accepted boundaries between right and wrong.

Moral Authority: Moral authority is patterned metaphorically on parental authority, where parents have a young child's best interests at heart and know what is best for the child. Morality is obedience. Just as the good child obeys his or her parents, a moral person obeys a moral authority, which can be a text (like the Bible or the Koran), an institution, or a leader.

Moral Essence: Just as physical objects are made of substances which determines how they will behave (e.g., wood burns, stone doesn't), so people are seen as having an essence—a "character"—that determines how they will behave morally. Good essential properties are called virtues; bad essential properties are called vices. When we speak of someone as having a "heart of gold" or as "not having a mean bone in his body" or as "being rotten to the core," we are using the metaphor of moral essence. The word "character" often refers to moral strength seen as an essential moral property. To "see what someone is made of" is to test his character, to determine his moral essence. The logic of moral essence is this: Your behavior reveals your essence, which in turn predicts your future behavior.

Moral Health: Immorality is seen as a disease that can spread. Just as you have a duty to protect your children from disease by keeping them away from diseased people, so you have a duty to protect your children from the contagion of immorality by keeping them away from immoral people. This is part of the logic behind urban flight, segregated neighborhoods, and strong sentencing guidelines for nonviolent offenders. Since purity and cleanliness promote health, morality is seen as being pure and clean.

Moral Wholeness: We speak of a "degenerate" person, the "erosion" of moral standards, the "crumbling" of moral values, and the "rupture" or "tearing" of the moral fabric. Wholeness entails an overall unity of form that contributes to strength. Thus Moral Wholeness is attendant on moral strength.

We can see these metaphors at work in the conservative worldview, in conservative rhetoric, and especially in social policy. The "three strikes and you're out" law, which is popular with conservatives, is a reflection of the metaphor of moral essence: Repeated criminal behavior reveals an essence that is "rotten to the core." If a person has an immoral essence, you will keep performing immoral acts that can be predicted even before they are performed. Locking you up for twenty-five years, or for life, may seem like punishment for metaphorically predicted crimes, but if you believe in Moral Essence, then it is simply protection for society.

The metaphors of Moral Boundaries, Moral Health, and Moral Wholeness can be seen clearly in conservative views of pornography and sexually explicit art. Pornography should be banned to stop the contagion of immoral behavior (Moral Health). If pornography is allowed, then it marks out new paths of sexual behavior as normal, and the old, clear paths and boundaries that define right and wrong become blurred (Moral Bounds). Sexually explicit art defies the edifice of traditional sexual values, leading those values to "crumble" or "erode" (Moral Wholeness). Indeed, deviant behavior of any kind challenges all these metaphors for morality, as well as the metaphor of Moral Authority, according to which deviance is disobedience.

From the perspective of these metaphors, multiculturalism is immoral, since it permits alternative views of what counts as moral behavior. Multiculturalism thus violates the binary good-evil distinction made by Moral Strength. It violates the well-defined moral paths and boundaries of Moral Bounds. Its multiple authorities violate any unitary Moral Authority. The multiplicity of standards violates Moral Wholeness.

This cluster of metaphors—what I will call the "strength complex"—defines the highest priorities in conservative moral values. There is another metaphor that serves these priorities—the metaphor of Moral Self-Interest. It is based on a folk version of Adam Smith's economics: If each person seeks to maximize his own wealth, then by an invisible hand, the wealth of all will be maximized. Applying to this the metaphor that Well-being is

Wealth, we get: If each person tries to maximize his own well-being (or self-interest), the well-being of all will be maximized. This metaphor sees it as the highest morality when everyone pursues his own self-interest unimpeded.

In conservative thought, self-reliance (a goal defined by Moral Strength) is achieved through the disciplined and unimpeded pursuit of self-interest. In metaphorical terms, the complex of strength metaphors defines the moral goal, and Moral Self-Interest defines the means for achieving that goal. In moderate conservatism, the reverse is true. There, maximizing self-interest is the goal, and conservative values (defined by the strength complex) are the means. Thus the difference between strict and moderate conservatism is a matter of priorities. Strict conservatives are moralistic, giving highest priority to the conservative moral metaphors and seeing the pursuit of self-interest as the natural means for achieving conservative moral values. Moderate conservatives are more pragmatic and less moralistic, seeing conservative moral values as the natural means to achieve the pragmatic end of maximizing self-interest.

Consider for a moment what a model citizen is from the point of view of this moral system. It is someone who, through self-discipline and the pursuit of self-interest, has become self-reliant. This means that rich people and successful corporations are model citizens from a conservative perspective. To encourage and reward such model citizens, conservatives support tax breaks for them and oppose environmental and other regulations that get in their way. After all, since large corporations are model citizens, we have nothing to fear from them.

THE FAMILY

At this point, a natural question arises. What gives rise to the cluster of conservative moral metaphors? Why should these metaphors fit together as they do? The answer, interestingly enough, is the family. Conservatives share an ideal model of what a family should be. I will refer to this model as the strict-father model.

The Strict-Father Model

The strict-father model is that of a traditional nuclear family with the father having primary responsibility for the well-being of the household. The mother has day-to-day responsibility for the care of the house and details of raising the children. But the father has primary responsibility for setting overall family policy, and the mother's job is to be supportive of the father and to help carry out the father's views on what should be done. Ideally, she respects his views and supports them.

Life is seen as fundamentally difficult and the world as fundamentally dangerous. Evil is conceptualized as a force in the world, and it is the father's job to support his family and protect it from evils, both external and internal. External evils include enemies, hardships, and temptations. Internal evils come in the form of uncontrolled desires and are as threatening as external ones. The father embodies the values needed to make one's way in the world and to support a family: he is morally strong, self-disciplined, frugal, temperate, and restrained. He sets an example by holding himself to high standards. He insists on his moral authority, commands obedience, and when he doesn't get it, metes out retribution as fairly and justly as he knows how. It is his job to protect and support his family, and he believes that safety comes out of strength.

In addition to support and protection, the father's primary duty is to tell his children what is right and wrong, to punish them when they do wrong, and to bring them up to be self-disciplined and self-reliant. Through self-denial, the children can build strength against internal evils. In this way, he teaches his children to be self-disciplined, industrious, polite, trustworthy, and respectful of authority.

The strict father provides nurturance and expresses his devotion to his family by supporting and protecting them, but just as importantly by setting and enforcing strict moral bounds and by inculcating self-discipline and self-reliance through hard work and self-denial. This builds character. For the strict father, strictness is a form of nurturance and love—tough love.

The strict father is restrained in showing affection and emotion overtly and prefers the appearance of strength and calm. He gives to charity as an expression of compassion for those less fortunate than he and as an expression of gratitude for his own good fortune. Once his children are grown—once they have become self-disciplined and self-reliant—they are on their own and must succeed or fail by themselves; he does not meddle in their lives, just as he doesn't want any external authority meddling in his life.

This model of the family (often referred to as "paternalistic") is what groups together the conservative metaphors for morality. These metaphorical priorities define a family-based morality, what I will call "strict-father morality." Though many features of this model are widespread across cultures, the no-meddling condition—that grown children are on their own and parents cannot meddle in their lives—is a peculiarly American feature, and it accounts for a peculiar feature of American conservatism, namely, the antipathy toward government.

Conservatives speak of the government meddling in people's lives with the resentment normally reserved for meddling parents. The very term *meddling* is carried over metaphorically from family life to government. Senator Robert Dole, addressing the Senate during the debate over the Balanced Budget Amendment, described liberals as those who think "Washington knows best." The force of the phrase comes from the saying "Father knows best," which became the title of a popular TV sitcom. It appears that the antipathy to government shown by American conservatives derives from the part of the strict-father model in which grown children are expected to go off on their own and be self-reliant and then deeply resent parents who continue to tell them how they should live.

Despite the fact that strict-father models of the family occur throughout the world, this aspect of the strict-father model appears to be uniquely American. For example, in strict-father families in Spain or Italy or France or Israel or China, grown children are not expected to leave and go off on their own, with a proscription on parents playing a major role in guiding the life of the child. Similarly, conservative politics in such countries does not involve a powerful resentment toward the "meddling" of government.

The centrality of the strict-father model to conservative politics also explains the attitudes of conservatives to feminism, abortion, homosexuality, and gun control. In the strict-father model of the family, the mother is subordinated to running the day-to-day affairs of the home and raising the children according to the father's direction. It is the father who bears the major responsibility and makes the major decisions. The strict-father model is exactly the model that feminism is in the business of overthrowing. Hence the appropriate antipathy of conservatives to feminism (although there is the recent phenomenon of conservative feminists, namely, women who function with the values of conservative men such as self-discipline, self-reliance, and the pursuit of self-interest). The conservative opposition to homosexuality comes from the same source. Homosexuality in itself is inherently opposed to the strict-father model of the family.

The conservative position on abortion is a consequence of the view of women that comes out of the strict-family model. On the whole, there are two classes of women who want abortions: unmarried teenagers, whose pregnancies have resulted from lust and carelessness, and women who want to delay conception for the sake of a career, but have accidentally conceived. From the point of view of the strict-father model, both classes of women violate the morality characterized by the model. The first class consists of young women who are immoral by virtue of having shown a lack of sexual self-control. The second class consists of women who want to control their own destinies, and who are therefore immoral for contesting the strict-father model itself, since it is that model that defines what morality is. For these reasons, those who abide by strict-father morality tend to oppose abortion.

It is important to understand that conservative opposition to abortion is not just an overriding respect for all life. If it were, conservatives would not favor the death penalty. Nor is it a matter of protecting the lives of innocent children waiting to be born. If it were, conservatives would be working to lower the infant mortality rate by supporting prenatal care programs. The fact that conservatives oppose such programs means that they are not simply in favor of the right to life for all the unborn. Instead, there is a deep and abiding, but usually unacknowledged, reason why conservatives oppose abortion, namely, that it is inconsistent with strict-father morality.

The protection function of the strict father leads to conservative support for a strong military and criminal-justice system. It also leads to an opposition to gun control. Since it is the job of the strict father to protect his family from criminals, and since criminals have guns, he too must be able to use guns if he is to do his job of protecting members of his family against evil people who would harm them. Although the National Rifle Association talks a lot about hunting, the conservative talk shows all talk about protecting one's family as the main motivation for opposing gun control.

THE NATION-AS-FAMILY METAPHOR

What links strict-father family-based morality to politics is a common metaphor, shared by conservatives and liberals alike—the Nation-as-Family metaphor, in which the nation is seen as a family, the government as a parent, and the citizens as children. This metaphor turns family-based morality into political morality, providing the link between conservative family values and conservative political policies. The strict-father model, which brings together the conservative metaphors for morality, is what unites the various conservative political positions into a coherent whole when it is imposed on political life by the Nation-as-Family metaphor.

The strict-father model of the family, the metaphors that are induced by it, and the Nation-as-Family metaphor jointly provide an explanation for why conservatives have the collection of political positions that they have. It explains why opposition to environmental protection goes with support for military protection, why the right to life goes with the right to own machine guns, and why patriotism goes with hatred of government. To sum up, the conservative worldview and the constellation of conservative positions is best explained by the strict-father model of the family, the moral system it induces, and the common Nation-as-Family metaphor that imposes a family-based morality on politics.

LIBERALISM

The conceptual mechanisms I have just described are largely unconscious, like most of our conceptual systems. Yet conservatives have a far better understanding of the basis of their politics than liberals do. Conservatives understand that morality and the family are at the heart of their politics, as they are at the heart of most politics. What is sad is that liberals have not yet reached a similar level of political sophistication.

Liberal politics also centers on a family-based morality, but liberals are much less aware than conservatives are of the unconscious mechanisms that structure their politics. While conservatives understand that all of their policies have a single unified origin, liberals understand their own political conceptual universe so badly that they still think of it in terms of coalitions of interest groups. Where conservatives have organized for an overall, unified onslaught on liberal culture, liberals are fragmented into isolated interest groups based on superficial localized issues: labor, the rights of ethnic groups, feminism, gay rights, environmentalism, abortion rights, homelessness, health care, education, the arts, and so on. This failure to see a unified picture of liberal politics has led to a divided consciousness and has allowed conservatives to employ a divide-and-conquer strategy. None of this need be the case, since there is a worldview that underlies liberal thought that is every bit as unified as the conservative worldview.

The family-based morality that structures liberal thought is diametrically opposed to strict-father morality. It centers around the nurturant-parent model of the family.

The Nurturant-Parent Model

In the nurturant-parent model, the family is of either one or two parents. Two are generally preferable, but not always possible.

The primal experience behind this model is one of being cared for and cared about, having one's desires for loving interactions met, living as happily as possible, and deriving meaning from one's community and from caring for and about others. People are realized in and through their "secure attachments": through their positive relationships to others, through their contribution to their community, and through the ways in which they develop their potential and find joy in life. Work is a means toward these ends, and it is through work that these forms of meaning are realized. All of this requires strength and self-discipline, which are fostered by the constant support of, and attachment to, those who love and care about you.

Protection is a form of caring, and protection from external dangers takes up a significant part of the nurturant parent's attention. The world is filled with evils that can harm a child, and it is the nurturant parent's duty to ward them off. Crime and drugs are, of course, significant, but so are less obvious dangers: cigarettes, cars without seat belts, dangerous toys, inflammable clothing, pollution, asbestos, lead paint, pesticides in food, diseases, unscrupulous businessmen, and so on. Protection of innocent and helpless children from such evils is a major part of a nurturant parent's job.

Children are taught self-discipline in the service of nurturance: to take care of themselves, to deal with existing hardships, to be responsible to others, and to realize their potential. Children are also taught self-nurturance: the intrinsic value of emotional connection with others, of health, of education, of art, of communion with the natural world, and of being able to take care of oneself. In addition to learning the discipline required for responsibility and self-nurturance, it is important that children have a childhood, that they learn to develop their imaginations, and that they just plain have fun.

Through empathizing and interacting positively with their children, parents develop close bonds with children and teach them empathy and responsibility toward others and toward society. Nurturant parents view the family as a community in which children have commitments and responsibilities that grow out of empathy for others. The obedience of children comes out of love and respect for parents, not out of fear of punishment. When children do wrong, nurturant parents choose restitution over retribution whenever possible as a form of justice. Retribution is reserved for those who harm their children.

The pursuit of self-interest is shaped by these values; anything inconsistent with these values is not in one's self-interest. Pursuing self-interest, so understood, is a means for fulfilling the values of the model.

This model of the family induces a very different set of moral priorities, which can be characterized by another set of metaphors for morality. Here are these metaphors:

Morality as empathy: Empathy itself is understood metaphorically as as feeling what another person feels. We can see this in the language of empathy: "I know what it's like to be in your shoes. I know how you feel. I feel for you." To conceptualize moral action as empathic action is more than just abiding by the Golden Rule, to do unto others as you would have them do unto you. The Golden Rule does not take into account that others may have different values than you do. Taking morality as empathy requires basing your actions on their values, not yours. This requires a reformulation of the Golden Rule: Do unto others as they would have you do unto them.

Morality as nurturance: Nurturance presupposes empathy. A child is helpless. To care *for* a child, you have to care *about* that child, which requires seeing the world through the child's eyes as much as possible. The metaphor of morality as nurturance can be stated as follows:

- The Community is a Family.
- Moral Agents are Nurturing Parents.
- People needing help are Children needing care.
- Moral Action is Nurturance.

This metaphor entails that moral action requires empathy and involves sacrifices, and that helping people who need help is a moral responsibility.

Moral self-nurturance: You can't take care of others if you don't take care of yourself. Part of the morality of nurturance is self-nurturance: maintaining your health, making a living, and so on.

Morality as social nurturance: There are two varieties of moral nurturance— one about individuals and the other about social relations. If community members are to empathize with one another and help one another, then social ties must be maintained.

The metaphor can be stated as follows:

- Moral Agents are Nurturing Parents.
- Social ties are Children needing care.
- Moral Action is the Nurturance of Social Ties.

This entails that social ties must be constantly attended to, that maintaining them requires sacrifices, and that one has a moral responsibility to maintain them.

Morality as happiness: This is based on the assumption that unhappy people are less likely to be empathetic and nurturant, since they will not want others to be happier than they are. Therefore, to promote your own capacity for empathy and nurturance, you should make yourself as happy as possible, provided you don't hurt others in the process.

Morality as fairness: Fairness is understood metaphorically in terms of the distribution of material objects. There are three basic liberal models of fair distribution: (1) equal distribution; (2) impartial rule-based distribution; and (3) rights-based distribution. Metaphorical fairness concerns actions conceived of as objects given to individuals. One can act to the benefit of others equally, impartially and by rule, or according to some notion of rights. According to this metaphor, moral action is fair action in one of these ways.

Moral growth: Given that morality is conceptualized as uprightness, it is natural to conceptualize one's degree of morality as physical height, to understand norms for the degree of moral action as height norms, and therefore to see the possibility for "moral growth" as akin to physical growth. Where moral growth differs from physical growth is that moral growth is seen as being possible throughout one's lifetime.

These are the metaphors for morality that best fit the nurturant-parent model of the family, and accordingly they are given the highest priority in liberal thought. The metaphor of Moral Self-interest, here as in conservative thought, is seen as operating to promote the values defined by this group of metaphors. As in the case of moderate conservatism, moderate liberalism can be characterized by placing Moral Self-interest as the goal and seeing these metaphors as providing the means by which to help people seek their self-interest.

Applying the metaphor of the Nation as Family with the government as parent, we get the liberal political worldview:

Social programs: The government as nurturant parent is responsible for providing for the basic needs of its citizens: food, shelter, education, and health care.

Regulation: Just as a nurturant parent must protect his or her children, a government must protect its citizens—not only from external threats, but also from pollution, disease, unsafe products, workplace hazards, nuclear waste, and unscrupulous businessmen.

Environmentalism: Communion with the environment is part of nurturance, part of the realization of one's potential as a human being. Empathy includes empathy with nature. Caring for children includes caring for future generations. Protection includes protection from pollution. All of these considerations support environmentalism.

Feminism and gay rights: Nurturant parents want all their children to fulfill their potential, and so it is the role of government to provide institutions to make that possible.

Abortion: Women seeking abortion are either women who want to take control of their lives or teenage children needing help. Considerations of nurturance for both require providing access to safe, affordable abortions.

Multiculturalism: Nurturant parents celebrate the differences among their children, and so government should celebrate the differences among its citizens.

Affirmative action: Since women and minorities are not treated fairly in society, it is up to the government to do what it can to make sure that they have a fair chance at self-fulfillment.

The arts and the humanities: Knowledge, beauty, and self-knowledge are part of human fulfillment, and so the government must see to it that institutions promote such forms of human nurturance.

Taxation: Just as in a nurturant family it is the duty of older and stronger children to help out those who are younger and weaker, so in a nation it is the duty of citizens who are better off to contribute more than those who are worse off.

Again, what we have here is explanation—explanation of why liberal policies fit together and make a coherent whole: what affirmative action has to do with progressive taxation, what abortion has to do with affirmative action, what environmentalism has to do with feminism. Again, the explanation centers on a model of the family, the moral system that goes with that model, and the Nation-as-Family metaphor.

Unfortunately, liberals are less insightful than conservatives at recognizing that morality and the family lie at the center of their political universe. The cost to liberals has been enormous. Where conservatives have organized effectively in a unified way to promote all their values, liberals have misunderstood their politics as being about coalitions of interest groups and so have remained divided and unable to compete effectively with conservatives.

FILLING IN SOME DETAILS

As noted at the outset, this is a brief overview of a long study, and, as such, it has been drastically oversimplified. Some of these oversimplifications are so important that they must be addressed, if only in a cursory way.

All of us—liberals, conservatives, and others—make use of all of the metaphors for morality discussed here. The difference is in the priorities assigned to them. Thus conservatives also see morality as empathy and nurturance, but they assign a lower priority to them than liberals do. The result is that nurturance and empathy come to mean something different to conservatives than to liberals. In conservatism, moral nurturance is subservient to moral strength. Thus moral nurturance for a conservative is the nurturance to be morally strong. For conservatives, moral empathy is subservient to moral strength, which posits a primary good-evil distinction. That distinction forbids conservatives from empathizing with people they consider evil, and so empathy becomes empathy with those who share your values. Thus, where liberals have empathy even for criminals (and thus defend their rights and are against the death penalty), conservatives are for the death penalty and against decisions like *Miranda*, which seek to guarantee the rights of those accused of crimes.

Correspondingly, liberals too have the metaphor of Moral Strength, but it is in the service of empathy and nurturance. The point of Moral Strength for liberals is to fight intolerance and inhumanity to others and to stand up for social responsibility.

The resulting picture of the priorities of the strict-father and nurturant-parent moral systems is as follows:

Strict-Father Morality (Basic Conservative Morality)
   The Strength Complex
   Moral Self-Interest
   The Nurturance Complex

Nurturant-Parent Morality (Basic Liberal Morality)
   The Nurturance Complex
   Moral Self-Interest
   The Strength Complex

Here one can clearly see the opposition in moral priorities.

Of course, not all liberals are the same, nor are all conservatives. This model oversimplifies many divisions within the liberal and conservative ranks. First, there are moderate versions of both, pragmatic views in which Moral Self-Interest is put first:

Moderate Conservative Morality
   Moral Self-Interest
   The Strength Complex
   The Nurturance Complex

Moderate Liberal Morality
   Moral Self-Interest
   The Nurturance Complex
   The Strength Complex

Another source of variation on all these categories comes within the nurturance and strength complexes, where different kinds of liberals can assign different priorities to the morality metaphors there. For example, President Clinton, unlike most other liberals, assigns higher priority to the nurturance of social ties than to moral nurturance itself. That is, he sees it of the utmost importance to compromise for the sake of trying to bring people together. This makes him seem like a waffler to liberals for whom the nurturance of social ties has a lower priority. The point is that these are rich systems, with lots of room for variations of all sorts. In addition, there are many other factors that are not part of this analysis that distinguish other political positions. This analysis, after all, is not intended to account for everything there is in politics.

It is important to understand that one can have different family-based moralities in personal and political life. Thus one can have strict-father morality at home and nurturant-parent morality in politics—and the reverse. Finally, the strict-father model does not rule out strict mothers. Though it is based on a masculine family model, women can use that model. Though I have used the gender-neutral term *nurturant parent*, that model ultimately derives from a woman's model of the family. In short, the models are ideal and the general tendencies are simple, but in practice there are extremely complex variations on these models.

CONSEQUENCES

If this analysis is right, or even close to right, then a great deal follows. Liberals do not understand what unifies their own worldview and so are helpless to deal effectively with conservatism. Not only is there no unified liberal political structure, but there is no overall effective liberal rhetoric to counter the carefully constructed conservative rhetoric. Where conservatives have carefully coined terms and images and repeated them until they have entered the popular lexicon, liberals have not done the same. Liberals need to go beyond coalitions of interest groups to consciously construct a unified language and imagery to convey their worldview. This will not be easy, and they are thirty years behind.

If this analysis is right, there are implications not just for contemporary politics, but also for the long-term philosophical study of moral systems. I have argued that perhaps the most important part of any real moral system is the system of metaphors for morality and the priorities given to particular metaphors. If I am correct, then vital political reasoning is done using those metaphors, and it is usually done unconsciously. This means that the empirical study of metaphorical thought must be given its appropriate place in ethics and moral theory, as Mark Johnson (1993) has argued.

Finally, there are major consequences for social research itself. Social research these days tends not to take into account empirical research on conceptual systems done within cognitive science in general and cognitive linguistics in particular. Cognitive explanations, like those given here, are not the norm. Instead, explanation has tended to be based on economics, or class, or the rational-actor model, or models of power. I would like to suggest that the study of conceptual systems is a major tool for explanation in social research, a tool so vital in our current situation that it cannot be ignored.

NOTE

This chapter is a significantly reduced version of an article that appeared in *Social Research* 62, no. 2 (Summer 1995). For a fuller treatment of these issues, see my *Moral Politics: What Conservatives Know That Liberals Don't* (Chicago: University of Chicago Press, 1996).

1. For an introductory survey of basic results in the theory of metaphor, see Lakoff 1993. Other suggested readings include Gibbs 1994; Lakoff and Johnson 1980; Johnson 1987; Lakoff 1987; Sweetser 1990; Turner 1987; Lakoff and Turner 1989; Winter 1989; and Lakoff and Johnson, 1999.

REFERENCES

Gibbs, Raymond W., Jr. 1994. *The poetics of mind: Figurative language, thought, and understanding*. Cambridge: Cambridge University Press.

Johnson, Mark. 1987. *The body in the mind*. Chicago: University of Chicago Press.

———. 1993. *Moral imagination*. Chicago: University of Chicago Press.

Lakoff, George. 1987. *Women, fire, and dangerous things: What categories reveal about the mind*. Chicago: University of Chicago Press.

———. 1993. The contemporary theory of metaphor. *Metaphor and thought*, ed. A. Ortony, 2nd ed. 202–251. Cambridge: Cambridge University Press.

Lakoff, George, and Mark Johnson. 1980. *Metaphors we live by*. Chicago: University of Chicago Press.

———. 1990. *Philosophy in the flesh: The embodied mind and its challenge to western thought*. New York: Basic Books.

———. 1996. *Moral politics*. Chicago: University of Chicago Press.

Lakoff, George, and Mark Johnson. 1999. *Philosophy in the flesh*. New York: Basic Books.

Lakoff, George, and Mark Turner. 1989. *More than cool reason: A field guide to poetic metaphor*. Chicago: University of Chicago Press.

Sweetser, Eve. 1990. *From etymology to pragmatics: Metaphorical and cultural aspects of semantic structure*. Cambridge: Cambridge University Press.

Turner, Mark. 1987. *Death is the mother of beauty: Mind, metaphor, criticism*. Chicago: University of Chicago Press.

Winter, Steven L. 1989. Transcendental nonsense, metaphoric reasoning, and the cognitive stakes for law. *University of Pennsylvania Law Review* 137.4.

Language as a Weapon of Hate
Rae A. Moses

One has only to open the newspaper to find evidence of violent prejudice. Hutus kill Tutsis. Croats murder Moslems. A small group of indigenous people in Mexico are slaughtered by their neighbors. Ethnic, religious, and racial hatred are a historical ubiquity. Romans fed Christians to their lions for sport; Jews and Gypsies have long suffered exclusion and genocide. The history of the United States is littered with racial hatred from its early persecution of indigenous populations to its acceptance of slavery and the resulting discrimination of the past 150 years. In addition, we have successively treated each of our immigrant groups with disdain, suspicion, and hatred. There is something about the human social condition that appears to make group hatred universal—common to all times and groups of people.

Hate is often expressed by violent actions, but a common vehicle for prejudice is language. Derogatory ethnic labels like *chink, kike, nigger*, or *spic* are ways that language is used to express prejudice. Language is used to evaluate, stereotype, distance, and make subtle allusions about differences or threaten mayhem. Verbal expressions of hate often accompany or act as a prelude to violence. The early brutality toward the indigenous population in the United States was reflected in the phrase "The only good Indian is a dead Indian," a saying that dates back to the colonial period. American English is littered with the labels and phrases that provide linguistic evidence of our mistreatment of Americans of African descent. More recently, the Nazi genocide was accomplished in the midst of an abundance of anti-Semitic, anti-Slavic, and homophobic rhetoric. Language appears to universally license brutality toward groups and the killing of hated populations in war by designating members of a target group as subhuman.

Language is a defining characteristic of the human species. Linguists believe that humans are innately endowed with this symbolic capacity and that all of the languages of the world share broad structural similarities that derive from a biologically universal template. If all the languages of the world can be used to express hate, are there specific features of language that predispose it to be used for this purpose? Before attempting to answer this question, let us examine what scholars know about hate speech.

The classic scholarly work on prejudice, *The Nature of Prejudice* (1954) by the social psychologist Gordon Allport, devotes an entire chapter to verbal prejudice. He points to the symbolic nature of verbal labels and argues that the symbolic nature of verbal labels permits generalized classifications. Because there is a difference in the potency of various types of labels, one label may take on stronger meaning than others. Allport uses the example of a person who is described as a human, a philanthropist, Chinese, a physician, and an athlete. While the person may have all five of these characteristics, it is the ethnic identity that is the most potent. If we add that our philanthropist is blind, that will probably be a more salient characteristic than her ethnic identity (though I have probably undermined your gender expectations by using the feminine pronoun). Allport argues that certain words that classify people carry inherent value judgments. Words like *insane, alcoholic,* and *pervert* gain extra salience because they point to deviance. In the same way, he suggests, words that call attention to differences like *negro, mulatto,* and *chinaman,* or, for that matter, *whitey* or *white-eyes* (a common ethnic label used by Asians for Europeans), carry powerful negative meaning. The saliency and power of an attribute is determined by how well it characterizes difference.

Social psychologists regard ethnic and racial hate as products of stereotyping and the identification of out-groups, distinguishing them from more powerful in-group members. Linguists, on the other hand, have been concerned with the development and function of the slang nicknames that are used to express difference and hate. Irving Allen, a sociolinguist and lexicographer, in his book *The Language of Ethnic Conflict* (1983), attributes ethnic slang nicknames to the "anxiety and aggression arising from structural strains of society" (23). He cites the size and the density of populations as factors that determine these lexical inventions. His study offers a wealth of examples of how ethnic slurs are derived. Ethnic labels, which are the most prevalent form of prejudiced language, are derived in a variety of ways. In some cases they are forms of the proper name of the group, for example, *hebe* (sometimes *heeb*) from *Hebrew,* or *polack,* which refers derogatorily to both male and female people of Polish descent and derives from the nonderogatory Polish word for a Polish male. Frequently, some physical characteristic is used: *slant-eye* for Asians, *redskin* for Native Americans, and *hooked-nose* for Jews. Traditional ethnic foods can inspire nicknames: *Tamale* or *beaner* for Mexicans, *fortune cookie* or *ricer* for Chinese, or *kraut* for Germans.

Allen notes that while ethnic labels are nouns that refer directly to ethnic groups, prejudiced speech can also use the proper name of a group as an adjective or verb: *Italian perfume* for garlic, *Irish twins* as siblings less than a year apart, or a *Turkish medal* for an undone fly button. Verbs such as *to welsh, to gyp, to go dutch*, or *to french kiss* go beyond slang and have become standard English usage. Other forms of ethnic slurs include nominal forms that use ethnicity as a metaphor, for example, *a young turk* for a person who wishes to challenge the establishment. Verbal abuse also takes the form of proverbs like "The only good Indian is a dead Indian," mentioned earlier. It can also occur in the form of ethnic jokes (Allen 1983, 11).

In his second book on the subject, *Unkind Words* (1990), Allen argues that ethnic slurs are a pervasive kind of slang. He makes a distinction between more serious kinds of slurs, which he views as older, and newer labels based upon euphemism and code words that vary in pejoration from "malicious and vicious to puerile and jocular" (7). For Allen, name calling is a "technique by which out-groups—'them' as opposed to 'us'—are defined as morally justified targets of aggression" (Allen 1990, 9). The Nazi rhetoric of the early part of the twentieth century labeled the out-group as *vermin, defective*, and *a threat to the supreme race* (the in-group), thereby justifying the Nazis' euphemized *final solution*.

A group of social psychologists has conducted experimental studies to understand the effects of derogatory ethnic labels. In their research, Jeff Greenberg, S. L. Kirkland, Tom Pyszczynski, and their colleagues (1988) have shown how the use of ethnic labels like *nigger* have separate effects on the target of the slur, the users, and those overhearing them. For the target, there is "rejection, then dejection and eventually anger and rage" (81). Users have increases in their self-esteem, but also in their anxiety and hostility. Those who overhear derogatory ethnic labels are encouraged to behave negatively toward them (85). The work of these social psychologists makes the dynamic of verbal prejudice clearer.

Teun van Dijk in his book *Communicating Racism: Ethnic Prejudice in Thought and Talk* (1987) takes a different approach to the issue of verbal prejudice. He compares the sources and form of prejudiced discourse in two communities, San Diego and Amsterdam. His thesis is that public and interpersonal racist dialogues allow racism to be acquired, shared, and socially accepted. His data are drawn from 180 interviews with White majority members about ethnic minorities. While they contain no ethnic slurs, he explains how a minority group can be represented negatively, for example, by referring to their country of origin: "They should be sent back"; their goals: "They take our jobs and houses"; their difference: "They treat women badly and have too many children"; and personal characteristics: "They are dirty, lazy, noisy." His work reveals that ethnic labels are but one means of conveying prejudice. Discourse is another powerful tool that supports the reproduction of racism. What, then, are the qualities of language that allow it to be used so universally as a weapon of ethnic hatred and discrimination?

Language has many qualities that make it especially adapted for the expression of human prejudice. Premier among the qualities is its *representational* nature. The symbolic properties of language allow it to express meaning through the use of categories. Words stand for things. The word *rabbit* stands for a member of the species of small furry mammals with long ears and a stubby tail. Language provides a way to distinguish one furry mammal from others by means of categories that are based upon prototypical characteristics. Rabbits' ears and their characteristic hop make them different from tail-wagging, barking, furry creatures we call dogs. Notice that language depends upon categories to convey meaning. The human capacity to represent is not unique to language. Other representational systems are based upon our senses, for example, vision and perhaps even the sense of smell. Note the fragrance "scratch and smell" advertising, where the fragrance of a whole line of merchandise is represented in a small patch. Verbal representation is but one of the ways humans categorize the world about them.

The *representational* quality of language allows it to be used to assign labels to categories of people whom we see as different. Thus labels can refer to Asians, the disabled, the aged, or female people who are then seen as a category because they share qualities. Categorization is a human capacity that is crucial to the expression of meaning. Most of the lexicon of our language is based on groups of hierarchically arranged related categories that reflect the human predilection for making categories. Notice how the following arrangement of nouns shows the relationship among the categories:

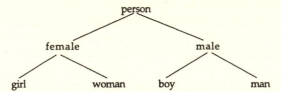

That is, there are two kinds of people, males and females, who can either be young (boys and girls) or adult (men and women). Of course, such a set of relationships is more complicated than this simple model. A more complicated model would have to account for the pairs *guy:girl* and *gentleman:lady* and maybe even *broad*.

While representational meaning can be modeled quite formally, there is another kind of meaning that is not captured easily in this way. All words also have *connotative* meanings. These derive from the social and cultural knowledge we have about our world. It is this kind of meaning that allows us to use or interpret metaphor or say things in new ways. If I were to use a completely novel sentence, for example, "It's a peanut and jelly kind of day," my intended meaning and the meanings that a listener would interpret would be based on what we know and believe about peanut butter and jelly. Whether my intention is to convey that the day is "a return to youth" or "a day when things must be done quickly and without ceremony" or "a day when dinner is not-so-good leftovers," I would be relying on our shared experience and the context to convey my meaning. The same kind of allusion is used in labeling groups. When Blacks are called *smoked Irish*, the phrase relies on the connotations of each word, namely, "darkened" and "ethnic." Similarly, referring to a Middle Easterner or a North African as a *camel jockey* makes use of our knowledge of the camel's territory and the allusion to riding found in the word *jockey*. Connotative meanings are subtle and highly coded. They allow the speaker to hide his or her hostility in metaphor.

While language represents meanings, it does so in a way that is *arbitrary*. What is called a *rabbit* in English will be *conejo* in Spanish, *lapin* in French, *sungura* in Swahili, and *tu zi* in Mandarin Chinese. The sounds and shapes of words have nothing to do with what they stand for. The link between the label and the object that is represented is not logical or necessary. Rather, words represent concepts because speakers share similar systems for producing and understanding words.

Dago, wop, paisano, eyetalian, spaghetti-bender, and *pinocchio* are all ethnic slurs that have been used for Italians. All have the same representational meaning (Italian), but they have very different connotations. *Dago* and *wop* are strongly derogatory, while *paisano* has a friendly ethnic quality. The remaining labels have a slightly playful connotation. It is the *arbitrary* nature of language and the *connotative* aspect of word meaning that allow for the fine tuning of meaning.

While the arbitrary and connotative aspects of language allow speakers to use weaponlike expressions, speakers also can create novel expressions, thereby adding to what language can represent. A speaker's capacity to add new expressions gives language an open-ended, *productive* quality. While I know the word *rabbit*, I can also use the word *bunny* for the same animal, or if I want to, I can make up a nickname, for example, *cottontail*. Of if these words do not please me, I can take some aspect of rabbithood, for example, their stereotypic carrot eating. Or an individual rabbit might lead to names like Carrot-crunch, Bugs, or Peter. The open-ended nature of language accounts for the fact that we have over one thousand documented words that refer to Americans of African descent. It allows the addition of derogatory labels that refer to a new group of immigrants.

Another feature of language that supports discriminatory language use is how we learn to talk. While van Dijk and other theorists of prejudice have pointed out the importance that the powerful and elite have in the genesis of hatred, the reproduction of prejudice relies on the ways in which attitudes are passed from generation to generation. Language is *culturally transmitted*. Children learn their language from the society around them. Prejudice is learned in the same way and at the same time. Children learn the vocabulary of prejudice in the same way they learn to hate—from their family and their community. Just as culture is taught to the young of any community, the early understandings of hatred and prejudice are acquired in the home, in the neighborhood, and in the community.

There are features of language that account for its natural use to express prejudice. The way language represents meaning by utilizing natural categories requires speakers to use defining characteristics to sort and differentiate. Prejudice is based on such sorting. That words have subtle connotations provides a way for encoding disturbing concepts. Its arbitrary nature makes language capable of distortion, since there is no necessary connection between a word and the thing it represents. The openness of the system assures that there will always be the possibility of expressing a new form of hostility. That young children learn their language norms in their community makes it certain that the ethnic hatred will be preserved by its community members.

But the negative communal effect of our capacity to talk does not mean that we must destroy or restrict our defining human characteristic—language—in order to undermine racial hatred. The same language that is used to form derogatory labels and racist discourse can be used in a dialogue of racial and ethnic reconciliation. Racist talk can be answered with verbal condemnation. Stereotypes can be challenged, and immigration policy can be debated. By understanding the qualities of language that facilitate ethnic categories and their use and transmission, and by responding with more language, we can begin to overcome the use of language as a weapon and the violence that too often is associated with such use.

REFERENCES

Allen, Irving Lewis. *The Language of Ethnic Conflict: Social Organization and Ethnic Culture*. New York: Columbia University Press, 1983.
———. *Unkind Words: Ethnic Labeling from Redskin to Wasp*. Westport, CT: Bergin and Garvey, 1990.
Allport, Gordon W. *The Nature of Prejudice*. New York: Doubleday, Anchor Books, 1954.
Greenberg, Jeff, S. L. Kirkland, and Tom Pyszczynski. "Some Theoretical Notions and Preliminary Research Concern Derogatory Ethnic Labels," in *Discourse*

and Discrimination, edited by Geneva Smitherman-Donaldson and Teun A. van Dijk. Detroit: Wayne State Press, 1988.

van Dijk, Teun A. *Communicating Racism: Ethnic Prejudice in Thought and Talk*. Newbury Park: Sage Publications, 1987.

LANGUAGE AND THE NEWS MEDIA: FIVE FACTS ABOUT THE FOURTH ESTATE

Colleen Cotter

The language of the news media intersects with our activities, relationships, and beliefs. It is daily. It is habitual. It is freely available. Although most of us are familiar with this language, the primary conduit for the media's messages, we may not be aware of what is systematic or characteristic of media communication, the features that make it distinctive and identifiable. Given the news media's power to persuade, sway, enlighten, frustrate, and inform, it is worth going deeper than the critiques and jokes that politicians, pundits, and comedians quite glibly deliver about what English statesman Edmund Burke called the Fourth Estate. (After the "estates" of the clergy, the nobility, and the common people in eighteenth-century English society came the Fourth Estate, the media.)

In this chapter, I present five propositions about news language, using the newspaper as my point of reference—five ways of looking at the language and communicative practices that inundate us daily. Most of these points concern the relationship between patterns of language use and the social dimensions of identity, meaning, values, and beliefs. We make these observations by looking not just at words, grammatical points, and meanings in isolation, but at language in a larger context. We will examine news media at the discourse level, looking at the exchange of information, social meaning, interaction, and discourse structure.

From the discourse perspective, our questions are these: what is being conveyed or talked about? Who is talking? What is the purpose of the exchange? Is there a relationship or order to the parts? These questions allow us to identify the parameters that define the discourse and to isolate the key factors that work to create the language patterns that constitute media language. Parameters such as topic, participants, goals, and ordering of elements contribute to our understanding of the position and relevance of communicative acts in the media and help us to see the systematicity in what we read or hear. The five points listed here reflect different sociolinguistic vantage points that help us understand how discourse processes create and are created by our social and linguistic realities.

1. *Discourse topics and relation building*: Media language is embedded in the context of social relationships. Just as the particular relationship between two people governs the topics they discuss and how those topics are framed—a boss and an employee do not talk about the same things as two siblings—subject matter and framings in the news media reflect a particular relationship between the media and their audience.

2. *Interactional norms and expected patterns of communication*: Much of what we find normal in everyday conversation is also normal in everyday news talk, with certain adaptations.

3. *Discourse organization and genre*: Behind news stories is a fairly predictable set of rules that manifest themselves in genres and subgenres. The rules are simple, but because the process of information gathering is multifaceted and stories are compiled by many participants, their output becomes complex.

4. *Language attitudes and the rules of style*: News-media practitioners see themselves as protectors of the language standards we associate with civility and education. In this approach, they part company with linguists, who want to describe, not prescribe against, variations and alterations in how we speak and write.

5. *Language change as a function of need and use*: The media are a rich repository of language history and demonstrate how living languages change to meet the contingencies of communicative needs.

POINT 1: MEDIA LANGUAGE IS EMBEDDED IN THE CONTEXT OF SOCIAL RELATIONSHIPS

Communication specialists often discuss the nature of mass communication in terms of information design, noting its flow from media source to many recipients and citing mass distribution and a lack of visibility and reciprocity as key features. But these models seldom account for the interaction-based nature of media writing and practice. From the opening pages of a journalism textbook to the daily news meetings where decisions about Page One stories are made, the readers or viewers are always explicitly referred to and made a vital part of the journalist's world.

Thus media language is not just a static artifact that exists in yellowed clips, microfilm, and television archives, but is the output of an interaction between journalists and the community they cover. News-media practitioners select topics or information to present to their readers and viewers, i.e., stories to write, by following principles with regard to incorporating assumptions about shared knowledge, maintaining a particular role, and considering what might be of interest or what people should know and what would offend or be proper—the same principles that govern inter-locutors in conversation. In short, the news media and their audience have a relationship of a particular kind, just as individuals engaged in conver-sation do.

The relationship exists whether it involves the country's premier news-paper of record, the *New York Times*, or a small-town media source like the *Corning* (California) *Observer*. The tiny *Corning Observer* and the mighty *New York Times* both have relationships with their respective com-munities of coverage that date back to the early days of that community's development. Both are important vehicles for collecting, reflecting, and transmitting community knowledge and identity through news and feature stories, editorials, and opinion pieces.

Another aspect of the discourse relationship between news media and the community of coverage is that in order to fulfill their function (and ensure their survival), the media must maintain the interest and attention of their readers. This means that a principle guiding story selection and framing is that the story should have immediate appeal. Accessible head-lines, lead or opening paragraphs that draw in the reader, short paragraphs, enticing layout, and use of photos, are all ways that newspapers strive to keep the dialogue going by keeping readers interested in what they have to say. (Readers, for their part, are not shy about writing, phoning, e-mailing, or coming in when the paper runs something that they disagree with or that does not suit them.)

Since the media reflect what is salient about the community, the topics of stories that are covered indicate what the paper perceives is important to the community. The topics are not just the ones that would be exchanged by neighbors over the fence, but are created in part by the journalism pro-fession's sense of what makes news. The stories on the front page of a recent *Corning Observer* both indirectly and explicitly reflect topics of in-terest and importance to the town of 10,000 as well as point to some characteristics of what "makes news" from the journalist's perspective:

- "PG&E starts improvement project"
- "Corning students will be questioned about drug use in upcoming survey"
- "ECO Resources wins awards . . . again"
- "Kerr purchases Hall Brothers Mortuary"

These headlines for January 28, 1998, relate important news that will affect or could affect a fair percentage of residents' lives and their percep-tions of where they live. They assume a shared knowledge among the community and its members (the names and acronyms would be opaque to anyone else not familiar with the town or region). A power project, a survey eliciting social behaviors of young people, news that the water and sewer service is in reputable hands, and reassurance that the mortuary's services will continue despite a new owner—the first in forty-six years—illustrate two of the most important defining characteristics of news: It is about proximity and about change. The language not only reports the news, but positions its impact in relation to the community.

The *New York Times* likewise has its own relationship with its community, functioning not only as the "local paper" but as the newspaper of record for the nation. The stories reflect its national role and status. The focal point is the nation. The Page One headlines point to an even more complex set of relationships between newspaper and community because the paper's scope goes beyond the geographical confines of New York City:

- "Charities Use For-Profit Units to Avoid Disclosing Finances"
- "U.S. Will Not Ask to Use Saudi Bases for a Raid on Iraq"
- "Canadian Indians Celebrate Vindication of Their History"
- "Resurrection Is Near for Lost Rail Station"

These headlines for February 9, 1998, show only one "local" story, the one about the Penn rail station (and even there a congressional connection is part of the news focus). The others show a scope that reflects the nation in relation to its states and institutions (the charities story), its world position (the Saudi bases story), and its neighbors, with whom certain issues of colonial expansion are shared (the Canadian Indians story). The *Times* stories illustrate three more of the most important defining characteristics of news: It is about impact, prominence, and currency.

In this way and others, the transmission of knowledge runs both ways: the media are informed by the community and the community is informed by the media. *Reciprocal transmission* is the operation behind the interplay of texts, creators, and audience and is what allows the media to engage with us on the community level as well as provide content that captures facts about our social worlds.

Besides developing a relationship through content, the media also relate to the community in the role they assume in delivering the content. One of the features that characterize the role assumed by the news media in relation to their audience is that of an authority, not like a parent or lawgiver but like a neighbor whose knowledge and good judgment can be counted upon. This means that in principle topics selected reflect the media's judgments about what their audience most needs to know. Stories about routine, local government meetings are notoriously uninteresting to the large portion of readers (television generally never covers them unless there is a big conflict involved), but they are always covered by "newspapers of record" because of the media's self-described role as a thorough and authoritative informant on all matters that fundamentally affect the community.

This also means that most mainstream news outlets that purport to be objective do not explicitly frame stories in terms of judgments or moral lessons to be learned but in an apparently more neutral way that allows readers to make judgments for themselves. Attribution of information to multiple sources or weak hedges like "allegedly" are intended to reinforce the news media's position as a cautious, reliable, and unbiased authority and reporter of what is happening in the world. Former television news anchor Walter Cronkite, as the "most trusted man in America," embodied this role.

Authoritativeness, however, is not the sole defining feature of the relationship between media and community. Both broadcast and print journalists want to maintain and express their solidarity and connection with the community they report on. (The phrase under the *Oakland Tribune*'s front-page nameplate is "Friend of the People It Serves.") Solidarity dynamics are often a feature of relationships between individuals when there is some social or phatic aspect to the exchange beyond the exchange of information. (Brothers Click and Clack, the celebrity radio car mechanics, tend to spend more time exchanging phatic talk with the callers to *Car Talk* than they do giving automotive advice.) Stories that focus more on quality of life (food, home, automotive, and style stories are good examples) tend to fulfill this solidarity function, providing "news you can use."

Of course, there is an inherent tension in maintaining an authoritative distance and a neighborly proximity. Typifying this paradox is an Oakland, California, reader who called his local paper "too gossipy" but the *New York Times*—his idea of how a paper should read—"not relevant." This tension can be expressed and resolved through language. For example, radio broadcasts have distinctive prosodic patterns, that is, stress and intonation conventions that influence how newscasts sound. Closer analysis reveals that broadcast prosody shares features of both spontaneous speech (e.g., pauses within grammatical units) and planned reading or public speaking (e.g., a faster speech rate) (Cotter 1993). This allows an announcer to be simultaneously professionally distant and conversationally connected to the unseen listener. The fine line between professional credibility, which is often associated with objectivity, and personal connection within the discourse relationship is always being negotiated with the linguistic resources available.

Any inventory of discourse parameters and linguistic habits that point to the audience focus that governs the media's orientation to the stories they run also underscores the asymmetries of the relationship. The media seldom explicitly refer to themselves or their members—they seldom talk about themselves—unless something extraordinary occurs, good, bad, or tragic: Pulitzer Prizes or other industry awards; the *New Republic* and *Boston Globe* dropping writers for fabrications in their stories; a television reporter's documentary about her breast-cancer fight; and the extremely personal coverage the *San Francisco Chronicle* gave to the June 1998 death of its respected political editor Susan Yoachum and to its venerated columnist Herb Caen in 1997.

POINT 2: MEDIA LANGUAGE HAS ROOTS IN OUR EVERYDAY COMMUNICATIVE PRACTICES

Much of what we find normal in everyday conversation (how we take turns, how we tell stories, how we display alliance) is also normal in everyday news talk, with some adaptations. The conventions of news language are not created in a vacuum, but rather are built upon conversational and communicative resources from everyday life. When we communicate, we employ underlying and culturally situated rules for taking turns, we structure our stories in predictable ways, we use language to create relationships of whatever degree, and we make extensive use of inference and implicature, the use of context to disambiguate meaning—a feature of language that allows us to convey meaning indirectly.

All human beings engage in "solidarity talk," that is, vocalizing or communicating to strengthen social ties, as British linguist Jean Aitchison (1997) puts it. Often our conversations are not so much to exchange information as to strengthen social bonds. Instances of what could be characterized as "solidarity talk" are also present in media venues. The banter that news anchors exchange on the evening news is a classic case (although it is more stylized and conventionalized than the banter we exchange in everyday situations, as are lighter feature stories in print venues (known as "brites" or "readers"—something that goes down easily but has something to say about another dimension of the community's face).

Television news gives us another example of the way media practitioners adapt everyday communicative strategies to their news contexts by way of its turn-taking routines. All cultures have formulated rituals surrounding turn taking in conversation. For example, the majority of North Americans have a "no gap, no overlap" rule of turn taking in which silence and interruptions are considered awkward or rude and are to be avoided. We use word, gesture, and meaningful pause to indicate that our turn is concluded. On television, the turn-taking transitions are much more explicit: "Back to you, Doreen." "Let's now hear from Sandy Trent in the field. Sandy?"

We also know the genres of our culture and the expectations that different speech activities entail. CBS anchor Connie Chung conducted a now-notorious interview in early 1995 with Kathleen Gingrich, the mother of the Republican Speaker of the House. The interview became well known because Chung got Mrs. Gingrich to say that her son regarded Hillary Clinton as a "bitch."

What happened here? Should Chung have been lambasted for violating the bounds of decorum in a news interview (her interview was criticized inside and outside the media)? Could this incident be accounted for in another way? If we consider the exchange from the discourse perspective, we can attribute the development of the exchange to the infinite range of social meanings that can be communicated on the discourse level. An important clue is that Chung did not ask the question outright, as we would expect of a journalist in an interview, but rather, she whispered to Mrs. Gingrich, simulating chum to chum, a change in register that allowed the interview relationship to change.

If we consider our speech within a "frame of interpretation," or context, then we can see how Chung exploited this shared cultural awareness of what is expected in a speech frame such as an interview or a friendly confidence. As a culture, we agree on what verbal behaviors belong in which place. But because language and communicative behaviors are malleable and accessible to multiple meanings, we can create subtle shifts in the communicative context by changing the subject, avoiding commitment to a topic, agreeing or disagreeing with our interlocutor without saying as much, and so on.

Chung's whispered question about Hillary Clinton acted to cue a change in footing (now we're just chums; I'm no longer journalist and you're no longer interviewee) and framing (this is now tête-a-tête, not a media interview) that enabled her to get Mrs. Gingrich to pass on a damning judgment. Like Chung, Gingrich also subverted the expectations of the speech frame to say what could not be said anywhere within the media context. Chung got a fresh response (a communicative goal of the journalist), and Gingrich made her point. The other implications and value judgments on the participants' behaviors were supplied by the societal peanut gallery, which is us.

POINT 3: BEHIND NEWS STORIES IS A FAIRLY PREDICTABLE SET OF RULES

News practitioners look at newspapers differently than the readers, seeing boundaries of genre, perspective, and function that are invisible to other eyes. For instance, they make many more discriminations between news and opinion and about where opinion should be placed and how it should be labeled ("news analysis" if the content is more personal opinion than reported content). They also speak of a "fire wall" between advertising and news, between the advertising and "editorial" sides. The person who writes the headline is different from the person who writes the story. Ultimately, reporters' and editors' professional behaviors, practices, and values have a bearing on the texts that they produce and that we read.

Behind news stories is a fairly predictable set of rules that affect both text and practices. These rules manifest themselves in genres and subgenres (the weather story, the day-after-Thanksgiving shopping story, and so on) and modes of practice (whom to call, dealing with deadlines, and what to do when). The rules of constructing stories are simple and shared, but because the process of information gathering is multifaceted and stories are compiled by many participants, their output becomes complex. (See also Raskin 1999 in *Language Alive in the Classroom* for discussion of cross-cultural differences.)

For the sake of illustration, here is an example of how the process works behind the scenes. Consider the following imaginary "news tip":

> Jack and Jill went up a hill
> to fetch a pail of water.
> Jack fell down and broke his crown,
> and Jill came tumbling after.

Then imagine the scenario after the call comes in to the newsroom. The reporter decides that he wants eyewitness quotes as well as information from the authorities at the scene and drives out to the hill, where many people are looking on. The location, the importance of the story, the desire for good quotes and information, and enough time until deadline are factored into a consideration of "newsworthiness."

He interviews Jack's companion Jill, the police sergeant at the scene (since a story like this needs attribution from the authorities), and an onlooker who witnessed the accident that sent Jack to the hospital with a head injury. Note the many contributors to the story. Because Jack and Jill are considered well-known actors (the news value of *prominence*) involved in the area's regional theater located in the town (the news value of *proximity*), which had just won a national award for a traveling children's troupe (news values of *currency* and *importance*), their story would matter to the community (the news value of *interest*).

The reporter writes the story back in the newsroom, calling the hospital for a condition report and the theater group's director for comment. He sends the story to the editors, where it is read for proper style, grammar, and punctuation. A copy editor deletes reference to Jack's theatrical "oeuvre" (unusual or foreign words are typically edited out) and attaches a "two-deck" headline:

> Blue Goose Founder in Coma Following Tumble at Hill;
> Water in Bucket Shifts, Throws Thespian Off Balance

After work, the reporter takes his notes to his freshman newswriting class at the local college. He has the students write the story themselves, critiquing their leads (twenty-five to thirty-five words maximum; grab the reader; show them why they should continue reading; and so on). He also asks them to select the best quotes and reminds them to attribute information, organize the story so the narrative builds logically and smoothly, provide sufficient background and context, and follow Associated Press style and punctuation rules—in twenty minutes.

This process is largely behind most types of news stories and results in the particular constellation of opening information, quotes, sentence and narrative structure, and informational thoroughness that characterizes a news story. Consider the opening paragraphs of this *Washington Post* story (August 10, 1998):

> Negotiators for Bell Atlantic Corp. and the Communication Workers of America union worked late last night to try to end the biggest strike against a regional telephone company since the breakup of the Bell system 14 years ago.
>
> More than 73,000 CWA members struck Bell Atlantic early yesterday in a job-security dispute that the union says will determine who gets the jobs of the future in the fast-expanding telecommunications industry: union or non-union workers.
>
> "This is really about the future. We're talking about the growth jobs of the information society," CWA spokesman Jeff Miller said.

The two most important tasks are to convey the importance of the story instantaneously and to provide all the information possible (much as the Jack-and-Jill nursery rhyme does). The finesse comes in choosing which elements to put in front order. Not only does the most important information generally come first, but the contextual information must support its importance.

In this story, the first two paragraphs answer the key questions: who (phone company and union), what (negotiations to end huge strike, now in its second day), when (last night), and the reason—why—behind the strike (jobs in the future). Where is implied, by absence of specifics, to be Washington; this is confirmed later in the story, when picketing outside Bell Atlantic's offices at 20th and L streets is mentioned—a detail that would have been distracting in its relative unimportance in the opening paragraphs. To enhance the news value and weight of the story, both paragraphs provide contextual information that situates the news for maximum importance (biggest strike since the historic Bell-system breakup; a determinant of future telecommunications jobs).

Quotes are generally inserted early in the story to give a sense of immediacy and freshness, and this strike story follows the form. In this case, the quote functions to underscore the proposition of the previous paragraph; provide attribution, which has been absent until now, before too much more is said; and introduce a voice that succinctly says what a reporter cannot. Quotes also break up the type and provide textual mile markers that readers can follow.

The ingredients are roughly the same for all stories, although the weight of the various components of information will affect organization on the micro level. While the rules of assembling and writing a story in practice are altered to fit various contingencies (could not confirm a fact, find a source, and so on), in theory they are shared and assumed by mainstream reporters whether in Alaska or Florida, in Corning or New York.

Rhetorical goals in newswriting include brevity, clarity, accuracy, objectivity, and balance. These goals work in tandem with other factors and constraints generated within the journalism profession as the filters, or discourse parameters, that help produce "news language." The following are some of these parameters:

- News values, or deciding what is prominent or newsworthy
- Story organization, in which the newest or most important or most interesting information is placed first and is followed by other information from sources
- Writing with the readership explicitly in mind
- Technical constraints, such as deadlines or the capabilities of the printing press
- Attribution practice, in which information that is not independently verifiable must be attributed to a person other than the journalist

Thus constraints on practitioners are simultaneously textual and ideological (as well as mechanical in that deadline pressures and equipment failures have a greater bearing on news outputs than most readers think). On the textual or discourse level, reporters are taught to write a certain way. They learn to write short sentences and short paragraphs (for ease of comprehension). They learn to be attentive to their recipient audience (to both serve and attract the reader). Stories are organized with the most salient or catchy information first, following the "inverted pyramid" style. Information that is not independently verifiable is to be attributed, and sources must reflect a balance of views. The importance of the lead, or first, paragraph gets special emphasis when crafting a story. What is most important comes first.

On the ideological level, the concept of "news values" governs choices of coverage, sources, and story placement. The importance of news values cannot be overestimated: it rules the content of the news pages. News values address the questions "What do people need to know?" and "What do people want to know?" Proximity, conflict, importance, currency, prominence, and interest are all factors that play a role in decision making about the value of news. These factors have been operational since the beginning of the century, when "modern journalism" practice developed out of the science-focused empirical models of the nineteenth century.

A good reporter or editor has good news judgment. This means that he or she knows what is salient within the profession and in relation to the community of coverage. Reporters and editors learn about news values from several sources: textbooks, teachers, peers, experienced journalists, trade publications, and conferences, as well as from the continuity and stability of the various genres that comprise the news (the crime story, the "first X," and so on). News values are handed down through the forms of the text, with their authors and creators in the process learning, reinforcing, and reproducing values that determine "newsworthiness." Many hands are involved in news production; a story that receives multiple edits and is built on reported speech technically does not have a single author. The collective authorial voice, then, becomes a collective reflection of the community.

POINT 4: NEWS LANGUAGE IS CONSERVATIVE

While some innovations in language use make it onto the news pages, generally news practitioners see their role as that of upholding the usage standards that the larger society values. They are fairly conservative in how they regard language, seeing themselves as protectors, not defilers, of the standards we associate—rightly or wrongly—with civility and education. In the 1986 edition of their classic editing textbook, Baskette, Sissors, and Brooks devote an entire chapter to "Protecting the Language." Early on they say: "The copy editor plays a major role in protecting the language against abuse. One who knows how to spell, makes certain a story is written in proper English, recognizes and clarifies fuzzy passages, and protects the meaning of words is a valuable member of the staff" (57). This attitude also reflects and reinforces the newspaper's role of authority in its relationship with readers.

While many people consider the media's handling of language an affront to good usage, linguists would characterize the media in fact as having a fairly prescriptive and conservative (rather than innovative) attitude toward language use. (Both conservation and innovation play a key part in the robustness and continuity of a language, a conundrum that experts who seek to revive dying languages deal with.) There is evidence of this linguistic orientation in, for example, the continued use of "he" instead of "they" whereas the rest of the culture, especially in spoken contexts, has largely adopted "they" as the generic form. Or denominalization practices (making a verb out of a noun, like "interface" or "beep") will persist in print while editors decry their very existence.

Next to good reporting, journalists like good writing, and the number of stylebooks, grammar guides, newsroom writing coaches, and articles on usage in well-respected industry periodicals like *Columbia Journalism Review* is an abundant indication of this orientation. (Of course, the articles do not pick linguists' brains about natural language-change processes, so a great deal of the change is viewed with alarm, just as it is by the larger society.) For example, writing clearly is emphasized. Liveliness is valued. Intensifiers are to be used sparingly, as is the passive voice. Redundancies and wordiness are explicitly despised. Correct use of *that, which*, and *whom*, subject-verb agreement rules, and removal of dangling modifiers and split constructions head the list of proper verbal practices. Whether the texts reflect this prescriptive, somewhat self-conscious orientation is another matter.

At the level of style, there is evidence through language that local, professional, and societal standards are enforced and replicated. For instance, most papers have rules against profanity, but since nearly all newswriting rules are locally interpretable, there is variation in rendering the rule. College papers or alternative papers sometimes have more relaxed restrictions on profanity than the mainstream, daily paper delivered to the home, in part because they have determined what their audience, their community of coverage, will allow.

Besides upholding societal notions of correct usage, print and broadcast media are also concerned with maintaining their own local and profession-specific style rules. At nearly every reporter's and editor's elbow is *The Associated Press Stylebook and Libel Manual* (also known as "the journalist's bible"; Goldstein 1994). Interspersed between grammar, punctuation, and capitalization rules are guidelines for language use that have broader social implications and that change as society changes. For example, *elderly*: "Use this word carefully and sparingly"; *handicap*: "It should be avoided in describing a disability"; *race*: "Do not use derogatory terms unless they are part of a quotation that is essential to the story."

Thus style decisions are not merely cosmetic, grammatical, or obvious ones, but can invoke a set of social meanings that relate to the community. Retired newswoman Lee Peters, who worked for a daily paper near Corning, recalled that the editor called her into his office to discuss her use of the phrase "objets d'art" in a story about new home decorations (Peters, personal communication). It wouldn't do, said he, a refugee from San Francisco, where historically they had plenty of objets d'art. The largely rural readership of ranchers and farmers who valued plain speech would think that the reporter was putting on airs with a French phrase. (She did come from "back East," after all.)

His solution was a translation from the French: art objects. This incident occurred in the 1950s, but even today, journalism textbooks advise adhering to local-community standards for language use. Plain language is always considered the better choice, even in the *New York Times*, whose own sparing use of "objets d'art" (thirteen times in 1997, compared with thirty-eight instances of "art objects") evidently follows the precept laid down by Baskette, Sissors, and Brooks (1986, 90): "Newspapers display an affectation when they use foreign words not readily understood by their readers."

POINT 5: THE MEDIA ARE A RICH REPOSITORY OF LANGUAGE HISTORY

The news media give us a snapshot of ourselves as users of language, especially if we take a long, systematic look at the pile of newspapers we usually throw into the recycling bin, or if we review news broadcasts from radio and television's infancy. The media afford us a glimpse into the dynamic construction of language in use as well as a way to chart the inevitable changes and alterations that language and society undergo over time.

The media function for us as time-lapse photography functions in a nature show: they show us the results of an ongoing process. Since language change is not observable in the immediate moment, looking back and comparing vocal or written style, semantics, syntax, and conventions of usage with the present shows what has changed and what has remained the same. It allows us to consider the point that language changes to meet the contingencies of communicative needs.

For example, the use of "and" and "but" connectives to start sentences began to occur more often in newspaper writing, first appearing occasionally in the 1940s in quoted material. This construction gradually flourished in subsequent decades and now is fairly routine, as in this example:

> The line of Barney toys due from Hasbro this summer is expected to generate $100 million in sales.
>   And to think, it all began on an expressway in central Dallas. (*San Francisco Chronicle*, March 5, 1993)

The old "don't start a sentence with a connective" rule, which has since been discarded in most grammar books although it is still very active in the minds of many journalists and students of English, prescribed against such a construction. This trend toward sentence-initial connective use, in an environment in which copy editors often flog reporters for their grammatical and stylistic sins, speaks to other motivations in language use.

The connectives in the news data are used primarily in the way we use such words in face-to-face discourse (Cotter 1996)—not so much semantically (for their logical meaning) as pragmatically (for their functional meaning). We do this in conversation when we want keep our turn—saying "and" and pausing is very useful for that purpose—or when we want to gain the floor, sometimes jumping in with a "but" to establish our presence in the conversational exchange.

This means that the connectives function pragmatically in the written-discourse context as well as the spoken level, allowing us with little effort to achieve coherence or to extend or change a turn of talk. An "and" offers another tool for creating coherence in a world of very short paragraphs. A "but" often signals the introduction of a new source or new point in a very elegant, simple, uncomplicated way.

In terms of the discourse relationship, the use of sentence-initial connectives, a characteristic of face-to-face spoken interaction, can be viewed as a way to minimize the distance the written modality imposes on the reader (Cotter 1996). So, too, Quirk (1986) mentions writers of an earlier century who once evoked conversational immediacy by calling on the "gentle reader"—also the habit of genteel syndicated columnist Miss Manners. Importantly, the presence of sentence-initial *and*s and *but*s in the newspaper means that the demands of communicating are superseding prescriptive rules, and that addressee-oriented goals of writing have taken precedence over other considerations.

The mechanics of the profession have also had a superficial impact on the language of the media. In the "old days" when the type was set by hand in hot lead, the physical-temporal limitations of setting type led to shorter-word spelling conventions (*employe* for *employee*, *cigaret* for *cigarette*) that the computer age has since eliminated. But even now, a deadline means getting the news out as quickly, completely, and accurately as possible. Reporters and editors rely on the routines they know, and that includes linguistic ones. These routines introduce the potential for gaps, inconsistencies, and errors, big and little, some of which are occasional and random, and some of which signal part of a larger pattern of language change.

These five facts about the Fourth Estate are meant to show that while the news media have their own culture and their own language patterns, they also participate in the communicative routines of the wider society in which they are embedded. The media provide insight into language behavior and processes of change at the same time that they attempt to standardize and constrain the unruly display of language as a social artifact. News language reflects norms and displays agendas and identities, actions that are accomplished through language and the reciprocal interaction of author, audience, and text.

REFERENCES

Aitchison, Jean. 1997. *The language web: The power and problem of words.* Cambridge: Cambridge University Press.
Baskette, Floyd, Jack Z. Sissors, and Brian S. Brooks. 1986. *The art of editing.* 4th ed. New York: Macmillan.

Cotter, Colleen. 1993. Prosodic aspects of broadcast news register. *Proceedings of the 19th Annual Meeting of the Berkeley Linguistics Society*, 90–100. Berkeley, CA: Berkeley Linguistics Society.

———. 1996. Engaging the reader: The changing use of connectives in newspaper discourse. *Sociolinguistic variation: Data, theory, and analysis*, Jennifer Arnold, et al., eds., 263–278. Stanford: CSLI Publications.

Goldstein, Norm, ed. 1994. *The Associated Press stylebook and libel manual*. Reading, PA: Addison-Wesley.

Quirk, Randolph. 1986. *Words at work: Lectures on textual structure*. Essex: Longman.

Raskin, Victor. 1999. Writing well in an unknown language: Linguistics and composition in an English department. *Language alive in the classroom*, Rebecca S. Wheeler, ed., 139–154. Westport, CT: Praeger.

LIFE ON MARS: LANGUAGE AND THE INSTRUMENTS OF INVENTION

Mark Turner and Gilles Fauconnier

On July the Fourth, 1997, a Martian admiring the night sky above the ancient floodplain of the Ares Vallis, now a desert, would have seen the Pathfinder space probe parachuting toward the ground in a protective cocoon of inflated air bags. A multimillion-dollar space beach ball, it bounced fifty feet high before dribbling to rest, where the bags deflated. The lander retracted the air bags, unfolded to release a small exploratory roving vehicle, and beamed pictures of rocks back to the Jet Propulsion Laboratory.

An American Earthling, sitting at home, might have seen those rocks on television, interspersed with images of space aliens accompanying news reports about the fiftieth anniversary of "the Roswell Incident." According to believers, space aliens had crashed in Roswell, New Mexico, fifty years earlier, and the U.S. Air Force had covered it up. The Air Force, which once dismissed these rumors as absurd, now, on the fiftieth anniversary, admitted that the believers were not actually crazy. They had merely seen desert wreckage of secret high-altitude balloon tests involving capsules and dummies.

As the Mars rover began to analyze the rocks, an anonymous spoof appeared on the Web:

> Valles Marineris (MPI)—A spokesthing for Mars Air Force denounced as false rumors that an alien spacecraft crashed in the desert, outside of Ares Vallis on Friday. Appearing at a press conference today, General Rgrmrmy The Lesser stated that "the object was, in fact, a harmless high-altitude weather balloon, not an alien spacecraft."
>
> The story broke late Friday night when a major stationed at nearby Ares Vallis Air Force Base contacted the Valles Marineris *Daily Record* with a

story about a strange, balloon-shaped object which allegedly came down in the nearby desert, "bouncing" several times before coming to a stop, "deflating in a sudden explosion of alien gases." Minutes later, General Rgrmrmy The Lesser contacted the *Daily Record* telepathically to contradict the earlier report.

General Rgrmrmy The Lesser stated that hysterical stories of a detachable vehicle roaming across the Martian desert were blatant fiction, provoked by incidents involving swamp gas. But the general public has been slow to accept the Air Force's explanation of recent events, preferring to speculate on the "other-worldly" nature of the crash debris. Conspiracy theorists have condemned Rgrmrmy's statements as evidence of "an obvious government cover-up," pointing out that Mars has no swamps.

We are guided to a blended story. The Roswell story itself has no Mars Pathfinder and no landing on Mars, while the Pathfinder story itself has no Martian Air Force, no Martian newspapers, and no sceptical public. These two stories share the scenario of a spacecraft landing in a desert, and they involve balloons. We must borrow parts of each of them to weave a blended story in which the Pathfinder lands on a Mars that has a government, rumors, newspapers, and an Air Force cover-up.

This selective borrowing, or rather, projection, is not merely compositional. Although the Air Force comes from the Roswell story, or more generally from knowledge of the United States, it is not projected blindly into the blend. The Air Force must be Martian, as must the Martians. To create them, we make use of pre-existing blended stories about fictional Martians, who are like us but not like us, who eat unhuman foods, who speak in unhuman languages, who live in subzero (Fahrenheit) temperatures, who communicate through extrasensory channels, who have roles and social organization, and so on.

We also make use of standard news reporting to give, in the blend, a Martian byline (Mars Press International) and a newsy prose style ("A spokesthing for Mars Air Force denounced as false . . . ," "But the general public has been slow to accept . . .").

The blend is a joke. Some of the humor comes from creative selective projection, bringing about, in the blend, telepathic denials, bizarre personal titles, and scare quotes for strangeness, inaccuracy, and incredulity placed around garden-variety and referentially accurate words. The punchline involves sophisticated leaps in the attribution of invention: at first we credit the *inventor* of the blend for having equipped it with telepathic Martians, an Air Force, conspiracy theorists, newspaper reporters, and swamp gas, but then, inside the blend, the Martians accuse the General of having invented the swamp gas—which proves, since it contradicts their knowledge (actually, our knowledge, projected to them) about the physical environment of Mars, that he must be lying. We, outside the blend, appreciating the entire network, can find this accusation funny, a clever invention by the network's inventor, but the Martians, living in the blend, cannot.

This blend has a logic. The Martians can't object, as we can, that they don't exist. The language of the news report presupposes that there are Martian spokesthings and that at least General Rgrmrmy is telepathic, so these facts are straightforward in the blend. Nonetheless, residents of the blend can object to the presupposition by General Rgrmrmy that there are Martian swamps, even though we, outside the blend, may believe that Martians could have no concept of swamps at all.

This spoof looks exotic, but it is the product of a basic, everyday cognitive operation which we call "conceptual integration." The principal statements of our research are Fauconnier and Turner (1998), Fauconnier (1997), and Turner (1996), but many other publications have appeared and many other people have contributed to the research program: Seana Coulson, Margaret Freeman, Douglas Hofstadter, Edwin Hutchins, Nili Mandelblit, Todd Oakley, Martin Ramey, Adrian Robert, Tim Rohrer, Douglas Sun, Tony Veale, Lawrence Zbikowski, and others.

We leave aside the structural and dynamic properties of blending, the competing optimality constraints on blending, the taxonomy of standard kinds of conceptual integration networks that result from those optimality constraints, and a range of other technical results. They can be pursued by investigating the Web page for blending and conceptual integration at <*http://www.wam.umd.edu/~mturn/WWW/blending.html*>. We will instead give a brief and intuitive explanation of blending, provide some examples, and illustrate ways in which linguistic constructions prompt us to create conceptual blends.

GHOSTS OF PREDATORS PAST

The Pathfinder blend is merely amusing, but blending often plays a role in the development and expression of scientific knowledge. The front page of the science section of *The New York Times* for Tuesday, December 24, 1996, carried a large photograph of a small American pronghorn chased by pen-and-ink prehistoric cheetahs and long-legged dogs. The American pronghorn is excessively faster than any of its modern predators. Why would evolution select for this costly excessive speed when it brings no additional reproductive benefit? The scientists propose that

the pronghorn runs as fast as it does because it is being chased by ghosts—the ghosts of predators past. . . . As researchers begin to look, such ghosts appear to be ever more in evidence, with studies of other species showing that even when predators have been gone for hundreds of thousands of years, their prey may not have forgotten them.

The ancient American pronghorn, in the historical story, barely outruns nasty predators like cheetahs and long-legged dogs. The modern American pronghorn, in the modern story, easily outruns all its modern predators. In the blend, the modern American pronghorn is being chased by nasty ancient predators, marked as "ghosts" to signal that they have no reference in the modern pronghorn's world. We are not confused by this felicitous blend: we do not expect to see ghosts chasing a real modern pronghorn; we do not think the modern pronghorn remembers the prehistoric predators. Instead, we know how to connect the blend to the story of the modern pronghorn: great speed was adaptive for the ancestors of the modern pronghorn, who faced nasty predators, and although those predators are now extinct, the instinctive capacity for speed survives.

The network of pronghorn stories is complicated by its use of generic stories for species—a species doesn't actually run, but we can think of the generic representative of the species: the cow chews cud; the pronghorn runs fast; and so on. How we connect the scene of an individual pronghorn to the generic story is an issue we leave aside. There are touches that make the blend seem natural: the existing phrase "ghost of Christmas past" gives a basis for "ghosts of predators past." As Fauconnier and Turner (1994) and Oakley (1995) show, "ghost" blends are frequent whenever an element from an earlier story has an effect but not an existence in a later story.

NON-EUCLIDEAN GEOMETRY

Blends can constitute basic scientific and mathematical knowledge. Consider hyperbolic geometry. As Kline (1972) and Bonola (1955 [1912]) survey, the laborious birth of non-Euclidean geometry took fifteen hundred years. Euclid had defined parallel lines as straight lines in a plane that, when extended indefinitely in both directions, never meet. He had presented a sequence of proofs independent of the parallel axiom that show that two straight lines are parallel when they form with one of their transversals equal interior alternate angles, or equal corresponding angles, or interior angles on the same side that are supplementary. But proving the converses of these propositions appeared to require the parallel axiom: "If a straight line falling on two straight lines makes the interior angles on the same side less than two right angles, the two straight lines, if produced indefinitely, meet on that side on which the angles are less than two right angles." This axiom seemed to many geometers, probably including Euclid, to lack the desirable feature of self-evident truth. Rather than assume it as an axiom, they sought to derive it from the other axioms and from Euclid's first twenty-eight theorems, none of which uses the parallel axiom.

Gerolamo Saccheri (1667–1733) made the crucial attempt, as Bonola reports. Saccheri focused on a quadrilateral ABCD where angle DAB and angle ABC are right angles, and where line segments AD and BC are equal:

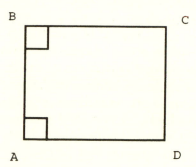

Without using the parallel axiom, it is easy to prove that angles BCD and CDA must be equal. Saccheri did this. If we assume the parallel axiom, BCD and CDA must be right angles. Therefore, if we deny that BCD and CDA are right angles, we thereby deny the parallel axiom. Saccheri did just this, in the hope of deriving a contradiction from the denial, which would prove the parallel axiom by reductio ad absurdum.

But if BCD and CDA are not right, they are still equal, and so they must be either obtuse or acute. Saccheri sought to show that, in either case, a contradiction follows. He assumed that they are acute; that is, he performed the following conceptual integration:

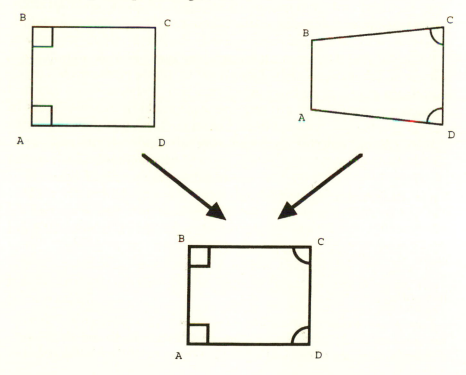

Both inputs are routine Euclidean figures. Both have a quadrilateral ABCD, equal line segments AD and BC, equal angles DAB and ABC, and equal angles BCD and CDA. The blend takes this structure from both inputs. But the first input has right internal angles DAB and ABC, and the second input has acute internal angles BCD and CDA. The blend takes the right angles from the first input and the acute angles from the second. The blend is impossible in Euclidean geometry, but Saccheri never really found a contradiction for this blend. He carefully drew many conclusions about this blend that he regarded as repugnant elaborations of the blend's inherent falsity but that today count as foundational theorems of hyperbolic geometry.

It is important to see that all of Saccheri's elaboration of the blend followed everyday procedures of Euclidean geometry. The input spaces are Euclidean and familiar; the elaboration procedures are Euclidean and familiar. The only thing new in the process is the selective, two-sided projection to create the blend. Saccheri's line of reasoning, far from being exotic, is the uniform strategy of all reductio argument in logic and mathematics: a system of inferential principles that is taken to be consistent is applied to a structure that may not be consistent. Saccheri imagined that he was conducting what could only be a reductio ad absurdum argument, and he hoped that the inevitable contradiction would be forthcoming. Those who came after him reinterpreted the same proofs not as reductio arguments but as steps in the development of a new and consistent branch of geometry.

It happens that there are many equivalent ways to produce a blend that delivers hyperbolic geometry. All that is needed is a blend that requires the interior angles of a triangle to sum to fewer than 180 degrees.

Saccheri is not credited with the invention of non-Euclidean geometry. As Kline summarizes and simplifies the history, "If non-Euclidean geometry means the technical development of the consequences of a system of axioms containing an alternative to Euclid's parallel axiom, then most credit must be accorded to Saccheri, and even he benefited by the work of many men who tried to find a more acceptable substitute axiom for Euclid's" (page 869). Credit is given instead to Gauss, Bolyai, and Lobatchevsky for recognizing (but not proving) that hyperbolic non-Euclidean geometry is mathematically consistent, and to Gauss for recognizing that physical space might be non-Euclidean.

BLENDING AND METAPHOR

If metaphor is the understanding of something in one conceptual domain, like business competition, by conceptual projection from something in a different conceptual domain, like boxing, then none of the blends we have seen so far is essentially metaphoric. The hyperbolic geometry network lies within the domain of geometry, and the two inputs are not related by metaphor. The pronghorn network lies within the domain of North American pronghorns, and the modern pronghorn is the evolutionary, not the metaphoric, counterpart of the historical pronghorn. The Pathfinder spoof lies within the domain of *spacecraft landing on a planet*. Its input stories have literal counterparts: planets, spacecraft, landings, and balloons.

Yet metaphoric projections also typically involve blending in ways that have gone unnoticed. Here is an example that forces us to notice the blending. As we write, the Dow Jones Industrial Average has rocketed past 8000, but just a few months ago, it stood at 6500 as investors had become cautious, even bearish. Reuters news service reported:

> U.S. stocks ended sharply lower on Wednesday after an attempt to extend a one-day rally was quashed. Market players said investors were unwilling to return to the market amid fears that rising interest rates would lead to further losses in the days ahead. "Everybody has their horns pulled in," said Arnie Owen, director of equities at Kaufman Brothers.

"Everybody has their horns pulled in" exploits a conventional metaphor in which a market charging up is a bull and aggressive investors with confidence in the market are also bulls. In the target story of investment, there is a linear scale of confidence in the market, linked as causal to a linear scale of investment. In the source story of bulls, a bull is a bull is a bull and the length of a bull's horns is fixed. But in the blend, length of horn is degree of confidence and investment, and so, in the blend, a bull/investor can increase or decrease the size of its horns.

Consider the standard view that metaphor and analogy make their contribution by projecting structure from the source to the target or by finding shared structure. The metaphor of "horns pulled in" does not fit this view. It does not project the nature of horns from the source onto the target or find structure they share. Instead, it works by creating a blend. The horns in the blend have a variable nature incompatible with the horns in the source. Certainly this is an example of metaphor, and the metaphor is certainly unidirectional—we understand investors by projection from bulls and bears, not bulls and bears by projection from investors—but the central inferential mechanism is neither projection from source to target nor detection of structure they share.

There can be multiple inputs to a blend, and an input can be covert. For example, it is possible that the "horns pulled in" blend has, for some readers, a covert input of "animal retracting its claws." In lucky cases, there is linguistic or conceptual evidence indicating the covert input, but not here. It would be useful to have psychological tests for detecting covert inputs.

The "horns pulled in" blend is noticeable, but for the most part, blending is itself a covert operation that escapes notice. Consider "that's a two-edged sword," used conventionally of arguments or strategies that are risky since they simultaneously help and hurt the user. In the domain of literal swords, two-edged swords are superb weapons, better for stabbing since both edges cut and better for slashing since both edges slash. Their superior performance explains their development and deployment despite the relative difficulty of manufacturing and maintaining them. But a two-edged sword in the blend is quite different: one edge of the sword/argument exclusively helps the user and the other edge exclusively hurts the user. It is not impossible for a literal warrior to be hurt by his own literal blade, the way it is impossible for literal bulls to retract their literal horns, but it is atypical, and even in the atypical scenario, it doesn't happen that one of the edges always hurts the user while the other always helps. If it did, the two-edged sword would be discarded for the one-edged model. This atypical scenario, recruited to the source under pressure from the target, still projects only selectively to the blend. The central inference of the metaphor still does not arise by projecting the structure of the atypical scenario to the target or finding structure they both share.

CHINESE FLAGS IN A CAPITALIST BREEZE

Metaphor often involves multiple blending:

> HONG KONG, Tuesday, July 1—As dawn rises for the first time over red Chinese flags officially fluttering here in a capitalist breeze, the most fascinating question is not how China will change Hong Kong but how Hong Kong will change China. (Nicholas D. Kristof, "Year of the Trojan Horse," *New York Times*, front page, 1997)

A flag is a metonymic symbol—for example, fifty stars for fifty states. Understanding a nation metaphorically as a physical object (e.g., "Austria was crushed during the negotiations") does not delude us into believing that the physical flag is actually the nation it represents, but blending may be at work in this metaphor. There are, now anyway, many American citizens with no political opinion about the burning of cloth, no visceral reaction to the expression "I despise America," and a firm belief in protected free speech who nonetheless become so distressed at the image of someone burning an American flag that they want to make the act illegal. They refer to the act not as "burning an American flag" but as "burning *the* American flag." In such a case, the flag may count as more than mere metonymic representation. In the blend, an attack on the flag is an attack on the nation. We are not trapped inside blends, but emotional reactions generated there can, like inferences generated there, leave their mark on reality.

The ceremony of raising a flag adds another metaphoric connection to this blend—*higher versus lower* maps to *governing versus governed*. In the blend, the raised flag is simultaneously a physical object, a flag, a higher physical object, a political entity, and a government. What it is raised above is simultaneously a geographical or architectural entity, a lower object, and a governed political or institutional entity.

The blend is useful in giving a concrete and realistic representation of government. We learn in grade school the fiction that the blend had legal causality: planting a flag on "discovered" land made it the territory of the "mother nation." The raising-the-flag blend, with its evident psychological and emotional power, was exploited during Britain's handover of Hong Kong to the People's Republic of China. The "handover" was portrayed to the world in a riveting and memorable scene in which the British flag was lowered and then the Chinese flag was raised.

"Raising the flag" is a standard blend in which power relations are given entirely by the fact that the flag is above. In this blend, there is no significance in which way the flag blows or even whether it blows at all. But in the *New York Times* flag blend, new structure has emerged: China, a nation, a government, a physical object, specifically a flag, is now affected by physical force, a breeze, capitalism, Hong Kong, the governed political entity. This new blend uses the standard metaphoric connection between physical forces and causation to give an odd inference: the higher, governing element is controlled by what it governs; China, the flag, is controlled by Hong Kong capitalism, the breeze. This irony is the point of the article. It is further elaborated in many interesting ways—if China had not taken over Hong Kong, had not raised its flag over Hong Kong, then Hong Kong, the breeze, would have had no opportunity to influence China, the flag.

There is a second interesting reversal in the *New York Times* blend. In a different standard flag blend, there is indeed significance in which way the flag blows and whether the flag blows at all. In this blend, the flag is not merely a physical object but also an animate agent: flag and nation are personified, or at least given some features of animacy. This blend underlies descriptions of the U.S. flag as "proudly snapping in the breeze" and of the "once-proud Soviet flag" now "drooping." In this blend, internal psychology of the flag/person/nation causes the movement/behavior of the flag. Appearance is the index of psychology. But in the *New York Times* blend, the movement/behavior of the flag/nation is caused not by China but by something else—Hong Kong, the breeze, capitalism.

Examples like these suggest that basic metaphors should be reanalyzed to determine whether they depend upon hidden conceptual blending. We have argued elsewhere (Fauconnier and Turner 1998) that basic metaphoric connections—such as the metaphoric connection between anger and heat, or between failure and death—give rise to conventional blends like "Steam was coming out of his ears" and "You are digging your own grave." In fact, even the most famous of all basic metaphors, the "conduit metaphor of communication," analyzed by Michael Reddy in 1979, requires conventional blending. In this basic metaphor, a sender (speaker) places an object (meaning) into a container (expression) and sends it (expresses it) to a receiver (hearer) who opens the container (processes the expression) to take out the object (understand the meaning). This metaphor underlies expressions like "I am trying to put my thoughts into words" and "I am not getting much meaning out of this poem."

But we can also use the conduit metaphor in saying, "Most of the meaning this poststructal critic finds in *Paradise Lost* simply isn't there." In the source domain of physical objects and containers, "finding" something presupposes its existence in the location where it is found, so it must be impossible to find a physical object in a container if it isn't in the container. But in the blend, the object/meaning depends for its existence upon the mental work of the receiver, so it can be there for the critic but not for the poet.

VISUAL BLENDS

Before we turn to language, it is best to emphasize that blending is not restricted to language. Blending is, for example, common in visual representation, from Renaissance and early modern paintings of the Annunciation to contemporary newspaper cartoons. An issue of *The New York Times, The Economist, The Washington Post, Le Figaro*, or any American news magazine will usually include many visual blends, or rather, visual representations that evoke conceptual blends.

Consider an advertisement for a Zip disk, a data-storage device in a squarish, flat hosing. The circular hole in the middle of the casing reveals a metal circle used in turning the disk mechanically. The ad shows the Zip disk standing up, its central circle transformed into a camera lens. A small flash bulb and a shutter release button have been added, and a photographic print is rolling out of its lower section as if the Zip disk were a Polaroid camera delivering a print. The ad asks us to think of a Zip disk as a digital photo album—the storage disk is camera-like not in taking the picture but in delivering the picture, and is album-like in serving as a repository of the image. The image can go back into this disk-camera-album and come back out as many times as you like.

Visual representations that prompt for blends often exploit accidental connections ingeniously. The divided Apple Computer Corporation is depicted as a quartered apple, with printed circuits for flat interior surfaces and computer chips for seeds. An illustration on the cover of *The Economist* for a story about the dangers of genetic explanations of behavior depicts an abstract human being controlled like a puppet by threads/chains that are double helixes. A Samsung all-in-one office machine is depicted as a Swiss Army knife with its blades out: the helical corkscrew is the helical phone cord, and so on. A news story, "Can Pepsi Become the Coke of Snacks? Using Fritos, Not Fizz to Conquer the World," shows distinctive snack foods pouring out of a Pepsi can. We are meant to construct a conceptual blend in which the Pepsi can is the Pepsi Corporation and the distinctive snack foods are produced by corporations owned by Pepsi.

An ad for the J. P. Morgan Company shows a man striding purposefully up the stairs. He is going to plummet, since the middle stairs are missing. But an enormous key—J. P. Morgan Company—is being pushed by three employees into place, its round head down and its blade in line with the stairs, so that its perfectly regular notches will serve as the missing stairs, arriving in place just as the man requires them to sustain his *ad astra* ascent into wealth. The caption for this visual blend exploits its unobvious nature—"Morgan means more than the obvious solution." In small print, "The obvious solution may not always be the one that takes you furthest." Visual blends like these are common, once you look for them.

CONCEPTUAL INTEGRATION AND LINGUISTIC CONSTRUCTIONS

Conceptual integration typically works below the horizon of observation. It is a general cognitive operation with many functions and wide application. It is routine, cognitively cheap, and not restricted to exceptional examples. It occurs dynamically in the moment of thinking, acting, and speaking, for local purposes, but its products can become entrenched. Often, it builds on those entrenched products to yield hyperblends. It interacts with other cognitive operations, such as analogy, metaphor, mental modeling, categorization, and framing.

Research on blending includes research on language. We have often argued (see, e.g., Turner 1991, 206), that expressions do not mean, but are prompts, usually minimal, to construct meanings by working with mental processes we already know. The meaning of an expression is never "right there in the words." Understanding an expression is never understanding "just what the words say"; the words themselves say nothing independent of the richly detailed knowledge and powerful cognitive processes we bring to bear.

Many expressions prompt for blending. To make this point, we have often cited the example of a modern philosopher saying in seminar, "I claim that reason is a self-developing capacity. Kant disagrees with me on this point. He says it's innate, but I answer that that's begging the question, to which he counters, in *Critique of Pure Reason*, that only innate ideas have power." In the blend, Kant and the philosopher are holding a debate. Words like "agree," "disagree," "retort," "answer," "respond," "counter," "yes," "no," "yes and no," and so on can be used to pick out elements in the blend, and we know the relation of that "debate" blend to the input story of Kant and to the input story of the modern philosopher.

"McJobs" asks us to think of a blend that constitutes an extended category of entry-level, low-paying, stultifying, impersonal, insecure jobs that offer little opportunity for advancement. Adjective-noun compounds like "artificial life" and "military democracy" have the same purpose. Noun-noun compounds like "house boat," "computer virus," "bond ghoul," and "same-sex marriage" also suggest obvious blends.

THE DITRANSITIVE CONSTRUCTION

It may be less obvious that clausal constructions can also prompt for blending. Consider the Ditransitive Construction in English, analyzed by Adele Goldberg (1995). A prototypical example is "Bill gave Mary a gift," with prototypical syntax

NounPhrase1–Verb–NounPhrase2–NounPhrase3.

By itself, the verb "give" evokes an abstract conceptual schema in which a causal agent, by some means, successfully causes the transfer of an object to a recipient. Call this schema "D" for "ditransitive schema." By itself, the verb "pour" does not evoke D ("The water poured out of the drain pipe"), yet when "pour" is used in the ditransitive syntax ("Bill poured Mary some wine"), the construction evokes schema D: Bill causes the transfer of a glass of wine to Mary.

For the complexities of the ditransitive construction and its relation to other constructions (e.g., "I baked Joe a cake" versus "I baked a cake for Joe"), we refer the reader to Goldberg. Our purpose here is to use the English ditransitive construction as an illustration of the way in which a clausal construction can prompt for blending, especially including two-sided blending.

The ditransitive construction prompts for a blend B that has two inputs, D and I. D is the abstract but highly integrated ditransitive schema. I is a set of unintegrated elements to which the words refer. The blend B is *two-sided*, by which we mean that B takes some of its organizing schema-level structure from each of its inputs, D and I. Although Goldberg does not use the model of conceptual integration, various two-sided blends are implicit in her analysis. The following is a restatement of her claims in the vocabulary of the network model, with some slight changes.

If D and I have organizing schemas that match closely, their blend takes its organizing schema from both D and I. This is the case for verbs that inherently signify acts of giving an object ("give," "pass," "hand," "serve," "feed," and so on), verbs of instantaneous causation of ballistic motion ("throw," "toss," "slap," "kick," "poke," "fling," "shoot," and so on), and verbs of continuous causation in a deictically specified direction ("bring," "take," and so on).

But if the verb is a verb of refusal ("refuse," "deny") as in "The boss denied Bill a raise," then the blend B takes the potential recipient and the potential patient from D but the causing of the not receiving from I, with the result that D is counterfactual with respect to B.

If the verb is a verb of giving with associated satisfaction conditions ("guarantee," "promise," "owe," and so on), then the blend takes from I kinds of casual structure for reception that are not in D.

If the verb involves a scene of creation ("bake," "make," "build," "cook," "sew," "knit," and so on) or of obtaining ("get," "grab," "win," "earn," and so on), then B takes from D intention to cause the recipient to receive the patient, and invites us to take success as well, but does not require it. If you "feed Joe a cake," he almost certainly receives it, but not so if you merely "bake Joe a cake" (and even less so if you "bake a cake for Joe").

If the verb is a verb of permission ("permit," "allow," and so on), then B takes enablement from I rather than successful causation from D.

If the verb is a verb of future transfer ("leave," "bequeath," "allocate," "reserve," "grant," and so on), then the blend takes future transfer from I rather than successful causation of present reception from D.

These blends fall into conceptual classes, each class with its own two-sided organizing schema, and each with its associated classes of verbs. These two-sided conceptual blends, and the use of the ditransitive construction to evoke them, can become conventional, so that the ditransitive can be associated not only with the prototypical schema D but also with these various abstract two-sided blends.

In fact, this only scratches the surface of the conventional conceptual integration that can be prompted by the English ditransitive construction. There are various metaphoric blends that have D as one input. Although Goldberg does not use the model of conceptual integration, there is a taxonomy of metaphoric blends implicit in her analysis, as follows:

(1) D is conventionally blended with an abstract schema for *causing an effect for an entity*. This produces a metaphoric blend in which the effect is an object and causing the effect for the entity is causing the object to come to the entity. This conventional blend inherits the ditransitive syntax from D, so one can say "The medicine brought him relief" and "She gave me a headache."

(2) D is conventionally blended with a schema for *communication*. This produces a metaphoric blend, analyzed by Reddy (1979), in which meaning is an object and communicating it to someone is giving it to a recipient. This conventional blend inherits the ditransitive syntax from D, so one can say "She told Jo a fairy tale."

(3) There is a conventional blend of *motion of an object toward a recip-*

ient with *perceiving*. In the blend, perceiving is reception of the "perception" by the recipient. This metaphoric blend is exploited as a basis for producing a more detailed metaphoric blend, with D as one input and *causing someone to perceive* as the other. In this more detailed blend, a perception is an object and causing someone to perceive it is transferring it to him. This blend inherits the ditransitive syntax from D, so one can say, "He showed Bob the view."

(4) D is conventionally blended with *directing an action at another person*. In this metaphoric blend, the action is an object and directing it at another person is transferring it to her as recipient. This blend inherits the ditransitive syntax from D, so one can say "She threw him a parting glance."

(5) There is a conventional metaphoric blend of *constructing an object out of parts* and *developing an argument*. In this blend, facts and assumptions used in arguing are parts used in constructing. This blend is exploited as a basis for a more detailed blend, of D and *granting facts and assumptions to an arguer*. In this more detailed blend, granting a fact or assumption to the arguer is transferring it to her as recipient. This blend inherits the ditransitive syntax from D, so one can say, "I'll give you that assumption."

There is an interesting final case. Goldberg observes correctly that in expressions like "Slay me a dragon," one of the input spaces has an agent performing an action for the benefit of someone else, and the first postverbal noun refers to the beneficiary while the second postverbal noun refers not to what the recipient receives but rather to what the causal agent acts upon. We offer the following explanation, which we think follows the spirit of Goldberg's analysis closely even though we use the model of blending and an array of input schemes that differs mildly from Goldberg's.

D inheres in a more detailed but highly conventional schema D'. In D', someone brings a benefit to someone by transferring an object to him. For example, "Bill gave me a dollar" is typically understood as meaning not only that a dollar was transferred but that a benefit (e.g., the ability to purchase) was conferred by means of the transfer. "Mary poured Bob a glass of wine" is typically understood as meaning not only that a glass of wine was poured with the intention of transfer but also that a benefit (e.g., wherewithal for pleasure or nourishment) was intended to be conferred by means of pouring and (intended) giving. Of course D is not always an instance of D': "My child handed me his banana peel" is probably D but not D', because there is no intended conferral of benefit. Nonetheless, the ditransitive syntax is attached not only to D but also to D', and, depending on vocabulary and context, it is usually a good strategy to try to interpret ditransitive syntax as evoking D'. In the ditransitive construction, the second postverbal noun always refers to the patient (metaphoric or not) of the causal agent's action, whether or not that patient is also the transferred object (metaphoric or not).

What happens in "Slay me a dragon," "Carry me two messages" (said by the Queen to her messenger), and "Slide me a bass trombone" (sung by James Taylor to the band) is a two-sided, selective projection to the blend, with D' as one input, as follows. From D', the blend takes a causal agent performing an action on an object (metaphoric or not) and the intended consequent conferral of a benefit on someone, but the blend does *not* take the reception of an object. The blend inherits the ditransitive syntax associated with D', and, as always in the ditransitive, the patient of the causal action (*a dragon, two messages, a bass trombone*) is assigned to the second postverbal noun.

THE XYZ CONSTRUCTION

The XYZ construction is specialized to evoke blending. "Money is the root of all evil" and "Brevity is the soul of wit" are examples of this construction, first noticed by Aristotle, in the following passage:

"As old age (D) is to life (C), so is evening (B) to day (A). One will accordingly describe evening (B) as the "old age of the day" (D + A)—or by the Empedoclean equivalent; and old age (D) as the "evening" or "sunset of life" (B + C). (*Poetics*, 1457B)

Consider "Vanity is the quicksand of reason." The XYZ syntax prompts for a conceptual mapping scheme involving conceptual integration.[1] The scheme is complicated: X (*vanity*) and Z (*reason*) are to be grouped into a single mental array; Y (*quicksand*) is to be placed inside a different mental array; some unspecified cross-domain mapping is to be found in which Y (*quicksand*) is the counterpart of X (*vanity*); an unmentioned W (e.g., *traveler*) is to be found in the Y (*quicksand*) domain such that W (*traveler*) can be the counterpart of Z (*reason*); X and Y are to be integrated (*vanity-quicksand*); W and Z are to be integrated (*reason-traveler*); the X-Z (*vanity-reason*) relation is to be integrated with the Y-W (*quicksand-traveler*) relation. A great deal—what the relevant conceptual domains are, their internal organization, what W and the other unmentioned counterparts might be, the nature of the relevant relations, and so on—must be constructed by the understander without further formal prompting.

The products of XYZ mappings are diverse:

Adams Morgan is the Greenwich Village of Washington, D.C.

He's the Babe Ruth of Hungarian kayaking.

Sex is the ancilla of art.

Sex is the poor man's opera.

Children are the riches of poor men.

The wages of sin is death.

In "Vanity is the quicksand of reason," the two mental arrays connected by the mapping (the *quicksand* space and the *reason* space) are radically unlike: one involves geographical travel while the other involves internal personal psychology. In contrast, "Adams Morgan is the Greenwich Village of Washington, D.C." has two mental arrays that share a specific conceptual frame: *city and its neighborhoods*. In "Paul Erdos is the Euler of our century," the mental arrays connected by the mapping share not only a frame (*mathematician*) but many details not standard for that frame: both Euler and Erdos were exceptionally prolific; both lived a long time; both worked in a number of fields; each was eminent but never quite attained the status of a mathematician like Gauss or Newton; and so on. "Erdos is the Euler of our century" feels quite different from "Vanity is the quicksand of reason," but they involve the identical syntactic form paired with the identical pattern of conceptual mapping.

SATAN, SIN, AND DEATH

Literary works frequently prompt for highly intricate blending. Milton's portrayal of Satan as father in the second book of *Paradise Lost*, analyzed in Turner (1987), is an extended display of two-sided blending.

The commonplace notion of Satan is already a blend for which a conceptual domain has been elaborated. Satan is a blend of individual human being—thinking, talking, desiring, intending, and so on—and theological ontology. In the theological space, there are eternal features (e.g., evil) as well as nonhuman powers and limitations. Satan is anthropomorphic, but he has theological features and unhuman conditions. The blended domain for Satan is quite elaborated—Satan has like-minded colleagues in the form of a cohort of devils; Satan and the devils form an intricate hierarchical organization of social groups; and so on. This blended domain is entrenched both conceptually and linguistically. Consequently, although the blend is in some ways two-sided, expressions like "The devil made me do it" or "Get thee behind me, Satan"—or even expressions based on further blending, such as the reference to a child as a "little devil"—do not feel especially figurative.

Milton extends this blend in ways that seem strikingly figurative and allegorical. Milton's theological space includes evil, disobedience, sin, death, and their relations, as well as the psychology of the prototypical sinner confronted with spiritual death. Milton's kinship space includes progeneration and kinship relations, especially the role *father*. He adds to the kinship space a pre-existing blend, of the birth of Athena from the brow of Zeus.

In Milton's blend, Satan conceives of the concept of sin; a fully grown woman, Sin, leaps from his brow. Satan is attracted to sin/Sin: he has sex with her. Although he does not know it at the time, his involvement with sin/Sin has a consequence, namely death—in the blend, Death is the male offspring of Satan's incestuous involvement with Sin. Death rapes his mother, causing her to give birth to a small litter of allegorical monsters.

After Satan has been sent to Hell and has decided to try to escape, he meets two characters at the gates of Hell who have been stationed there to keep him in. They are Sin and Death. He does not recognize them.

The mental spaces that contribute to this blended story—the kinship space and the theological space—correspond in some ways but not others. Milton draws from both of them, selectively, to create a two-sided blend. For example, he takes exclusively from the kinship space Sin's intercession between Death and Satan—father and son—when they are on the brink of terrible combat.

He takes exclusively from the theological space many central features, as follows. In the theological space, there is a sinful cast of mind that does not recognize spiritual death and mortality as the result of sin and that is at last appalled when it must acknowledge these consequences. Hence, in the blend, Sin is surprised to have conceived Death, and she finds her son odious. Next, in the theological space, mortality and spiritual death over-shadow the appeal of sin and are stronger than sin; acknowledging death devalues sin; willful, sinful desires are powerless to stop this devaluation. Hence, in the blend, Sin is powerless to stop her horrible rape by Death. In the theological space, the fact of spiritual death brings ceaseless remorse and anguish to the sinful mind, and the torments of hell bring eternal pun-ishment. Hence, in the blend, the rape of Sin by Death produces monstrous offspring whose birth, life, actions, and relationship to their mother are impossible for the domain of human kinship:

> These yelling Monsters that with ceasless cry
> Surround me, as thou saw'st, hourly conceiv'd
> And hourly born, with sorrow infinite
> To me, for when they list, into the womb
> That bred them they return, and howl and gnaw
> My Bowels, thir repast; then bursting forth
> Afresh with conscious terrors vex me round,
> That rest or intermission none I find.

Milton creates unobvious correspondences between the kinship space and the theological space. For example, he blends the unusual scenario of disliking a child with feeling horror at the fact of death. He blends the unusual scenario of a son raping a mother with the effect of death on sin.

Perhaps most ingeniously, he blends the unusual medical frame of traumatic vaginal birth that physically deforms the mother, making her less attractive, with the way sin becomes less attractive once death is acknowledged as its outcome:

> At last this odious offspring whom thou seest
> Thine own begotten, breaking violent way
> Tore through my entrails, that with fear and pain
> Distorted, all my nether shape thus grew
> Transform'd.

Although Milton's portrayal of Satan as a father is two-sided, it preserves considerable structure associated with *father* and *birth*. Consider first the paternity of Death. The "father" has human form and speaks human language, is excited by feminine beauty, and has anthropomorphic sex with an anthropomorphic female in a prototypical human scene. There is a birth through a vaginal canal. The son inherits attributes of both father and mother. Father and adolescent son have a conflict over authority. And so on. Now consider the paternity of Sin. The father again has human form and speaks human language. There is an offspring in human form, who emerges from a container-like body part and who develops into a sexual being.

Other examples, taken from *Death is the Mother of Beauty*, show a different projection from the space of *father* and *birth*. "Satan, liar and father of lies" does not take the anthropomorphic offspring. "The acorn is the father of the oak" takes neither anthropomorphic form nor anthropomorphic progeneration for either father or child. "Thy wish was father to that thought" (Shakespeare) does not take physical distinction for either father or child. Similar two-sidedness appears in "Fear, father of cruelty" (Ezra Pound), "Pain is the father of complaint" (Sidney), "Love's extremity is the father of foul jealousy" (Spenser), and "Pale desire, father of Curiosity" (Blake).

Consider as a final example the XYZ expression "The Child Is Father of the Man" (Wordsworth). The two inputs—father-and-child versus child-growing-to-man—come from the same conceptual domain, human life. But the example feels figurative, for the following reasons. First, the cross-space connections are highly resisted because they run counter to usual categories: *Immature child* in the first input has as its counterpart *father* in the second input, and *grown man* in the first input has as its counterpart *immature child* in the second input. Second, the blend must integrate frame-level structure from both inputs in a particularly surprising way. The chronological *child* in the blend takes from the input of father-and-child the relative influence (and even causal role) of the father, but it takes from the input of child-to-grown-man the relative *youth* of the child. The chronological *man* in the blend takes from the input of child-to-man the maturity of the man, but it takes from the input of father-and-child the dependency of the child.

The oddness of its counterpart connections and the extensive two-sidedness of its blend help make Wordsworth's line feel figurative. But the syntax and mapping scheme of "The Child Is Father of the Man" are the same as the syntax and the mapping scheme of "John is the father of Mary." Both evoke a conceptual mapping scheme involving conceptual blending.

THE SCOPE OF BLENDING

The cognitive study of language, which seeks an approach to language fitting the empirical facts, goes beyond both a philological interest in the history of words and a formal interest in the patterns of grammar to a cognitive scientific interest in basic mental operations that underlie language and that are indispensable to human understanding. Conceptual blending is a basic mental operation. It plays a role in grammar, semantics, discourse, meaning, visual representation, mathematics, jokes, cartoons, and poetry. It is indispensable to the poetics of literature because it is fundamental to the poetics of mind.

NOTE

1. For the original work on the XYZ construction, see Mark Turner, *Reading Minds*, chapter nine, "The Poetry of Connections, III"; and Gilles Fauconnier and Mark Turner, 1994, "Conceptual Projection and Middle Spaces."

REFERENCES

Aristotle. *Poetics*. 1995. In *Aristotle*, volume 23, edited and translated by Stephen Halliwell. Cambridge: Harvard University Press [Loeb].

Bonola, Roberto. 1955 [1912]. *Non-Euclidean geometry: A critical and historical study of its development*. Translated by H. S. Carslaw. New York: Dover Publications.

Fauconnier, Gilles. 1997. *Mappings in thought and language*. Cambridge: Cambridge University Press.

Fauconnier, Gilles, and Mark Turner. 1994. Conceptual projection and middle spaces. UCSD Cognitive Science Technical Report 9401. San Diego. [Available from *http://cogsci.ucsd.edu* and from *http://www.wam.umd.edu/~mturn*]

———. 1996. Blending as a central process of grammar. In *Conceptual structure, discourse, and language*, Adele Goldberg, ed. Stanford: Center for the Study of Language and Information.

———. 1998. Conceptual integration networks. *Cognitive Science* 22:2 (April–June 1998), 133–87.

Goldberg, Adele. 1995. *Constructions: A construction grammar approach to argument structure*. Chicago: University of Chicago Press.

Kline, Morris. 1972. *Mathematical thought from ancient to modern times*. New York: Oxford University Press.

Oakley, Todd. 1995. Presence: The conceptual basis of rhetorical effect. University of Maryland dissertation.

Reddy, Michael. 1979. The conduit metaphor. In *Metaphor and thought*, edited by Andrew Ortony, 284–324. Cambridge: Cambridge University Press.

Turner, Mark. 1996. *The Literary Mind*. New York: Oxford University Press.

———. 1991. *Reading minds: The study of English in the age of cognitive science*. Princeton: Princeton University Press.

———. 1987. *Death is the mother of beauty: Mind, metaphor, criticism*. Chicago: University of Chicago Press.

Turner, Mark, and Gilles Fauconnier. 1995. Conceptual integration and formal expression. *Metaphor and Symbolic Activity* 10:3, 183–203.

Laughing at and Laughing with: The Linguistics of Humor and Humor in Literature

Victor Raskin

Humor research, or humor studies, is a relatively new multidisciplinary area. The flagship journal of the field, *Humor: International Journal of Humor Research* (of which, by a mere coincidence, I happen to be editor-in-chief) currently lists some twenty contributing disciplines, from philosophy to anthropology to medicine. Those fields that are typically represented in a large English department include linguistics, literary criticism, rhetoric and composition, creative writing, and English education. The first two of these areas have so far yielded much more scholarship on humor than the others, and this chapter will focus accordingly on the interaction and cooperation between linguistics and literary studies within an English department in the study of humor.

After reviewing the nature of humor research as an area of study and the way linguistics and literary criticism contribute to it, this chapter will deal with the nature of the overlap and some interesting theoretical and practical issues that go beyond humor. Readers who look for examples of jokes they have not heard yet (are there any?) may be disappointed: humor research is not about telling jokes but rather about understanding how they work. As humor researchers keep reminding interested outsiders, this is a serious area of investigation into an important and universal human faculty.

HUMOR RESEARCH

While scholars have commented on humor for millennia, humor research is primarily a twentieth-century field of study, pioneered by the French philosopher Henri Bergson (1899) and the Austrian psychiatrist Sigmund

Freud (1905) and jump-started by a multidisciplinary group of scholars in the early 1980s. Humor research focuses on such general issues as the nature of humor, the taxonomy of humor, humor techniques, reasons for humor, its relation to personality traits, and the role of humor in society, history, and politics.

Each contributing discipline from that ever-growing list of twenty-plus applies its ideas and methods to humor as a way both to gain insight into humor and to use humor material as a testing ground in pursuit of its own theoretical and methodological concerns. The interaction between each discipline and humor research has proven to be quite productive and mutually enriching for both sides.

The current frontier in humor research is to go from these well-established dyads into triads and larger groupings: in other words, for two or more disciplines to get together and look at humor in an amalgamated way. Some inroads have been made in this respect between linguistics and psychology (Ruch, Attardo, and Raskin 1993), and the results have been most promising, but such efforts are very difficult and expensive. It is believed, however, that the field of humor research can be strengthened and unified only as a result of such concerted efforts.

LINGUISTICS OF HUMOR

When linguistics jumped into the fray, its theoretical thrust and formal, rigorous apparatus seriously contributed to the reemergence of humor research as the high-powered scholarly effort it is today. Developed since the late 1970s (Raskin 1979, 1985; Attardo 1994), the linguistics of humor is seen as the most theoretically developed aspect of humor research. It has been widely emulated in and applied to other aspects of the field as well. The reason for this advanced state is primarily the theoretical and methodological edge that linguistics has over the other contributing disciplines. On the other hand, this comes paired with serious theoretical and methodological constraints—the usual price for formal rigor. In other words, linguistics delivers a great deal, but when the consumers' appetites are whetted, they demand more, and linguistics cannot—and should not be expected to—deliver more.

In the center of the linguistics of humor lies the script-based semantic theory of humor (Raskin 1985). An application of a formal semantic theory to humor, it is based on the central concept of script, an enriched, structured chunk of semantic information, associated with word meanings and evoked by specific words. Thus, described informally, the script of eating goes far beyond the standard dictionary definition of *eat* as ingesting by mouth. The script will include information on what is edible and what is not, on tables, chairs, plates, and forks (but probably not napkins or monogrammed napkin rings from Neiman-Marcus, though why not?—back to the drawing board of script theory), and on meals, cooking, and so on.

Each word comes with its script, and special rules combine the scripts evoked by the individual words in the sentence together to derive the meaning of the whole sentence as well as adding and subtracting the semantic material outside of the sentence. What also happens in the process is called disambiguation. If you have recovered from the shock inflicted by this awful word and are ready to read on, it is a mechanism for getting rid of ambiguity. Most words have more than one meaning and come with more than one script—each meaning evokes its own script. When words are put together in a sentence, most of the ambiguity usually disappears because the incompatible scripts cancel each other out.

Thus the English word *bill* can mean a dollar bill, a legal bill, an invoice, and even a part of a bird's anatomy (the beak). The sentence "This is a bill" leaves all the ambiguity in place. Normally, when we talk, we try to avoid ambiguity for fear of misunderstandings and the crippling legal bills that stem from misunderstandings these days. So a sentence like "Here is your bill, Sir, but you don't have to pay all of it at once" pretty much gets rid of the ambiguity. Only a Jim Carrey movie would associate this sound track with a picture of a dead flamingo served to his character on a silver tray by a maitre d' (don't rush to the video store yet—I just made this movie up). The normal intended meaning is, of course, that of an invoice.

This is the attitude to ambiguity in normal, nonhumorous discourse: down with ambiguity! The main hypothesis of the script-based semantic theory of humor is that the text of a joke is compatible, in full or in part, with two opposing combinations of scripts, and that there are only a few such standard oppositions—about twenty, as a matter of fact. Let us try to figure out what the previous sentence means; the fact that I wrote it gives me a slight edge.

The first half says, correctly, that verbal humor is based on deliberate ambiguity. In regular discourse, we trash ambiguity. In humor, we value it (and we value it a lot: Jerry Seinfeld has amassed a fortune of over 100 million dollars at this writing). If you think of the bottom-rung verbal humor, the pun, the ambiguity hits you on all exposed surfaces. Salvatore Attardo's (1994) favorite one is this: Why did the cookie cry? Because its mother was a wafer so long. (Got it? A wafer = away for? Truly side-splitting, isn't it?) But much more sophisticated humor is usually based on some sort of ambiguity also.

To anticipate a question, no, we are not on the second part of that sentence. Ambiguity alone doth (doest?) not a joke make, though. The already-familiar sentence "This is a bill" is ambiguous in at least four ways, but it is not funny. It gets to be funny only when the scripts are opposed in a funny and unexpected way. These oppositions usually contrast normal, expected views of reality with abnormal, unexpected, and often outright impossible ones. I am writing this about two weeks before Mother's Day (don't ask me what year—I am not telling on the publisher's expediency), so I will tread very cautiously here: the last time I had a cookie, which was at least 3.1 minutes ago, it did not have a mother—in fact, I don't think it was crying either: I have a real aversion to crying food.

So, the main tenet (I like this word) of this theory of humor is that there is built-in ambiguity, and it involves very starkly and unexpectedly contrasting oppositions of scripts evoked by the text. When such ambiguity and opposition are discovered in the course of normal linguistic analysis of a text, the text is declared to be a joke. In fact, it is only a potential joke: whether it will "fire" or not depends on a number of additional factors.

Here is an example of a very funny text for some people and not so funny for others, including most of you: A Mercedes 600 and a beat-up old Soviet tinny car collide. Four big Russian mafia types, in red Armani jackets, jump out of the Mercedes. A decrepit old man crawls out of the tin box. "Well, grampa," the Armani-clad Mercedes driver declares, "now we'll beat you up!" "That's unfair," says the old man, "there are four of you, strong young men, and look at me!" After a brief consideration, the driver agrees. "You are right there!" he says. "Okay, Boris and I will fight on your side against Ivan and Nick here!"

Let us figure out what is happening in this story. No matter how much or how little we know about the world of the post-Soviet Russian mafia and its victims, the behavior of the four mafiosi is absurd, isn't it? If they consider themselves aggrieved parties, they should simply attack their opponent. Dividing into two parties of two, one of them to side with the enemy, is counterproductive. Who will fight whom for what? There is a tension here, an opposition between the normal, expected, real situation and the abnormal, unexpected, and unreal situation described in the text. This kind of opposition is the basis of almost all verbal humor, according to my hugely overrated script-based semantic theory of humor that you can find written up in every new linguistic, pragmatic, anthropological, or philosophical encyclopedia (believe me, I am the one who put it there).

My book (Raskin 1985) distinguished fewer than twenty different script oppositions, such as good: bad, real: unreal, money: no money, and life: death. It is truly amazing how many jokes from diverse cultures are based on so few standard oppositions. Exceptions are not impossible, but they are very hard to come by—they have to be specially constructed to falsify the theory, and believe me, while I have occasionally succeeded in doing that, it is not easy at all, and the resulting jokes are pretty poor.

What we have in the new Russian joke is one of the standard oppositions, real:unreal, and the text that makes it work. But how does it make the opposition work? The theory may be basically correct, but it leaves too much distance between the underlying opposition and the actual text of the joke. There are too many choices to make between these two poles of the joke, the one all there on the surface and the other completely hidden from view and requiring sophisticated analysis to unearth it.

To bridge this distance, the theory has been revised to become more adequate (Attardo and Raskin 1991), and everybody hates the new, improved version because it is not as simple as the old one. Interestingly and significantly, even these later developments in the theory have not added new oppositions. They did add four more "knowledge resources" to complement the language of the joke and the script opposition underlying the joke as the two "old" resources. The new resources are narrative strategy, target, situation, and logical mechanism. It was the new and improved theory that was tested in a sophisticated psychological experiment (Ruch, Attardo, and Raskin 1993) and largely validated.

Let us see what these resources add. Script opposition remains the most abstract underlying level of joke analysis. We start the analysis on the surface, with the standard, not even specially humor-oriented analysis of the meaning of the text. At the same time, we note the rhetorical structure of the text, that is, its narrative strategy. The strategy is that of a straightforward chronological exposition, as opposed to any one of several alternatives. Many jokes, for instance, are presented as questions, conundrums, or unanswerable riddles. Others often follow the standard "triple structure," especially favored in American humor: "on the first day . . . ," "on the second day . . . ," "on the third day . . ." or "the first man . . . ," "the second man . . . ," "the third man . . . ," and the punch line is delivered the third time around. The author of the text made a deliberate choice here, just as he or she did in wording the story in a certain way on the language level.

The target of the joke is the new Russian mafia, complete with their Mercedes luxury cars and Armani jackets, but remaining the crude and stupid fist-happy moujiks they have always been. The target is presented as a bunch of dumb people. This class of jokes is very popular around the world, with various minorities selected as targets, usually quite arbitrarily. It is the Polish Americans in the United States, the Irish in Britain, the Ukrainians in Western Canada, the Newfoundlanders in Eastern Canada, the Belgians in France, the policemen in Moscow, and so on (see Davies 1990 for a superb analysis of "dumb" and all other kinds of ethnic humor). Again, the author of the joke made a deliberate choice of one particular target, among many possible ones, as well as of a laughable trait ascribed to the target.

The situation, which we learn from the meaning analysis, is that of a literal collision, a car accident, involving an expensive new Russian car and a tin box that miraculously outlived its Soviet times. The situation suggests to us various commonsensical ways of expected behavior, one of which is a fist fight. It is the logical mechanism of the joke that subverts the situation by distorting it from a four-against-one fight, corresponding to the two parties to the conflict, to a two-against-two-plus-one fight, corresponding to nothing and leading to nothing. There are many situations the author could choose and, actually, several alternative logical mechanisms.

There is more to these levels of joke analysis, such as their pretty strong interdependence. It is expressed in the linear order of choices the author has to make. The script-opposition choice limits the choice of a logical mechanism, which limits the choice of the situation, which limits the choice of target, which limits the choice of narrative strategy, which seriously limits the choice of the actual language (text) of the joke. In other words, the deeper the level, the more choice there is. We have validated that supposition in the psychological experiment I mentioned before, but that does not mean that we know everything there is to know about verbal humor. Still, it is something, and it is reasonably well defined as well as constructively derivable from rigorous linguistic analysis. This amount of knowledge and the degree of its certainty by far exceed the results from other academic disciplines contributing to humor, which explains why the linguistics of humor has so quickly gained a dominant position in humor research.

HUMOR IN LITERATURE

The literary study of humor precedes the linguistics of humor by decades, if not centuries. In literary studies, humor is typically explored in the process of a topical investigation—of a single book, a single author, a single period, or a single genre. Thus a course or a publication on Mark Twain will deal with humor because everything this author wrote was—or at least was intended to be—funny. A course on Shakespeare may look at his comedies as well as his tragedies. A course on American humor will combine the funny writings of various humorists. A course on any nonfunny author, such as, say, Theodore Dreiser, will still note any presence of humor, irony, or satire, intended or unintended, whether sanctioned by the U.S. Communist party (i.e., the old Russian mafia) or not.

The study of humor in literary studies typically follows the school of critical thought practiced by the instructor/scholar, and, in this sense, the treatment of humor does not differ from that of "serious" stuff. In any case, the literary study of humor is still rarely affected by humor research, let alone other disciplines participating in humor research. Only a minority of literary scholars are also humor scholars (see, for instance, Mintz 1988 or Lewis 1989), and their analysis of literary humor reflects the latest achievements and results in humor research outside of literary studies proper, such as linguistic, sociological, or psychological aspects of humor research, humor taxonomy, and the information-conveying aspect of humor.

Thus, if a contemporary Russian author quotes the new-mafia joke that we analyzed earlier, the literary scholar will be interested to know if it is used by the hero or the villain and will interpret accordingly where the author stands with regard to the highway-robbery type of cronyist capitalism unleashed in Russia after the collapse of the Soviet Union. The scholar will recognize the joke as "dumb" and will characterize the target accordingly. He or she will also absorb as factual the information that the new Russian mafiosi wear red Armanis, drive Mercedes sedans, and like to fight for fun if not for any real purpose.

Then the literary scholar will use this information to support his or her favorite literary theory as well as to question the opposing one(s). This brings up the turf-related issue of a fine line between two types of writings on the use of humor in fiction and (rarely) poetry. The humor-research type uses the material to gain new insights into one of the problems of, you guessed it, humor studies. The literary-studies type is interested in humor only in order to establish mutual influences among authors, periods, genres, and/or theories.

LINGUISTICS-LITERATURE COOPERATION IN THE STUDY OF HUMOR

A simple and obvious way for a linguist and a literary faculty to cooperate is to team-teach a course, say, on Mark Twain. The first half of the semester will be taught by a linguist of humor and the second half by a literary scholar. Will such a course be useful for a student? The answer is yes, but only because the student received two mini- or half-courses under the guise of one, and getting two different perspectives of the same phenomenon is always instructive.

Can an article or a book be written the same way? The answer is in the affirmative again, but with the same qualification: it will be two articles or two books under the same cover. This kind of cooperation may be useful also from the point of view of interprogram relations within the department and should not be dismissed. Intellectually, however, this "additive" mode is inferior to true cooperation between the two disciplines.

True cooperation evokes a triad: linguistics, literary studies, and humor research. This is much more difficult than just applying one established discipline to humor research. The ideas and methods of linguistics and of literary studies are very different. How does one go about amalgamating them and applying the combined results to humor? The best way to proceed is by identifying the common interests.

One such interest, straight from the hottest-item menu on the humor-research agenda, is the analysis of long humorous texts. You may have noticed already that we analyzed linguistically a very short joke. This is what the linguistics of humor does well. Literary scholarship always focuses on long forms—and anything, even the shortest fable, is longer than a typical joke—but it does not have the theory or methodology for figuring out what makes a long text funny. A heroic attempt was made very early in the script-semantics invasion of humor research to interpret a short story as a sequence of jokes (Chlopicki 1987). Each such joke, of course, could be—and was—analyzed separately, and even some links among these consecutive jokes could be observed, such as repeating or mutually supportive script oppositions. Nevertheless, even the author of that brilliant study was left with a sense of underachievement: the sum of the jokes did not add up to the story.

This work is being followed up by Chlopicki himself as well as by Attardo, who is trying, in a book he is preparing, to utilize the battery of high-level linguistic pragmatic techniques, such as presuppositions, speech acts, Grice's cooperative principle, and implicatures, for linguistic analysis of long humorous texts. This work is quite exciting, but it is proceeding very slowly because the linguists are out of their turf there. They desperately need the help of literary scholars, with all of their knowledge and techniques of interpreting longer texts. Aren't literary scholars interested in that kind of joint endeavor? Aren't they interested in understanding what exactly makes a Mark Twain story funny on the humor-research side? If they are not, they should be, and the rapidly growing number of literary-studies submissions to *Humor: International Journal of Humor Research* may be seen as an indication that such cooperative, exciting, and mutually beneficial efforts may be just a few years down the road.

LINGUISTIC AND LITERARY THEORY

An even more intriguing and promising venue for linguistics-literature cooperation in the study of humor may lead to results that will have rather little to do with humor, and that is the interface between linguistic and literary theory. If this happens, an application of both disciplines to humor will "back-influence" the applied fields in a fundamental way.

The poststructuralists, deconstructionists, and postmodernists in literary criticism often invoke linguistics and linguistic theories in their writings. Since Derrida (see, for instance, 1976), these mentions have stricken hard-core linguists as much less than honorable: it is hard for a linguist to recognize his or her own field or to identify any of the quoted findings in linguistics from those writings. The frustrating result is mutual dismissal.

Now, if both these literary theories and linguistics find themselves dealing with the same humor material, it will emerge that linguistics uses semantic methodology that may underlie the process of deconstruction and, in fact, provide some "harder" methodology for it. Obviously, there are risks involved: an attempt to reinforce deconstruction methodologically may expose it as a primitive and highly tendentious form of semantic interpretation. On the other hand, to be fair, even if I don't believe a word that follows, perhaps deconstruction evokes a higher-rung linguistic knowledge that linguistics has yet failed to deliver. Such intertheory cooperation remains, nevertheless, a highly challenging and far-reaching goal, and progress in this direction, stimulated by joint humor research, may change the direction of both linguistics and literary studies and put them on a more converging course. Which must be good, no?

REFERENCES

Attardo, Salvatore. 1994. *Linguistic theories of humor*. Berlin: Mouton de Gruyter.

Attardo, Salvatore, and Victor Raskin. 1991. Script theory revis(it)ed: Joke similarity and joke representation model. *Humor* 4.3–4: 293–347.

Bergson, Henri. 1899. Le rire: Essai sur la signification du comique. *Revue de Paris*, February 1, February 15, and March 1. English translation in *Comedy*, ed. by Wylie Sypher, 59–190. Garden City, NY: Doubleday, 1956.

Chlopicki, Wladislaw. 1987. An application of the script theory of semantics to the analysis of selected Polish humorous short stories. M.A. thesis, Department of English, Purdue University, West Lafayette, IN.

Davies, Christie. 1990. *Ethnic humor around the world*. Bloomington: Indiana University Press.

Derrida, Jacques. 1976. *Of grammatology*. Baltimore: Johns Hopkins University Press.

Freud, Sigmund. 1905. *Der Witz und seine Beziehung zum Unbewussten*. Leipzig: Deutke. Translated as *Jokes and their relation to the unconscious*. New York: Norton, 1960.

Lewis, Paul. 1989. *Comic effects: Interdisciplinary approaches to humor in literature*. Albany: SUNY Press.

Mintz, Lawrence E. (ed.). 1988. *Humor in America*. Westport, CT: Greenwood Press.

Raskin, Victor. 1979. Semantic mechanisms of humor. *Proceedings of the fifth annual meeting of the Berkeley Linguistics Society*, ed by. C. Chiarello et al., 325–35. Berkeley: University of California Press.

———. 1985. *Semantic mechanisms of humor*. Dordrecht: D. Reidel.

Ruch, Willibald, Salvatore Attardo, and Victor Raskin. 1993. Towards an empirical verification of the general theory of verbal humor. *Humor* 6.2: 123–36.

Women and Men in Conversation
Deborah Tannen

I was addressing a small gathering in a suburban Virginia living room—a women's group that had invited men to join them. Throughout the evening, one man had been particularly talkative, frequently offering ideas and anecdotes, while his wife sat silently beside him on the couch. Toward the end of the evening, I commented that women frequently complain that their husbands don't talk to them. This man quickly concurred. He gestured toward his wife and said, "She's the talker in our family." The room burst into laughter; the man looked puzzled and hurt. "It's true," he explained. "When I come home from work I have nothing to say. If she didn't keep the conversation going, we'd spend the whole evening in silence."

This episode crystallizes the irony that although American men tend to talk more than women in public situations, they often talk less at home. And this pattern is wreaking havoc with marriage. The pattern was observed by political scientist Andrew Hacker in the late '70s. Sociologist Catherine Kohler Riessman reports in her book *Divorce Talk* that most of the women she interviewed—but only a few of the men—gave lack of communication as the reason for their divorces. Given the current divorce rate of nearly 50 percent, that amounts to millions of cases in the United States every year—a virtual epidemic of failed conversation.

In my own research, complaints from women about their husbands most often focused not on tangible inequities such as having given up the chance for a career to accompany a husband to his, or doing far more than their share of daily life-support work like cleaning, cooking, social arrangements and errands. Instead, they focused on communication: "He doesn't listen to me," "He doesn't talk to me." I found, as Hacker observed years before, that most wives want their husbands to be, first and foremost, conversational partners, but few husbands share this expectation of their wives. In short, the image that best represents the current crisis is the stereotypical cartoon scene of a man sitting at the breakfast table with a newspaper held up in front of his face, while a woman glares at the back of it, wanting to talk.

How can women and men have such different impressions of communication in marriage? Why the widespread imbalance in their interests and expectations? Stanford University's Eleanor Maccoby reports the results of her own and others' research showing that children's development is most influenced by the social structure of peer interactions. Boys and girls tend to play with children of their own gender, and their sex-separate groups have different organizational structures and interactive norms. I believe these systematic differences in childhood socialization make talk between women and men like cross-cultural communication, heir to all the attraction and pitfalls of that enticing but difficult enterprise. My research on men's and women's conversations uncovered patterns similar to those described for children's groups as summarized by Daniel Maltz and Ruth Borker.

For women, as for girls, intimacy is the fabric of relationships, and talk is the thread from which it is woven. Little girls create and maintain friendships by exchanging secrets; similarly, women regard conversation as the cornerstone of friendship. So a woman expects her husband to be a new and improved version of a best friend. What is important is not the individual subjects that are discussed but the sense of closeness, of a life shared, that emerges when people tell each other their thoughts, feelings, and impressions.

Bonds between boys can be as intense as girls', but they are based less on talking, more on doing things together. Since they don't assume talk is the cement that binds a relationship, many men don't know what kind of talk women want, and they don't miss it when it isn't there. Boys' groups are larger, more inclusive, and more hierarchical, so boys must struggle to avoid the subordinate position in the group. This may play a role in women's complaints that men don't listen to them. Some men really don't like to listen, because being the listener makes them feel one-down, like a child listening to adults or an employee to a boss.

But often when women tell men, "You aren't listening," and the men protest, "I am," the men are right. The impression of not listening results from misalignments in the mechanics of conversation. The misalignment begins as soon as a man and a woman take physical positions. This became clear when I studied videotapes of children and adults talking to their same-sex best friends. I found that at every age, the girls and women faced each other directly, their eyes anchored on each other's faces. At every age, the boys and men sat at angles to each other and looked elsewhere in the room, periodically glancing at each other. They were obviously attuned to each other, often mirroring each other's movements. But the tendency of men to face away can give women the impression they aren't listening even when they are. A young woman in one of my classes was frustrated: Whenever she told her boyfriend she wanted to talk to him, he would lie down on the floor, close his eyes, and put his arm over his face. This signaled to her, "He's taking a nap." But he insisted he was listening extra hard. Normally, he said, he looks around the room, so he is easily distracted. Lying down and covering his eyes helped him concentrate on what she was saying.

Analogous to the physical alignment that women and men take in conversation is their topical alignment. The girls in my study tended to talk at length about one topic, but the boys tended to jump from topic to topic. The second-grade girls exchanged stories about people they knew. The second-grade boys teased, told jokes, noticed things in the room and talked about finding games to play. The sixth-grade girls talked about problems with a mutual friend. The sixth-grade boys talked about 55 different topics, none of which extended over more than a few turns.

Switching topics is another habit that gives women the impression men aren't listening, especially if they switch to a topic about themselves. But the evidence of the 10th-grade boys in my study indicates otherwise. The 10th-grade boys sprawled across their chairs with bodies parallel and eyes straight ahead, rarely looking at each other. They looked as if they were riding in a car, staring out the windshield. But they were talking about their feelings. One boy was upset because a girl had told him he had a drinking problem, and the other was feeling alienated from all his friends. When a girl told a friend about a problem, the friend responded by asking probing questions and expressing agreement and understanding. But the boys dismissed each other's problems. Todd assured Richard that his drinking was "no big problem" because "sometimes you're funny when you're off your butt." And when Todd said he felt left out, Richard responded, "Why should you? You know more people than me." Many women perceive such responses as belittling and unsupportive. But the boys seemed satisfied with them. Whereas women reassure each other by implying, "You shouldn't feel bad because I've had similar experiences," men do so by implying, "You shouldn't feel bad because your problems aren't so bad."

There are even simpler reasons for women's impression that men don't listen. Linguist Lynette Hirschman found that women make more listener-noise, such as "mhm," "uhuh," and "yeah," to show "I'm with you." Men, she found, more often give silent attention. Women who expect a stream of listener noise interpret silent attention as no attention at all.

Women's conversational habits are as frustrating to men as men's are to women. Men who expect silent attention interpret a stream of listener noise as overreaction or impatience. Also, when women talk to each other in a close, comfortable setting, they often overlap, finish each other's sentences and anticipate what the other is about to say. This practice, which I call "participatory listenership," is often perceived by men as interruption, intrusion and lack of attention.

A parallel difference caused a man to complain about his wife, "She just wants to talk about her own point of view. If I show her another view, she gets mad at me." When most women talk to each other, they assume a conversationalist's job is to express agreement and support. But many men see their conversational duty as pointing out the other side of an argument. This is heard as disloyalty by women, and refusal to offer the requisite support. It is not that women don't want to see other points of view, but that they prefer them phrased as suggestions and inquiries rather than as direct challenges.

In his book *Fighting for Life*, Walter Ong points out that men use "agonistic" or warlike, oppositional formats to do almost anything; thus discussion becomes debate, and conversation a competitive sport. In contrast, women see conversation as a ritual means of establishing rapport. If Jane tells a problem and June says she has a similar one, they walk away feeling closer to each other. But this attempt at establishing rapport can backfire when used with men. Men often take too literally women's ritual "troubles talk," just as women often mistake men's ritual challenges for real attack.

These differences begin to clarify why women and men have such different expectations about communication in marriage. For women, talk creates intimacy. Marriage is an orgy of closeness: you can tell your feelings and thoughts, and still be loved. Their greatest fear is being pushed away. But men live in a hierarchical world, where talk maintains independence and status. They are on guard to protect themselves from being put down and pushed around.

This explains the paradox of the talkative man who said of his silent wife, "She's the talker." In the public setting of a guest lecture, he felt challenged to show his intelligence and display his understanding of the lecture. But at home, where he has nothing to prove and no one to defend against, he is free to remain silent. For his wife, being home means she is free from the worry that something she says might offend someone, or spark disagreement, or appear to be showing off; at home she is free to talk.

The communication problems that endanger marriage can't be fixed by mechanical engineering. They require a new conceptual framework about the role of talk in human relationships. Many of the psychological explanations that have become second nature may not be helpful, because they tend to blame either women (for not being assertive enough) or men (for not being in touch with their feelings). A sociolinguistic approach by which male-female conversation is seen as cross-cultural communication allows us to understand the problem and forge solutions without blaming either party.

Once the problem is understood, improvement comes naturally, as it did to the young woman and her boyfriend who seemed to go to sleep when she wanted to talk. Previously, she had accused him of not listening, and he had refused to change his behavior, since that would be admitting fault. But then she learned about and explained to him the differences in women's and men's habitual ways of aligning themselves in conversation. The next time she told him she wanted to talk, he began, as usual, by lying down and covering his eyes. When the familiar negative reaction bubbled up, she reassured herself that he really was listening. But then he sat up and looked at her. Thrilled, she asked why. He said, "You like me to look at you when we talk, so I'll try to do it." Once he saw their differences as cross-cultural rather than right and wrong, he independently altered his behavior.

Women who feel abandoned and deprived when their husbands won't listen to or report daily news may be happy to discover their husbands trying to adapt once they understand the place of small talk in women's relationships. But if their husbands don't adapt, the women may still be comforted that for men, this is not a failure of intimacy. Accepting the difference, the wives may look to their friends or family for that kind of talk. And husbands who can't provide it shouldn't feel their wives have made unreasonable demands. Some couples will still decide to divorce, but at least their decisions will be based on realistic expectations.

In these times of resurgent ethnic conflicts, the world desperately needs cross-cultural understanding. Like charity, successful cross-cultural communication should begin at home.

NOTE

© Deborah Tannen. Reprinted by special permission of the author.
This chapter was previously published under the title "Sex, Lies, and Conversation" in *The Washington Post*, June 24, 1990, Sunday, Final Edition. It is based on the author's book, *You Just Don't Understand: Women and Men in Conversation*.

REFERENCES

Hacker, Andrew. 1979. Divorce à la Mode. Rev. of Husbands and Wives: A Nationwide Survey of Marriage by Anthony Pietropinto and Jacqueline Simenauer. *The New York Review of Books*, May 3, 1979, p. 24.

Hirschman, Lynette. 1994. Female-male differences in conversational interaction. *Language in Society* 23:3, 427–442.

Maccoby, Eleanor. 1990. Gender and relationships: A developmental account. *American Psychologist* 45:4, 513–520.

Maltz, Daniel N., and Ruth A. Borker. 1982. A cultural approach to male-female miscommunication. *Language and social identity*, ed. by John J. Gumperz, 196–216. Cambridge: Cambridge University Press.

Ong, Walter J. 1981. *Fighting for life: Contest, sexuality, and consciousness*. Ithaca: Cornell University Press.
Riessman, Catherine Kohler. 1990. *Divorce talk: Women and men talk about divorce*. New Brunswick, NJ: Rutgers University Press.

Breaking Mythical Bonds: African American Women's Language

Denise Troutman

African American women of this century have found that they must repeatedly take on the words of Sojourner Truth to claim inalienable rights, whether or not they are related to economics, jobs, education, or, in the case of the present chapter, even language:

> Nobody eber helps me into carriages, or ober mud-puddles, or give me any best place. And Ar'n't I a woman? Look at me. Look at my arm. I have plowed and planted and gathered into barns, and no man could head me—and Ar'n't I a woman? I could work as much and eat as much as a man (when I could get it), and bear de lash as well—and A'r'n't I a woman? I have borne thirteen chillen, and seen 'em mos' all sold off into slavery, and when I cried out with a mother's grief, none but Jesus heard—and Ar'n't I a woman? (Mabee 1993, 76)

Here, Sojourner Truth expresses a conundrum still applicable to African American women today: exclusion. Just as Sojourner Truth was not considered "a woman" with regard to nineteenth-century women's suffrage because of her race, African American women still are not considered "women" as a result of their large omission in descriptions of "women's language." The 1990s have elucidated that there is no monolithic African American person or African American experience; the social construct of "woman" is not monolithic as well. Yet research conducted in the area of language and gender continues to establish monolithic womanism, failing to examine the interrelationship between language, gender, race, and class. Due to this failure, significantly as we enter into the twenty-first century,

African American women must still ask, "Ain't I a woman? Where is the perspective that considers my being?"

Although the language patterns of the African American speech community have been described, beginning in the late 1960s, even these descriptions have excluded African American women, focusing primarily on African American male speakers (see, e.g., Labov 1969, 1972; Kochman 1972; Smitherman 1977, 1994; Baugh 1983). Even Smitherman, my sister, the world-renowned African American English authority and author of the widely cited *Talkin and Testifyin* (1977), incorporates language samples generated primarily by African American male speakers. As Morgan (1991b) notes, African American women's linguistic data "are essential if we are to understand how the community expresses its reality, because women have historically been responsible for the language development of their children and therefore their community" (7).

This chapter is a response to a void in sociolinguistic studies. It examines the language patterns of African American women in twentieth-century conversational settings and in one film depiction, regardless of social class. Questions to be addressed in this chapter are these: Do African American women use the purported "women's style" of language? What features are distinctive for the African American speech community of women?

WOMEN AND LANGUAGE

Robin Lakoff was a professor of linguistics at Berkeley in 1973 when she first presented her ideas on "women's language" in a paper. Lakoff's publication of that paper, *Language and Woman's Place* (1975), created a "wave effect" in subsequent research conducted on women's language. She claimed not only that women and men use language differently, but also that such a difference stems from their assignment to particular cultural roles, subservient roles for women and crucial roles for men. Thus Lakoff identified features of women's language very similar to those identified by Jespersen (1922), yet Lakoff's rationale for such differences went beyond ad hominem arguments or blaming women for apparent innate illogicality. Women, Lakoff argued, use a trivial, weak style because they have been socialized into trivial, weak cultural and political roles. Lakoff asserted that particular linguistic features (see table 17.1) descriptive of and restricted in use to women alone establish a separate "women's language," which is evident, at least in English, at all levels of the grammar. Specific lexical and syntactic items (for example, women use specific words to denote colors, *aquamarine* versus *blue*; also, women use specific types of sentence structures, such as tag questions, "That program was interesting, wasn't it?"), among others, both describe women's use of language and are restricted to use by women.

Although Lakoff advanced the idea of a distinct women's language and even though subsequent scholarship has affirmed that differences exist be-

Table 17.1
A Partial List of Features Characterized as "Women's Language"

Polite, cheerful intonational levels

Rising intonation on statements

Prestigious linguistic variables (- *ing* versus- *in*; postvocalic *r*)

Vocabulary reflective of women's spheres of existence: sewing, housework, cooking, childrearing

"Empty" adjectives ("precious," "cute," "sweet")

Hedges ("you know," "kinda," "sorta," "well")

Intensifiers ("so," "so much," "such")

Tag questions ("That was a good movie, wasn't it?")

Superpolite forms ("Would you mind closing the door?") (Lakoff 1975, 1990; Coates 1986)

tween women's and men's language, the latter work finds that those differences are quantitative, not qualitative; sex-preferential tendencies exist (where one gender tends to use certain forms more frequently than the other), not sex-exclusive differences (Cameron 1990; Coates 1986; O'Barr and Atkins 1980; Thorne and Henley 1975a).

Despite the twenty-three-year research track established for women and language studies, researchers have viewed the construct "woman" with myopic vision. African American women researchers have begun to point out that existent descriptions have focused mainly on European American middle-class women, excluding the voices and experiences of other women. Houston Stanback (1985b), in fact, titled one of her papers "Language and Black Woman's Place," conveying clearly the omission of African American women as a speech community from research on language and gender. Thorne and Henley noted in 1975 that "whole areas of study . . . have been virtually untouched, for example, the communication patterns of all-female groups, and of populations other than the white, middle class" (1975a, 30). West, Lazar, and Kramarae made this same point twenty-two years later in their 1997 publication "Gender in Discourse": "Much of what we 'know' about gender and discourse is really about white, middle-class, heterosexual women and men using English in Western societies. Studies like Etter-Lewis's (1991a), Goodwin's (1990) . . . and Nichols's (1983) [which focus on African American females] are the exceptions, rather than the rule" (137).

AFRICAN AMERICAN WOMEN AND LANGUAGE

In language samples collected and in conversations observed, I have found similarities and differences in African American and European American women's language. African American women use some of the same features indicated by the data for European American women, as listed in table 17.1. Specifically, they use polite, cheerful intonational levels, "empty" adjectives ("precious," "cute," "sweet"), hedges ("you know," "kinda," "sorta," "well"), and intensifiers ("so," "so much," "such"). Also, their conversational style is marked by collaborative and supportive exchanges, as already documented in the literature on "women's language." Tannen (1990), for example, discusses differing conversational styles for women and men in *You Just Don't Understand*. According to her, collaborative and supportive exchanges occur between women engaged in conversation, in contradistinction to hierarchical and competitive exchanges of men engaged in conversation (although men and women may use other conversational strategies also).

The transcription in language sample 1 demonstrates one example of the collaboration and support that occur among African American women in their conversations (see the Appendix to this chapter for an explanation of the transcription notations). Two African American women who have established a long-term friendship hold an informal conversation without interference from the researcher or others. The women discuss African American men in this conversation:

(1) Example of Supportive Speech

Dee: Am I right Leslie?

Leslie: You're right absolutely

Dee: Am I right ⌐

Leslie: ⌊ Yeah absolutely ⌐

Dee: ⌊Take for
           instance (2.4) Who can we take for instance

Leslie: Black man aren't happy with ((???))

Dee: They really   ⌐ aren't

Leslie: ⌊ The majority of them aren't = I'm not gonna
           say all Black men 'cause there are a few ⌐

Dee: ⌊ that are ⌐

Leslie: ⌊ that are⌐

Dee: ⌊ you
           right

Leslie: It ain't a whole **lot** now ⌐

Dee: ⌊ you right

The language sample in (1) shows the two women supporting each other's contributions and collaborating in the construction of the conversation. Dee seeks support for an assertion that she has made, which Leslie provides readily in the form of confirmation. Not only does Leslie agree with Dee's assertion verbally, but she also shows support through a conversational device calling latching. When Dee asks if she is right the second time ("Am I right"), Leslie latches Dee's speaking turn (indicated by a Z-shaped symbol). Latches, in this conversation, signify support since one speaker takes a speaking turn without interrupting or overlapping a conversational partner, allowing the partner a full and rightful turn at speaking. Thus Leslie shows support through her words ("You're right absolutely"; "Yeah absolutely") and through her timing in producing the second response, speaking precisely at the end of Dee's question. Dee reciprocates the support, latching Leslie's "Yeah absolutely" and confirming Leslie's statements with "You right."

The conversation displays collaboration through the co-construction of dialogue. In one instance, Leslie helps Dee construct a topic for discussion when Dee appears at a loss for ideas ("Who can we take for instance"). Here, competition (as one possible type of interaction) does not arise, yet cooperation occurs. Dee seeks help and receives it. Further, Dee acts on Leslie's suggested topic by responding to it ("They really aren't"), which shows acceptance and support for Leslie's contribution. In a second instance, Dee "puts words in Leslie's mouth" ("that are") without intruding on Leslie's speaking turn. Here, the two women engage in the conversational exchange as if playing instruments in a musical duet.

To sum up, this analysis of a real conversation documents that there are similarities between African and European American women's speech behavior. Members of both speech communities collaborate and give support during conversations. Data that I have analyzed from Spike Lee's *Jungle Fever* show that African American women's language is different also.

CHARACTERISTICS OF AFRICAN AMERICAN WOMEN'S LANGUAGE

African American women researchers, for example, Houston Stanback (1985b), Morgan (1991a), and Troutman (1995, 1996), have identified features of African American women's language (hereafter AAWL) not discussed previously in work on women's language. Some features of AAWL include "smart talk" (Houston Stanback 1985b), reading dialect (one form of signifying; Morgan 1996), culturally toned diminutives (Troutman 1996), assertiveness (Houston Stanback 1985b; Troutman 1995), diminutives and use of African American English (hereafter AAE) (Etter-Lewis 1991), and performance (Foster 1995). Only four of these features receive attention here.

Smart Talk

Houston Stanback coined the term and discussed the use of "smart talk." Based on her derivation, "smart talk" is an umbrella term encompassing a number of features of AAWL, not all of which have been identified or described, as of yet, in scholarly work. Signifying is one example of "smart talk." Within the African American speech community, signifying is a *game* of verbal wit. Smitherman (1977), the internationally known scholar on AAE, defines signifying as an indirect form of ritualized insult in which "a speaker puts down, talks about, needles—signifies on—the listener" (118). Signifying, in other regions of the United States, may also be referred to as "soundin," "cappin," "siggin," or "joanin" (Smitherman 1977, 119). Clearly, the word *signify* within the African American speech community has a specific historical origin and derivational meaning that varies from the broader speech community's use of the word. African Americans have taken this word and applied their own definition. Smitherman attaches the following characteristics to signifying (van Dijk et al. 1997, 151):

indirection, circumlocution

metaphors, . . . images rooted in the everyday real world

humor, irony

rhythmic fluency

"teachy" but not "preachy"

directness with respect to person(s) present in the speech situation (signifiers do not talk behind your back)

puns, word-play

For example, Mitchell-Kernan (1972) engages in signifying with a young man in his early twenties. Two other young men of the same age group are present also (323):

Young man:	Mama, you sho is fine.
Mitchell-Kernan:	That ain't no way to talk to your mother.
	(Laughter)
Young man:	You married?
Mitchell-Kernan:	Um hm.
Young man:	Is your husband married?
	(Laughter)

Here, signifying occurs due to the indirection of the discourse and the implied meaning. First of all, Mitchell-Kernan picks up on the young man's use of "Mama," basing her comment on the premise that "if I am your mama, that is no way to talk to her" ("That ain't no way to talk to your mother.") The group enjoys Mitchell-Kernan's repartee (as the pause for laughter indicates) because it is clever and because she plays right along with the young man, showing her mental agility. The young man fires back with the question "You married?" After Mitchell-Kernan responds ("Um hm"), the young man now scores a point with the question, "Is your husband married?" Here again, indirection occurs. The young man accepts Mitchell-Kernan's "um hm" reply that she is married, yet he queries more importantly whether Mitchell-Kernan's husband accepts, believes, and behaves as though he is married. (Touché!) The young man shows great skill in signifying with this witty response. Significantly here, none of the conversationalists get angry, not even the researcher. The exchange ends in laughter because the participants know that a game has been played for fun.

Reading Dialect

"Reading dialect" (Morgan 1996) is another form of language use that fits under "smart talk." Morgan borrows one portion of her phrase from the broader African American speech community. To "read someone" means to denigrate a person verbally because of some inappropriate action or words. Less commonly used expressions within the African American speech community are "She read him" or "Who you trying to read?" In contrast to the broader U.S. speech community, this application of reading is negative for the African American speech community because "to read someone" means that pages to person B's life are opened (or attempted to be opened) by person A in an explosive manner with the goal of exposing information that hearers may not be privy to. The act is an insulting one.

According to Morgan (1996), reading dialect is a means of contrasting two dialects, specifically, AAE and American English (AE), through the use of words, sentences, or discourse structures in order to signify on that person. Since AAE and AE have some words, grammar rules, sentences, and discourse features that are similar, speakers select one dialect or the other due to a distinct feature that it possesses in order to communicate an unambiguous point and most importantly to "read" a conversational partner. Thus Morgan (by a device called semantic extension) extrapolates the use of "reading someone" to "reading dialect."

For example, speaker B, in a particular situation where speaker A has extended a greeting using AE, has a number of choices to select from in responding to the greeting. Two possible choices are "How are you doing?" (AE) or "Whazzup?" (AAE). In order to convey a point (perhaps of dissatisfaction or power), speaker B, in this exchange, consciously selects the second choice, greeting speaker A with "Whazzup?" In this instance, Speaker B "reads dialect."

Among African American women, a common way of reading dialect is through use of the expression, "Miss Thang." During a conversation, one speaker may want to "read" another person due to the latter's inappropriate behavior. In order to communicate dissatisfaction, then, the first person may refer to the targeted receiver as "Miss Thang": "We were doing alright until Miss Thang decided she didn't want to go along with the program." In this instance, the first person "reads dialect" using AAE, communicating a negative point about the targeted receiver. The expression "Miss Thang" within African American women's speech community is a direct put down of a targeted receiver. The broader African American speech community, as well as the African American women's speech community, interprets *thang* negatively since a thing is an object, lacking an identity and other human qualities. (Smitherman and Troutman-Robinson 1998, 65)

Assertiveness

Houston Stanback (1985b) was the first scholar to claim that African American women communicate in an assertive, outspoken way just as African American men do, partially because of African American women's work in public spheres. African American women, however, must curtail their outspokenness as a result of community standards, which allow assertiveness only to a particular point for women, Houston Stanback explains. (Perhaps this restriction has historically given rise to the African American expression "Don't be so womanish." Or the restriction may be a product of African American women's code of feminine politeness, established through historical and social exigencies.)

In an analysis of the discourse style of Anita Hill during the Hill-Thomas Senate Judiciary Committee hearing, I found that Hill used an assertive style when under fire from Senator Arlen Specter (Troutman 1995). Hill interrupted Specter more often than the reverse, used syllogistic reasoning more skillfully than Specter (thus winning more verbal bouts), and used more latches (again, a turn-taking mechanism that occurs at the end of a conversational partner's turn, avoiding interrupting or overlapping a conversational partner's speech.) Latches, in the Hill-Specter analysis, conveyed readiness on Hill's part of "setting the record straight." Two examples demonstrate Hill's assertive style. Language sample 2 shows latching, while language sample 3 shows Hill's skill in quick reasoning (syllogistic argumentation):

(2) **Example of Assertiveness through Latching**

Specter: His words are that you said quote the most
           laudatory comments unquote. ⌐

Hill: ⌐ I have no
           response to that because I don't know exactly
           what he is saying.

(3) Example of Assertiveness through Quick Reasoning

Specter: Well (.) I'll repeat the question again.
          Was there any substance in Ms. Berry's **flat**
          statement that (.) quote (.) Ms. Hill was
          disappointed and frustrated that Mr. Thomas did not
          show any sexual interest in her?

Hill: No (.) there is not. There is no substance
          to that. He did show interest and I've
          explained to you how he did show that interest.
          (.) Now (.) she was not aware of that. If
          you're asking me (.) Could she have made that
          statement. (.) She could have made the
          statement if she wasn't aware of it. (.) But she
          wasn't aware of everything that happened.

Performance

Foster (1995) defines performance as "a special kind of communicative event in which there is a particular relationship among stylized material, performer, and audience" (333). Based on her collected data in a community-college classroom, Foster essentially found instances of teacher and student interactions that actively communicated the teaching point. Performances, in Foster's analysis, served as a different instructional vehicle. Instead of lecturing to convey salient points, the African American female teacher "performed" the teaching point, with students assisting in the construction of the performance. Foster gave the example that follows. The instructor of the course in which Foster collected data wanted to make sure that her class understood, realistically, what a budget is, and she uses performance to clarify the concept (335):

Instructor: you have a master plan to beat this economic system?

Student: no not yet (laughs)

Instructor: well, that's what a budget is

Student: I was referring to budgeting money to for payin' the bills runnin'
           my my house

Teacher: unhuh that's a budget

           . . .

           somebody else who wanna share their ideas about budget I want
           to make sure everybody understands what a budget is before we
           go on yes, Miss Goins

Both the teacher and the students constructed a performance of the teaching point in the example. Instead of giving a "liturgical" definition of the word *budget*, the instructor opted for a more concrete method of defining budget;

thus she engaged her students in a co-constructed performance of the word. They performed (or enacted) the meaning of budget. According to Foster, "A teacher was most likely to 'break into performance' when attempting to clarify a concept that students had encountered in a text or a lecture" (334). Performing essentially enabled the instructor to make concepts concrete.

In my study of the social construction of African American women's language and the analysis of films, specifically Spike Lee's *Jungle Fever*, all four features of African American women's language occurred, as identified by the researchers previously cited. To examine these occurrences more closely, I present one sample of the language along with its context in sample 4; then I present a discussion of each feature.

The conversational exchange in (4) takes place in a "soul food" restaurant. The lead character, Flipper (Wesley Snipes), has had an affair with an Italian American woman, Angie (Annabella Sciorra), his temporary secretary at an advertising firm. Flipper pursues the relationship with Angie, taking her out to dinner. In this scene, the restaurant is filled primarily with African American customers and serviced by African American employees. The waitress for Flipper and Angie's table has not waited on the couple, although thirty minutes have passed and although customers around them have received service. Flipper finally hails down the approaching waitress:

(4) Language Sample from *Jungle Fever*

Flipper: Excuse me Miss (.) Miss (.) may we order please.

Waitress: ((Walks over to table calmly; avoids eye contact; uses a low, calm tone of voice)) Yes (.) may I take your order.

Flipper: Is this your station?

Waitress: Yes ((establishes eye contact with Flipper)) this is my station (.) unfortunately ((looks down to write on ticketing pad; bats eyes))

Flipper: Look (.) you can take my order (.) matter of fact ((pointing finger)) you could've taken my order thirty minutes ago when I sat my black ass ⌜in this chair.

Waitress: ((Looks at Angie))   ⌞Can I take **your** order?

Angie: ((Surprised and speechless; stares back at waitress))

Flipper: ((Jumps in)) Excuse me (1.0) uhm do you have a problem?

Waitress: Yes (.) I do have a problem to be honest with you (1.0) Fake (.) tired brothers like you coming in heah. Dass so typical.
           . . .

Flipper: Let me tell you something (.) first of all Miss Al
           Sharpton (.)   ⌜you don't have (.)

Waitress: ⌞Why don't you pa:rade (0.1)

Flipper: It's not your busi ⌐ness (0.1)   ⌐who I bring in
        here   │   │

Waitress: └Why don't you parade (0.1) └your white friend
        somewhere else okay?

Flipper: It's not your business (.) you are a waitress (.) your job is to **wait**.

Waitress: (0.3) ((Resumes soft, calm tone; goes into a routine recitation.
        Looks up, rolls eyes, looks down at pad)) Today's specials are
        the Maryland crabcakes (.) Creole shrimp (.) gumbo and
        blackened catfish (.) ((speaks to Flipper, directly)) I suggest
        you have the **blackened** catfish.

The discussion that follows focuses primarily on the language used by the African American waitress. In the backdrop of the scene, the waitress, played by Queen Latifah, has obviously summed up the situation with Flipper and Angie; as a result, she makes a conscious decision not to give them service. Spike Lee captures the avoidance behavior of the waitress before any conversational exchange occurs. The waitress is shown serving customers at a nearby table, graciously and contentedly giving information and taking orders. Angie conveys exasperation nonverbally as the waitress walks away from their seated area to take care of other food orders, yet Angie does not voice her exasperation, partially because of the territory that she is in. Flipper continues with small talk, yet the next time the waitress passes their area, he gets her attention ("Excuse me Miss (.) Miss (.) may we order please.")

In language sample 4, the waitress demonstrates adeptness in language usage as gauged by African American standards. Quick-wittedness, humor, and spontaneous and apt retorts are marks of superior verbal acuity within the African American speech community. The waitress measures up to these standards superbly.

Performance occurs twice, as a result of obligatory behavior. Once the waitress is called upon in her official capacity, she carries out her duties perfunctorily. She performs, hiding her true feelings and speaking initially in a very calm and controlled tone of voice: "Yes (.) may I take your order." The waitress, in fact, gives the impression that she is ready to "take care of business." She is compelled to perform because this is her station, this is her job, and she does have an obligation to serve customers in her area. In order to fulfill her obligations, although she does not like the idea of a "brother" bringing a European American woman into African American territory, the waitress performs as though no problem exists: "((Walks over to table calmly; avoids eye contact; uses a low, calm tone of voice)) Yes (.) may I take your order." Her tone suggests humility, yet that suggestion is short-lived. Flipper's next question ("Is this your station?") brings out an element of "smart talk" (discussed later), and the first performance ends.

The second instance of performance occurs following a combative exchange. After the waitress and Flipper hurl invective, she temporarily resumes her duties of waitressing, aloofly: "Today's specials are the Maryland crabcakes (.) Creole shrimp (.) gumbo and blackened catfish." Performance occurs here because the waitress again puts on an act, performing as a gentle, acquiescent server, indicated by her tone, volume, and behavior. She assumes a calm tone, routinely reciting the day's specials. She puts on an act that things are okay and business can proceed. The waitress does not bite her tongue for long, though. Before this speaking turn is over, "smart talk" occurs a second time: "I suggest you have the **blackened** catfish."

Fear of repercussions does not appear to stop the waitress from responding "smartly." Although in both instances of "smart talk" she initially holds her peace, shortly thereafter she asserts her position directly and boldly, regardless of jeopardizing her job or conceivably her life:

Flipper: Is this your station?

Waitress: Yes ((establishes eye contact with Flipper)) this is my station

→ (.) unfortunately.

. . .

Waitress: (0.3) ((Resumes soft, calm tone; goes into a routine recitation. Looks up, rolls eyes, looks down at pad)) Today's specials are the Maryland crabcakes (.) Creole shrimp (.) gumbo and blackened catfish (.) ((Speaks to Flipper, directly))

→ I suggest you have the **blackened** catfish.

The word "unfortunately," included as part of the answer, demonstrates an instance of "smart talk" since the waitress gives an answer that does not suit her position (she is accountable to the customers whom she serves and is expected to watch her behavior, including her language). Within the African American community, children and youth typically are warned about using "smart talk." Grandmothers, mothers, and aunts train the young folk in this mode of discourse: those instances when particular speech behavior amounts to "smart talk," when speech treads too closely to being "smart talk," when young folks should avoid "smart talk," and even when "smart talk" may be used appropriately. The waitress knows these rules of the speech community and violates the usage in order to communicate her point.

During the second use of "smart talk," the waitress appears not to be concerned about fulfilling her tasks. She has conveyed her disapproval of Flipper's actions prior to this exchange and does not "cease and desist." She again boldly communicates her feelings ("I suggest you have the **black-**

ened catfish"). The emphasis on the word "blackened" seems to suggest that Flipper is African American superficially, only on the outside.

Finally, the waitress "reads" Flipper, switching from AE to AAE. She only stops at Flipper and Angie's table because she is called upon. This action pulls her into an obligatory performance of her duties, which she performs (although perfunctorily) using AE. When asked if she has a problem, the waitress "reads" Flipper his "rights," according to her law:

Flipper: ((Jumps in)) Excuse me (1.0) uhm do you have a problem?

Waitress: Yes (.) I do have a problem to be honest with you (1.0)

→   Fake (.) tired brothers like you coming in heah. Dass so typical.

Here, the waitress "reads dialect" by signifying on Flipper and by using phonological and lexical AAE features. Indirectly, she puts Flipper down; she does not say directly, "You are fake and tired." Instead, she signifies by associating him with other brothers who are fake and tired. "Reading dialect" occurs phonologically with "that" pronounced as "dass" and "here" pronounced as "heah." Also, the waitress uses lexical items (words) specific to the African American speech community:

tired: noncontributing African Americans; individuals who take re-
            sources away from the community instead of giving to and
            building the community

brothers: African American males collectively, who are not necessarily
            blood related

Even though the language sample in (4) occurred in a film, one produced, directed, and written by a male, the language represented there for African American women has social reality, especially as legitimated by the research on African American women's language.

CONCLUSION

This chapter documents the language patterns of African American women in particular, because study of their language usage has been omitted within sociolinguistic research. The language samples included here help to answer the two questions posed earlier. African American women use some of the features labeled as "women's language," situating them within the broader, generalized construct of "woman." They also use features of language not identified previously as used by African American men or women in general. These linguistic features reflect the social construct of "African American woman."

APPENDIX: TRANSCRIPTION NOTATIONS

(1)   Numbers in parentheses preceding the transcribed text indicate examples.

(1.2)   Numbers in parentheses within the transcribed text indicate silences in seconds
             and tenths of seconds.

(.)   A period enclosed in parentheses marks silences that were too short to time
             precisely.

⌐   A large Z-shaped symbol shows that latching occurs; little or no gap occurs
└   between the end of the current speaker's turn and the beginning of the next
             speaker's turn.

[A left bracket indicates overlapped speech; the next speaker begins a turn prior
└   to the end of the current speaker's turn.

=   An equals sign shows that there was no silence or pause discernible within one
             speaker's utterances.

.   A period indicates falling intonation, not grammar.

?   A question mark indicates rising intonation, not grammar.

bold   Boldfaced letters show emphasis, conveyed either by increased volume or pitch
             changes.

:   A colon marks the lengthening of the sound it follows.

(( ))   Double parentheses relay transcriber comments, not transcribed text. ((???)),
             for example, indicates indecipherable language for the transcriber.

→   An arrow marks a key example of the feature under discussion.

REFERENCES

Baugh, John. 1983. *Black street speech*. Austin: University of Texas Press.

Cameron, Deborah, ed. 1990. *The feminist critique of language*. New York: Rout-
        ledge.

Coates, Jennifer. 1986. *Women, men, and language: A sociolinguistic account of
        sex differences in language*. New York: Longman.

Etter-Lewis, Gwendolyn. 1991a. African American women's legacy. *Discourse &
        Society*, 2(4): 425–437.

———. 1991b. Black women's life stories: Reclaiming self in narrative texts.
        Women's words: The feminist practice of oral history, ed. by Sherna Berger
        Gluck and Daphne Patai, 43–58. New York: Routledge.

———. 1993. *My soul is my own: Oral narratives of African American women in
        the professions*. New York: Routledge.

Foster, Michele. 1995. "Are you with me?": Power and solidarity in the discourse
        of African American women. *Gender articulated: Language and the socially
        constructed self*, ed. by Kira Hall and Mary Bucholtz, 329–350. New York:
        Routledge.

Giddings, Paula. 1984. *When and where I enter: The impact of Black women on
        race and sex in America*. New York: William Morrow and Co.

Goodwin, Marjorie Harness. 1990. *He-said-she-said: Talk as social organization among Black children.* Bloomington: Indiana University Press.

———. 1993. Tactical uses of stories: Participation frameworks within girls' and boys' disputes. *Gender and conversational interaction*, ed. by D. Tannen, 110–143. New York: Oxford University Press.

Hill, Alette Olin. 1986. *Mother tongue, father time: A decade of linguistic revolt.* Bloomington: Indiana University Press.

Houston, Marsha. 1997. When Black women talk with White women: Why dialogues are difficult. *Our voices: Essays in culture, ethnicity, and communication*, ed. by Alberto Gonzalez, Marsha Houston, and Victoria Chen, 2nd ed., 133–139. Los Angeles: Roxbury.

Houston Stanback, Marsha. 1985a. Black women's talk across cultures. Paper presented to the Speech Communication Association, Denver, Colorado.

———. 1985b. Language and Black woman's place: Evidence from the Black middle class. *For alma mater: Theory and practice in feminist scholarship*, ed. by P. A. Treichler et al., 177–193. Urbana: University of Illinois Press.

Jespersen, Otto. 1922. The Woman. *Language: Its nature, development and origin*, 237–254. London: George Allen and Unwin Ltd.

Kochman, Thomas, ed. 1972. *Rappin' and stylin' out.* Urbana: University of Illinois Press.

Labov, William. 1969. The logic of non-standard English. *Linguistic-cultural differences and American education.* Special edition of the *Florida Foreign Language Reporter* (Spring/Summer).

———. 1972. *Language in the inner city.* Philadelphia: University of Pennsylvania Press.

Lakoff, Robin. 1975. *Language and woman's place.* New York: Octagon Books.

———. 1990. *Talking power: The politics of language in our lives.* New York: Basic Books.

Mabee, Carleton. 1993. *Sojourner Truth: Slave, prophet, legend.* New York: New York University Press.

Mitchell-Kernan, Claudia. 1972. Signifying, loud-talking, and marking. *Rappin' and stylin' out*, ed. by Thomas Kochman, 315–335. Urbana: University of Illinois Press.

Morgan, Marcyliena. 1989. From down south to up south: The language behavior of three generations of Black women residing in Chicago. Ph.D. dissertation, University of Pennsylvania.

———. 1991a. Indirectness and interpretation in African American women's discourse. *Pragmatics* 1.4: 421–52.

———. 1991b. Language and communication style among African American women. *UCLA Center for the Study of Women Newsletter* 7 (Spring): 13.

———. 1996. Conversational signifying: Grammar and indirectness among African American women. *Interaction and grammar*, ed. by Elinor Ochs, Emanuel Schegloff, and Sandra Thompson, 405–434. Cambridge: Cambridge University Press.

O'Barr, William, and Bowman Atkins. 1980. "Women's Language" or "Powerless Language." *Women and Language in Literature and Society*; ed. by Sally McConnell-Ginet, Ruth Borker, and Nelly Furman, 93–110. New York: Praeger.

Nelson, Linda Williamson. 1990. Code-Switching in the Oral Life Narratives of African-American women: Challenges to Linguistic Hegemony. *Journal of Education* Vol. 172 (3): 142–155.

Nichols, Patricia. 1983. Linguistic options and choices for Black women in the rural South. *Language, Gender and Society*; edited by Barrie Thorne, Cheris Kramarae, and Nancy Henley, 54–68. Boston, MA: Heinle and Heinle Publishers.

Penelope, Julia. 1990. *Speaking freely: Unlearning the lies of the fathers' tongues.* New York: Pergamon Press.

Smitherman, Geneva. 1977. *Talkin and testifyin: The language of Black America.* Boston: Houghton Mifflin.

———. 1994. *Black talk: Words and phrases from the hood to the amen corner.* Boston: Houghton Mifflin.

Smitherman, Geneva, and Denise Troutman-Robinson. 1998. Black women's language. *The reader's companion to U.S. women's history*, ed. by Wilma Mankiller, Gwendolyn Mink, Marysa Navarro, Barbara Smith, and Gloria Steinem. 65–66. Boston: Houghton Mifflin.

Tannen, Deborah. 1990. *You just don't understand.* New York: William Morrow and Co.

———. 1993. The relativity of linguistic strategies: Rethinking power and solidarity in gender and dominance. *Gender and conversational interaction*, ed. by D. Tannen, 165–188. New York: Oxford University Press.

Thorne, Barrie, and Nancy Henley. 1975a. Difference and dominance: An overview of language, gender, and society. *Language and sex: Difference and dominance*, ed. by Barrie Thorne and Nancy Henley, 5–42. Rowley, MA.: Newbury House Publishers.

———. eds. 1975b. *Language and sex: Difference and dominance.* Rowley, MA: Newbury House Publishers.

Troutman, Denise. 1996. Culturally toned diminutives within the speech community of African American women. *Journal of Commonwealth and Postcolonial Studies* 4.1 (Fall): 55–64.

Troutman-Robinson, Denise. 1995. Tongue and sword: Which is master? *African American women speak out on Anita Hill–Clarence Thomas*, ed. by G. Smitherman, 208–223. Detroit: Wayne State University Press.

van Dijk, Teun, Stella Ting-Toomey, Geneva Smitherman, and Denise Troutman. 1997. Discourse, ethnicity, culture, and racism. *Discourse as social interaction*, ed. by Teun A. van Dijk, 144–180. London: Sage Publications.

West, Candace, Michelle Lazar, and Cheris Kramarae. 1997. Gender in discourse. *Discourse as social interaction*, ed. by Teun A. van Dijk, 119–143. London: Sage Publications.

Index

About the Editor and Contributors

BAS AARTS is Senior Lecturer in English Language and Director of the Survey of English Usage at University College London. He has published books and articles on English syntax, both from a descriptive and theoretical point of view, including *Small Clauses in English: The Nonverbal Types* (1992) and *The Verb in Contemporary English: Theory and Description* (edited with Charles F. Meyer, 1995). His most recent publication is *English Syntax and Argumentation* (1997). With David Denison and Richard Hogg at the University of Manchester, he edits the journal *English Language and Linguistics*, founded in 1995. He has lectured at a number of foreign universities.

COLLEEN COTTER is an Assistant Professor at Georgetown University, dividing her time between the Department of Linguistics and the Communication, Culture, and Technology (CCT) master's program. She is currently completing a book on news discourse from the perspective of the community of practitioners, provisionally entitled *Making News: An Ethnographic Approach to Language and the Media*. She has also done research on the use of broadcast media to promote minority- or endangered-language development, focusing primarily on the case in Ireland.

DAVID CRYSTAL is Honorary Professor of Linguistics at the University of Wales, Bangor. Formerly Professor of Linguistics at the University of Reading, he now works from his home in Holyhead, North Wales, as a writer, editor, lecturer, and broadcaster. His authored works are mainly in the field of language, including *The Cambridge Encyclopedia of Language* and *The Cambridge Encyclopedia of the English Language*. He was founder-editor of the *Journal of Child Language, Child Language Teaching and Therapy*, and *Linguistics Abstracts* and has edited several book series, such as Penguin Linguistics and Blackwell's Language Library. He is also the editor of several general encyclopedias.

BETHANY K. DUMAS has taught linguistics courses as an Associate Professor of English at the University of Tennessee at Knoxville since 1974. Prior to joining the faculty at UTK, Dumas had taught at Trinity University (San Antonio), Southern University, and Southwest Missouri State University. Dumas received her J.D. degree from the University of Tennessee College of Law in 1985, her Ph.D. in English linguistics from the University of Arkansas in 1971, and her B.A. in English from Lamar University in 1959. She edits an electronic journal of language and law, *Language and the Judicial Process* <*http://ljp.la.utk.edu*>. She is currently completing a textbook on American English dialects and is conducting research on warning labels.

GILLES FAUCONNIER, trained in mathematics, philosophy, languages, science, and engineering, received his Ph.D. in linguistics in 1971 from the University of California at San Diego (UCSD). He served as Professor and Chair of the Department of Language Sciences at the University of Paris VIII and as Directeur d'Etudes at the Ecole des Hautes Etudes en Sciences Sociales in Paris. From 1981 to 1984 Fauconnier was Chair of the Graduate Program in Linguistics and Language Sciences at the Ecole, and from 1986 to 1988, he was Director of the C.E.L.I.T.H. Research Center. He was invited to present his work on cognitive domains and mental spaces in Italy, Brazil, Morocco, the United States, and Belgium. At the invitation of Umberto Eco, he and Philip Johnson-Laird were featured at Eco's lecture and discussion series on mental spaces and mental models in San Marino. Since 1993, Fauconnier, in collaboration with Mark Turner, has explored the general cognitive process of conceptual integration and blending. His latest book is *Mappings in Thought and Language*. Fauconnier is presently, or has been, on the consulting editorial boards of *Cognition, Cognitive Science, Cognitive Linguistics, Journal of Semantics, Linguistic Inquiry, Linguisticae Investigationes, Linguistics and Philosophy, Recherches Linguistiques*, and *Semantikos*. He is a coeditor of the book series *Cognitive Theory of Language and Culture*. Gilles Fauconnier currently serves as Chair of the Department of Cognitive Science at UCSD.

GEORGE LAKOFF is Professor of Linguistics at the University of California at Berkeley. He is the author of *Metaphors We Live By* (with Mark Johnson); *Women, Fire, and Dangerous Things: What Categories Reveal about the Mind; More Than Cool Reason: A Field Guide to Poetic Metaphor* (with Mark Turner); *Moral Politics: What Conservatives Know That Liberals Don't*; and *Philosophy in the Flesh: The Embodied Mind and Its*

Challenge to Western Thought (with Mark Johnson). He is now completing *Where Mathematics Comes From: How the Embodied Mind Creates Mathematics* (with Rafael Nunez).

LYNN S. MESSING has held a postdoctoral research fellowship with the Gesture and Movement Dynamics Laboratory of the University of Delaware and the Alfred I. duPont Hospital for Children. Messing currently teaches computer courses at Delaware Technical Community College. She received her bachelor's degree in computer science from the Pennsylvania State University and earned her doctorate in linguistics at the University of Delaware. She has coedited *Gesture, Speech, and Sign*, a book on the relationships among gesture and spoken and signed languages. She is also working on projects involving computer sign recognition and synthesis.

RAE A. MOSES teaches linguistics and women's studies at Northwestern University. Her work concerns how our social identity is represented by the ways we use language. In her teaching she is especially keen to present the applications of linguistics to real-world activities, especially for nonlinguists, in courses like Language and Medicine, Language and Prejudice, Language and Gender, and Language and Social Policy.

SALIKOKO S. MUFWENE is Professor and Chair in the Department of Linguistics at the University of Chicago. He has published several studies on the morphosyntax of Gullah and African American English, but most of his research of the past decade has been on the development of creoles and other contact-language varieties. He is associated with the "complementary hypothesis" of creole genesis and is currently developing an approach to the subject matter that is inspired by population genetics, as sketched in his article "The Founder Principle in Creole Genesis" (*Diachronica* 1996). He has (co)edited *Africanisms in Afro-American Language Varieties* (1993), *African-American English: Structure, History, and Use* (1998), *Issues in Creole Linguistics* (special issue of *Linguistics* 28, 1990), and *Symposium on Pidgin-to-English Continua* (special issue of *World Englishes* 16, 1997). He was the Columnist (1986–88) and the Associate Editor (1989–95) of the *Journal of Pidgin and Creole Languages*.

GERALD NELSON is a Research Fellow at the Survey of English Usage, University College London, where he has been responsible for the British component of the International Corpus of English since the start of the project. His research interests include corpus linguistics and English syntax, on which he has published widely. He is the author of the Internet Grammar of English.

GEOFFREY NUNBERG is a principal scientist at the Xerox Palo Alto Research Center and Professor of Linguistics at Stanford. He is also Usage

Editor of the *American Heritage Dictionary*. His most recent book is the collection *The Future of the Book*.

STEVEN PINKER is Professor of Psychology and Director of the McDonnell-Pew Center for Cognitive Neuroscience at the Massachusetts Institute of Technology. He is an experimental psychologist who has studied language development and visual cognition. His most recent books are *The Language Instinct* (1994) and *How the Mind Works* (1997).

GEOFFREY K. PULLUM is Professor of Linguistics at the University of California at Santa Cruz, where he has taught since 1981. He has published over 150 articles on a wide range of topics from syntax to phonetics and from English to Amazonian Indian languages. He was a coauthor of *Generalized Phrase Structure Grammar* (1985) and is widely known in linguistics for his collection of satirical commentaries on the discipline, *The Great Eskimo Vocabulary Hoax* (1991). His commentary on African American English, "Language That Dare Not Speak Its Name," appeared in *Nature* in 1997.

VICTOR RASKIN is Professor of English and Linguistics at Purdue University, where he also chairs the Interdepartmental Program in Linguistics. Educated at Moscow State University in Moscow in what was then the USSR (B.A., 1964; M.A., 1966; Ph.D., 1970, all in linguistics), he taught there until his emigration to Israel in 1973, where he taught both at the Hebrew University of Jerusalem and at Tel-Aviv University until his move to Purdue in 1978. He has been a visiting professor at the University of Michigan and a visiting speaker at many Soviet, Israeli, British, Dutch, Belgian, Canadian, Italian, and U.S. universities and research centers. He has published 16 books and over 200 articles in linguistic and semantic theory, linguistic applications, computational linguistics, the linguistics of humor, and other related areas. He has been Editor-in-Chief of *Humor: International Journal of Humor Research* since its inception in 1988.

MARI RHYDWEN now works as a consultant from her liveaboard yacht off the Australia coast, after several years teaching and researching linguistics at Murdoch University and the University of Western Australia. She became interested in language loss whilst doing her doctoral work on the English-based creole spoken in the Northern Territory by Aboriginal people, most of whom have lost their ancestral languages. Brought up in Wales, she stopped speaking Welsh when she attended school, where English was the medium of instruction.

DEBORAH TANNEN is on the faculty of the Department of Linguistics at Georgetown University, where she is one of only four who hold the distinguished rank of University Professor. She has been McGraw Distinguished Lecturer at Princeton University and was a fellow at the Center for Advanced Study in the Behavioral Sciences in Stanford, California, following a term in residence at the Institute for Advanced Study in Princeton, New Jersey. She has published sixteen books and over seventy articles on such topics as spoken and written language, doctor-patient communication, cross-cultural communication, modern Greek discourse, the poetics of everyday conversation, and the relationship between conversational and literary discourse. Among her books are *Talking Voices, Gender and Discourse*, and *Conversational Style*. She received her Ph.D. in linguistics from the University of California at Berkeley.

DENISE TROUTMAN is Associate Professor of American Thought and Language and Linguistics at Michigan State University. She teaches writing to first-year students and linguistics to undergraduate and graduate students. Currently, she is working on descriptions and theoretical explanations of African American women's language, which she has presented in special lectures and at conferences such as Black Women in the Academy: Defending Our Name, 1894–1994 (1994), Conference on College Composition and Communication (1998), New Ways of Analyzing Variation in English (NWAVE, 1996), the Sixth International Pragmatics Conference (1998), and the State of the Art Conference on Ebonics (1998). Holding appointments in two departments, she publishes articles on both writing and linguistics. Some key publications include "Tongue and Sword: Which Is Master?" in *African American Women Speak Out on Anita Hill–Clarence Thomas* (1995); "The Power of Dialect: Ebonics Personified" in *Lessons to Share on Teaching Grammar in Context* (1998); "Whose Voice Is It Anyway? Marked Features in the Writing of Black English Speakers" in *Writing in Multicultural Settings* (1997); and "Discourse, Ethnicity, Culture, and Racism" in *Discourse Studies: A Multidisciplinary Introduction* (coauthored with Teun van Dijk, Stella Ting-Toomey, and Geneva Smitherman; 1997).

MARK TURNER is Professor of English Language and Literature at the University of Maryland. He is a member of the faculty of Maryland's doctoral program in neuroscience and cognitive science and External Research Professor at the Krasnow Institute for Advanced Study in Cognitive Neuroscience. His Ph.D. in English and his M.A. in mathematics are from the University of California at Berkeley. His books include *The Literary Mind, Reading Minds: The Study of English in the Age of Cognitive Science*, and *Death Is the Mother of Beauty*. He has been a fellow of the Institute for Advanced Study, the Guggenheim Foundation, the Center for Advanced Study in the Behavioral Sciences, the National Humanities Center, and the National Endowment for the Humanities. In 1996, the Académie française

awarded him the Prix du rayonnement de la langue et de la littérature françaises.

REBECCA S. WHEELER is Assistant Professor of English at Christopher Newport University, in Virginia, where she teaches grammar, linguistics, writing and fiction. In the environment of an undergraduate English Department, she has become interested in helping students (as well as the lay public) steer their way clear around the often wild claims about language that fill our editorial pages, social hours, and even university hallways. Her research interests have centered on the nature of meaning in language, ambiguity, polysemy, and the interface between syntax and semantics. Recent publications include *Language Alive in the Classroom* (Praeger 1999); "Will the Real Search Verbs Please Stand Up?"(1996); " 'Understand' in Conceptual Semantics" (1995); and "Beyond 'Try to Find': The Syntax and Semantics of 'Search' and 'Analyze' " (1995). Wheeler, who received her Ph.D. in Linguistics from The University of Chicago in 1989, has been appointed to the Undergraduate Program Advisory Committee of the Linguistic Society of America.

ISBN 0-275-96245-8

90000>

EAN

9 780275 962456

HARDCOVER BAR CODE